NORWAY

Oslo

SWEDEN

Stockholm

FINLAND

Helsinki

Tallinn

ESTONIA

Kashin

Moscow

DENMARK

Copenhagen 20

Baltic
Sea

Riga 4

LATVIA

RUSSIA

Hamburg

Neuengamme ○Ravensbruck
Sachsenhausen ○

BERGEN-
BELSEN ■ Berlin

GERMANY

Dora ○
Buchenwald

Oederan ○

Danzig

Stutthof 12

LITHUANIA

Kovno 10

VILNA LAND

Vilna
11 12

Minsk

Rubzewitz 19

POLAND

2 Bialisk

TREBLINKA ▲

CHELMNO ▲ 1

Warsaw

Lodz 14

Gross
Rosen ○

14 22 23

Kielce

7

SOBIBOR ▲

Maidanek ▲

Kiev

UKRAINE

SUDETEN
LAND

Flossenbürg ○

6 8 13

■ TEREZÍN

BOHEMIA

Prague ●

AUSCHWITZ

9 16

Cracow ●

BELZEC ▲

Lvov

5

EASTERN
GALITIA

Mühldorf

MORAVIA

SLOVAKIA

Dachau ○○

Munich ●

Lenzing ○

8 ▲ Vienna

Mauthausen

AUSTRIA

SLOVENIA

HUNGARY

Budapest ●

18

9

Nagyvarad ●

ROMANIA

Odessa

Venice ●

■
FOSSOLI
DI CARPI

Florence ●

ITALY

Rome ●

Zagreb ●

CROATIA

Sarajevo ●

SERBIA

Belgrade ●

MONTE-
NEGRO

Bucharest ●

BULGARIA

Sofiya ●

Black Sea

Istanbul

Tyrrhenian
Sea

ALBANIA

GREECE

Aegean
Sea

TURKEY

18 to Israel

Adriatic Sea

Children in the Holocaust and World War II

∞

Their Secret Diaries

Children in the Holocaust and World War II

Their Secret Diaries

LAUREL HOLLIDAY

Pocket Books
New York   London   Toronto   Sydney   Tokyo   Singapore

From *Heroic Heart: The Diary and Letters of Kim Malthe-Bruun* by Kim Malthe-Bruun. Copyright © 1955 by Random House, Inc. Reprinted by permission of Random House, Inc.

From *Hannah Senesh: Her Life and Diary* by Hannah Senesh, trans. by Marta Cohn. Intro by Abba Eban. Text copyright © 1971 by Nigel Marsh. Introduction copyright © 1972 by Schocken Books, Inc. Reprinted by permission of Schocken Books, published by Pantheon Books, a division of Random House, Inc.

POCKET BOOKS, a division of Simon & Schuster Inc.
1230 Avenue of the Americas, New York, NY 10020

Library of Congress Cataloging-in-Publication Data

Children in the Holocaust and World War II : their secret diaries/
    [compiled by] Laurel Holliday.
        p. cm.
    Includes bibliographical references
    ISBN: 0-671-52054-7
    1. Holocaust, Jewish (1939–1945)—Personal narratives. 2. Jewish
children—Diaries. I. Holliday, Laurel, 1946–.
D804.3.C45   1995
940.53'18—dc20   95-3211
                                                                           CIP

First Pocket Books hardcover printing May 1995

10 9 8 7 6 5 4 3 2 1

POCKET and colophon are registered trademarks of
Simon & Schuster Inc.

Printed in the U.S.A.

Acknowledgments

I would like to thank the Interlibrary Loan staffs of the University of Washington's Suzzalo Library and the Seattle Public Library and the Ballard Branch librarians who have assisted me by obtaining hundreds of books from around the world. I would also like to thank librarian Rebecca Alexander of Temple de Hirsch Sinai, in Seattle, for her help with finding children's diaries and with Hebrew translation.

I would like to acknowledge the contribution of Christine Lienhart Nelson to this anthology. Her patient help with selecting excerpts from Macha Rolnika's diary and translating it from the French is very much appreciated.

And, finally, I would like to thank my agent, Sarah Jane Freymann, and my editor, Paul McCarthy, for their love of the children's diaries, their belief in the importance of this anthology, and their encouragement and support through the publishing process.

I think of nothing: not what I am losing, not what I have just lost, not what is in store for me. I do not see the streets before me, the people passing by. I only feel that I am terribly weary, I feel that an insult, a hurt is burning inside me.

YITSKHOK RUDASHEVSKI
Vilna Ghetto
Age 14

(Yitskhok's photograph appears on the front cover.)

Contents

Introduction

This is the first anthology of the diaries children wrote during World War II and the Holocaust. From the ghettos of Lithuania, Poland, Latvia, and Hungary, to the Terezín and Stutthof and Janowska concentration camps, to the bombed-out streets of London and Rotterdam, to a Nazi prison in Copenhagen, these diaries tell us what it was like for children to live each day with the knowledge that it could be their last.

A third of the diarists were twelve years old or younger when they decided to record the historic events that would so drastically change their own lives and those of everyone around them. The nine boys and fourteen girls in this collection, Jews and gentiles alike, described what the Nazis did to their families and their towns without guarding their feelings or mincing words. They wrote with courage—even humor—and they wrote very well.

Unfortunately, many of the children's diaries have been all but lost to history. Either they were never published in book form or there are only a handful of copies left in the world's major libraries. It is astonishing that, even though most of them are as powerful and well-written as Anne

Frank's diary, they have remained obscure while hers has been thought of as *the* child diary of the Holocaust.

Perhaps it is so painful to think about the impact of the war on children—particularly their mass executions—that we have not wanted to read about it, even when that has meant refusing to hear from the children themselves. Maybe it was as much as we could bear to designate Anne Frank the representative child of the Holocaust and to think, then, only of her when we thought about children in World War II.

But, in some ways, Anne Frank was not representative of children in the war and the Holocaust. Because she was in hiding, she did not experience life in the streets, the ghettos, the concentration camps, as it was lived by millions of children throughout Europe.

Through these boys' and girls' writings we learn about the external realities of children's wartime lives as well as their innermost thoughts and feelings. The diaries portray what it was like to live with constant Gestapo harassment, the daily grind of searching for the basic necessities, and the terror of seeing friends and relatives deported to their deaths. And they depict the ways some of these children fought back against their oppressors, not the least of which was to write what they personally witnessed of Nazi brutality as a historical record.

To write as frequently and as much as these children wrote was no simple matter. To begin with, they needed to find materials for writing. Pens and paper were difficult to obtain in the concentration camps and ghettos. Those children who were under Nazi guard also needed to find a place where they would not be observed writing. And, once they had written their stories, the children had to find suitable hiding places for their work so that it would not be confiscated during Gestapo searches.

Even for the gentile children, who lived neither in concentration camps nor in ghettos, writing with bombs falling all around them could not have been easy. Given these physical and psychological difficulties, why did the children persist in keeping their diaries, in some cases for the entire length of the war?

The boys and girls themselves reflect on this question. Some say they wrote from loneliness. Separated from their friends and/or family members, they had no one with whom to share what they were going through. Sixteen-year-old Moshe Flinker, a Jewish boy whose family had fled to Belgium from Holland when the war began, said that he wrote because he had discovered "the need to pour out one's heart to a friend."

Eva Heyman, a thirteen-year-old Jewish girl incarcerated in a Hungarian ghetto, used her diary to give her the courage to go on in the face of inhuman conditions and torture. She called her secret book "my best friend," and its safety was just as important to her as that of her canary Mandi.

Mary Berg, a fifteen-year-old who was living in Warsaw at the time of the Nazi occupation, kept one of the most detailed and expansive diaries of all the children. She wrote, she said, as a way of testifying to the unspeakable evils perpetrated by the Nazi criminals in the Warsaw ghetto. For her, to write in her diary was to resist the humiliation and oppression she was subject to every day. "I will tell everything," she declared, "about our sufferings and our struggles and the slaughter of our dearest, and I will demand punishment for the German murderers and their Gretchens in

Berlin, Munich, and Nuremberg who enjoyed the fruits of murder, and are still wearing the clothes and shoes of our martyrized people."

Some of the children wrote for more individual reasons. Seventeen-year-old Zionist Hannah Senesh viewed her diary as a tool for "self-analysis." By writing all she could about her thoughts and feelings, she was able to come to firm decisions about emigrating from Hungary to Israel and, eventually, about joining the British partisans as a parachutist.

Joan Wyndham, a sixteen-year-old living in London, used her diary to study her own maturation and how it was impacted by the war. Her account of her romantic adventures in bomb-scarred London is unique in its bold depiction of war's effect on adolescent sexuality.

Their diaries served most of the children as outlets for anger and rage. On paper, they could make threats against the Germans—call them forbidden names and promise to blow them into high heaven as bomber pilots or saboteurs—without the risk of being laughed at or punished. In this secret place, they could release the explosive anger they felt without upsetting and endangering their families.

The children also kept diaries as a way of finding meaning and purpose in the chaos with which they were surrounded. As they struggled to comprehend the horrors they were living through, their diaries allowed them an opportunity to acknowledge their pain and to try to make sense of it.

Some of the children monitored and recorded specific psychological states in their diaries. "I am nearly hysterical," wrote Mary Berg after the Jewish police burst into her house warning of a pogrom. Yitskhok Rudashevski gave a concise and accurate description of psychological dissociation when he said, "I think of nothing ... I do not see the streets before me, the people passing by." Kim Malthe-Bruun, a Danish boy in solitary confinement in a Nazi prison, wrote after being tortured, "I suddenly understood what insanity must be, but I knew that this was like everything else which has happened to me, and in a couple of days I'll be myself again."

All of the diaries provide an inside look at how children experience and survive trauma. It is clear that the children retained their sanity, their insight, and even humor while living in life-threatening conditions. Many of them gratefully acknowledged that their diaries helped them to do this.

Even if they had served no other purpose, the diaries gave the children the sense that they, as young as they might have been, had a right to express themselves about what was happening in their world. As psychologist Victor Frankl has said in his writings about his own concentration camp experience, the difference between those prisoners who went insane and those who were able to keep their mental health was a spirit of resistance and a focus on trying to be of service to others. Those who survived psychologically intact had to believe that what they did on a daily basis could make at least some small difference to someone else. Many of the children believed that their diaries would speak for them after the war was over and tell the story of "the final solution" so that humankind would not allow such a thing to happen again.

It cannot be overemphasized that the very act of writing in their diaries was a form of resistance for most of these children. With the exception of two of the children who were living in London, these boys and girls were performing private acts of heroism whenever they wrote because, had any of these diaries come to the attention of the Nazis, they could have been shot on the spot. They were speaking out with all their strength against Fascism and this very outcry may have been the secret to their psychological survival.

It seems almost any emotional trauma can be endured as long as one does not view oneself as a helpless victim and continues to cry out against injustice and oppression. Although the children occasionally lost hope, their diaries are clear evidence that they picked themselves up and went on to write the next day.

In addition to revealing how writing was a powerfully healing means of resistance, the diaries show the depth of thinking and the wisdom of which these children were capable. Many of them realized that not all Germans were Nazis and that not all Allies were their friends. In fact, a surprising number of the children wrote that they thought America was dragging its heels about entering the war and saving the Jews of Europe in part because of antisemitism—a suspicion that eventually proved to be true.

Some of the children also showed remarkable wisdom for their years by looking beyond their own anger and rage and realizing that if they followed their instincts to bomb the hell out of the German people, just as the Germans were bombing civilian targets all over Europe, this would devalue their own humanity.

In addition to their discernment, wisdom, and depth of reflection, these diaries reveal the children's resilience and their willingness to extend themselves to others. Despite the Nazi nightmare, they did all they could to rise above their own terror and to ease the suffering of those around them.

Child after child tells how he or she tried to save others—either by giving them food and first aid or by actively fighting Nazism as partisans. Three of the children gave the ultimate gift—their own lives—while defending those they loved.

Although all of these children were surrounded by war and deprivation, none of them lost touch with their interior lives and the self that was taking shape before the war began. As we read each of their diaries, we can hear a distinct personality that may have wavered when forced to adapt to circumstances, but did not disappear. Although certainly less naive, innocent, and trusting, the children seem to have espoused the same set of values and personal ethics at the end of the war as they had when it began. Rather than being irreparably damaged, as we might imagine children would be under such horrific circumstances, those who survived seemed to care even more deeply about those they loved and to have a stronger sense of purpose for their own lives.

In short, these boys and girls did not become the mindless automatons that the Nazis might have wished them to be. I believe that diary writing helped preserve a core sense of personal identity and integrity even for those whose names were replaced with numbers and who had dog tags hung around their necks. As we read these diaries today, it is my hope that the children's courage and integrity will inspire us to clarify our own values and to fight prejudice and injustice wherever we see it.

Some readers may hesitate to expose themselves, or their children, to these children's vivid descriptions of what they suffered. Out of a sincere desire to protect ourselves and our loved ones, we might want to turn away. After all, haven't we been led to believe that exposure to violence causes nightmares and warps the sensitive psyche?

These children's diaries are testimonies to the fact that telling the truth about violence is not harmful. In fact, one wonders how much greater harm these boys and girls would have suffered had they *not* written about the horrific events they were experiencing. Far more dangerous than reading about atrocities, I believe, is the pretense that atrocities do not occur. To turn our eyes away and refuse to see, or to let children see, what prejudice and hatred lead to is truly to warp our collective psyche. It is important for all of us— adults and children alike—to acknowledge the depths to which humankind can sink.

The children teach us, by sharing their own direct experience of oppression, that nothing is more valuable than human freedom. This lesson alone is reason enough to read, and to encourage children to read, these diaries.

To provide as full a picture as possible, the excerpts for this book have been drawn from as many as a hundred of each child's diary entries. Of necessity, however, much was omitted since most of the diaries are long enough to comprise full-length books. And because of space limitations, children's diaries that are readily obtainable, like Anne Frank's, have not been included in this anthology. These more accessible diaries are listed in the bibliography, on page 403.

In the interest of authenticity, I have not corrected the children's punctuation, grammar, and spelling. Nor have I changed the various names the children used for geographical locations. Some children called the transport camp near Prague Terezín, for example, while others called it Theresienstadt. The Vilna ghetto is also called Vilnius ghetto, and the death camp at Ponar is sometimes referred to as Ponarai. These variant place names simply reflect the fact that the children lived in different countries and spoke a variety of languages.

Many of the children's diary entries were undated. When possible, I have deduced dates from the content of the writing and enclosed these dates in brackets.

The ages given for the children indicate how old they were when they wrote the first excerpt and are not necessarily the ages they were when they began their diaries. The diaries are arranged by age—youngest to oldest.

—Laurel Holliday
1995

Janine Phillips

POLAND ∞ 10 YEARS OLD

*J*anine Phillips began her diary on her tenth birthday, in May of 1939. She was living in the Polish countryside with her large, well-to-do family who had fled Nazi oppression in nearby War-saw. Although the family had to accustom themselves to a simpler way of living, it is clear from Janine's writing that their suffering was nothing like what Mary Berg describes as going on in the city of Warsaw. With a certain amount of ingenuity, the family and all the relatives who were living with them were able to eat three hearty meals a day, to attend Mass every Sunday, and to enjoy a certain number of ordinary pleasures like fishing and celebrations of feast days.

Nevertheless, they were constantly aware of how precari-ous their situation was. The family listened to an illegal radio set for every hint of what was happening in the rest of Europe and in War-saw. Janine was an avid reporter of all the news on the domestic as well as the international fronts. In her diary, she boldly described *people's peculiarities and peccadillos in such a humorous manner that it is hard to remember that the family was living in war-torn Poland and that the reason she had so much time to write was that it was unsafe for her to go to school. Janine filled a one-thousand-page notebook the year she was ten. Then, when she was eleven, she left off diary writing and returned to school in Warsaw.*

In the epilogue to her diary, Janine says that during her four years in Nazi-occupied Warsaw she attended an illegal school where Polish history and literature were taught. When the Warsaw Ghetto Uprising occurred, she did her "duty" as a Girl Guide and set up a first aid station for the wounded. For this, she was arrested and taken to Germany as a prisoner of war. She was released, in 1945, when she was sixteen and she continued her education. Janine became a chemist and eventually worked as a researcher for a large company in London. She married and then returned home for a visit in 1965, twenty-one years after she had left Poland.

During this visit one of her aunts handed her a box containing her childhood diary. Janine translated it into English and it was published, in London, in 1982.

23rd August 1939

Papa says that war is inevitable. I asked Papa why Hitler wants to attack us and Papa said because he's a greedy bully. I only hope he knows that peaceful people don't think him very nice. Grandpa went to see Father Jakob and asked him to say a mass to save us from war. Grandpa remembers many wars and he says that a war not only kills people but it also kills people's souls. That's why Grandpa feels that God ought to intervene, because there won't be many souls left in His Heaven. I quite agree with Grandpa.

1st September 1939

Hitler has invaded Poland. We heard the bad news on the wireless a few minutes after spotting two aeroplanes circling around each other. Just before breakfast, about ten minutes to ten, I was returning from the privy when I heard aeroplanes in the sky. I thought it was manoeuvres. Then I heard some machine-guns and everybody came out from the house to see what was happening. Grandpa said, "My God! It's war!" and rushed indoors to switch on the wireless. The grave news came in a special announcement that German forces have crossed the Polish border and our soldiers are defending our country. Everybody was stunned. With ears glued to the loudspeaker we were trying to catch the fading words. The battery or the accumulator, or both, were packing up. When we could no longer even hear a whisper from the wireless set, Grandpa turned the switch off and looked at our anguished faces. He knelt in front of the picture of Jesus Christ and started to pray aloud. We repeated after Grandpa, "Our Father who art in Heaven, hallowed be Thy name . . ."

Soon after tea, Uncle Tadeusz, my new Aunt Aniela and Papa arrived from Warsaw with some more bad news. Papa said that we were not going back to Warsaw because it was safer to stay here, in the village. He arranged for a wagon to bring our winter clothes and other belongings. I wondered what will happen to our school, but Mama said that when a country is fighting for its survival, there is no time for schooling. All evening Papa has been trying to get the wireless going but did not succeed. Tomorrow, he'll try to get to

Warsaw and see what can be done about the set which is so vital to us just now. Please, Dear God, let our brave soldiers beat the nasty Germans.

3rd September 1939

Papa and Mama returned from Warsaw late last night together with our belongings. They hired a horse-drawn wagon and it took them several hours to get here. The roads were packed with soldiers and military vehicles. People in Warsaw are in high spirits and quite ready to fight. I wish I were in Warsaw too, because I can fight quite well when I set my mind to it. Papa brought a new battery, thank goodness, and is fiddling with the wireless at this very moment. Uncle Tadeusz and Aunt Aniela are coming back tomorrow or the day after because Uncle has been making arrangements for someone to mind his shop for him.

Magnificent news! England is going to thrash the Gerries in no time at all. Mr. Chamberlain said that England has declared war against Germany. This welcome news came from the loudspeaker like a blessing from Heaven. I am so glad that we have some good friends abroad. Papa said that Great Britain is a mighty power with a strong Navy and Air Force. Everybody is greatly relieved and we celebrated with a drop of our special vintage wine. I shall have to learn some English because I know only one word, "Goodbye," and that's hardly enough to carry on a conversation with English soldiers. Papa said in three or four weeks they'll be here. When they come, I should like to thank them for helping us to beat Hitler but if I haven't learnt sufficient English to say so, I'll just have to hug them and they'll know what I mean.

4th September 1939

We heard some heavy artillery fire. No-one seems to know where it was coming from. Grandpa took Mama and me to the market to get a stock of food but there was very little we could buy. The farmers are hanging on to their dairy produce and there were very few eggs left, and they have suddenly trebled in price. That also applies to wheat, flour and sugar. Anyway, we've managed to get a few kilogrammes of dry sausage and that will keep for many months. Mama went to see her friends and they sold her a large piece of pork belly and two kilogrammes of dripping. The Jewish shopkeepers are very frightened of Hitler and many have left their businesses and fled into the country. Grandpa promised to send them some vegetables. They were grateful and asked if we had a sufficient stock of oil and candles. It seems that Grandpa wants to buy anything he can lay his hands on. Grandpa knows from bitter experience that when there is a war, everything is in short supply.

Before sunset, Uncle Tadeusz and Aunt Aniela arrived bringing in a lot of valuable silver, glass, porcelain and other articles of sentimental value. Unfortunately, they also brought some bad news about our Baltic Corridor. The German Fourth Army has pushed through our defence lines. Uncle Tadeusz said that hundreds of Polish Cavalrymen lost their lives in a heroic battle. We were utterly sickened by this news. Grandpa suffered most. His empty eye-socket filled with tears. He blew his nose and went to the stable. Grandpa always goes to talk to Samson when things are bad.

13th September 1939

I very much hope that the thirteenth is more unlucky to the Gerries than it is to us. Warsaw is fighting back. We can hear explosions by day and see the red sky at night. Several shells have landed in nearby fields. Uncle Tadeusz decided that we'd have to build a shelter at the bottom of the garden. He thinks that our house might become a target for Nazi tanks. Having chosen a suitable place, Uncle Tadeusz got everybody he could grab hold of, including his wife, and formed us into a platoon. As the Commander-in-chief, he handed each of us a spade and told us to dig while he went elsewhere. Being next to Aunt Aniela, I could see that she is not a digger. Every time I dug a hole, she filled it in. After half-an-hour, which seemed like two hours, Uncle Tadeusz returned to inspect the hole. He was not pleased with our progress, and he said so. It is Uncle's nature to call a spade a spade and he did not mince his words on this occasion either. He wanted to know whether I and Aunt Aniela were, by any chance, digging for worms. I said that I was not, but Aunt Aniela said that she would much rather dig for worms than for Uncle Tadeusz. And to emphasize what she'd just said, she aimed her spade at the ground, but landed it on Uncle's foot. Uncle yelled and hobbled back towards the house in a huff. Aunt Aniela ran after him begging his forgiveness. We all agreed that it was a bad day for digging the shelter. We sank our spades in the ground and followed the Chief.

16th September 1939

Some good news today. The Germans have been repulsed on the Western Front. Our hopes rose and with them our moods improved. Uncle Tadeusz started to tease Mama and Aunt Stefa. He said that Mama puts on weight in front whereas Aunt Stefa does at the back, and it was quite out of character for identical twins to behave in such a contrary way. Aunt Stefa replied that he was a fine one to talk about other people's figures. Has he, meaning Uncle, by any chance, seen his own paunch? Uncle Tadeusz said he had, and it was not without purpose. Putting on weight around the middle kept him well balanced. Mama said that he was unbalanced because his head was too big. Everybody laughed, including Grandpa. Even Pempela wagged her tail. It was just like before the war. Mama made some cheese from the goat's milk. It looked delicious but nobody wanted to eat it. People just passed the cheese around and it came back to Mama untouched. She said it was the last time she was going to take the trouble to make cheese. Uncle Tadeusz, having made a sigh of relief, handed Mama pencil and paper and asked her to put it in writing. Everyone burst out laughing again, as if making the most of it before the next onset of doom.

18th September 1939

The shelter is ready. Uncle Tadeusz, having banished every female from the site, harnessed men to finish the job. Our shelter consists of a large hole in the ground which is lined with straw. The roof is made of logs, straw and earth. Papa said it was as depressing as a graveyard and a proper death-trap. And he, for one, won't be risking his neck by going in there. Uncle Tadeusz said that Papa might change his mind when a shell lands in his bed. Papa replied that he would much rather sleep with a shell than in Uncle's shelter. I said that I wanted to stay in the house too, but Mama ticked me off and said that I'll have to do what she says and not what I want to do. I felt cross with Mama and didn't like her just then. After ten-thirty in the evening, when the gun-fire intensified its rage, and when the moon climbed up the blue-black sky, we packed ourselves on the straw in the shelter like sardines. There was practically no room to lie down and not much air to breathe. The onion soup from supper was not a good idea, pointed out Uncle Tadeusz. At that moment he must have envied Papa, though he didn't say so. I asked Mama whether I could go back to my bed but she said "No", and in such a funny tone of voice that I did not dare to ask her again. Jurek complained that he couldn't breathe and Aunt Stefa told him to do without breathing. Every time somebody moved, a trickle of sand came down from the roof. Aunt Aniela said she felt like a mummy without having the advantage of being embalmed. Every quarter-of-an-hour somebody asked what was the time. By three in the morning, the atmosphere in the shelter got so heavy that if we stayed there a minute longer we would have suffocated. Aunt Aniela scrambled out first, saying that she'd much rather be blown to bits by a bullet than be poisoned by bad onions. We all followed, thankful for her courage. Mama could hardly stand up. She had a cramp in one leg and pins and needles in the other. We toddled off to the house, truly grateful for having a real roof over our heads and real beds to sleep in. Last night was the first time we used the garden shelter and it could well be the last. Very likely Uncle Tadeusz did not think much of his own architecture either, for he was just as pleased to get out of it.

19th September 1939

We are overwhelmed with sorrow. Polish resistance has collapsed. The Russians and the Germans have met near

Brest Litovsk. Warsaw is on its last legs. Papa said that they are short of ammunition and food. The German propaganda is pouring in from every wavelength. Papa's been trying to get the BBC on his secret wireless set which is somewhere in the attic. Papa often goes up there with Aunt Aniela. He fiddles with the knobs and she takes everything down. Then Tadek and Wojtek distribute the news around the village.

This afternoon, Father Jakob called to see how we are getting on. Grandpa was full of indignation about God allowing such injustice to prevail on Polish soil. Father Jakob had to stop Grandpa before he said something terrible. When Grandpa gets going and when he's het up no-one is safe, not even God. Having soothed Grandpa's nerves, Father Jakob said that we, the children of God, are not here to question His wisdom but to pray for help and peace. Grandpa said that's exactly what he's been doing and a lot of good it did. Father Jakob replied that God has been awfully busy lately with everybody praying at the same time. Grandpa nodded and agreed that it must be sheer hell in Heaven, just now.

20th September 1939

Great-Uncle Emil came to see Grandpa to discuss the matter of guns and other weapons in the village. Grandpa suggested hiding them under the hay in the barn. But Uncle Tadeusz pointed out that it was the first place the Germans would search. He said the safest place for all weapons was underground. Later in the morning, Great-Uncle Emil and Anton brought in at least a dozen different guns and buried them somewhere in the garden. I only hope Uncle Tadeusz can remember what is buried where.

Anton heard from a friend that he had met a shepherd

who had seen a German soldier near Zegrze. That's only three kilometres from us. So I went to a nearby field to see if I could spot any German soldiers. I saw nothing but heard enough to last me a long time. When I got about three hundred metres from the house, I heard bullets whistling around me. At first I didn't realise what was happening, until I saw puffs of dust in the road. Someone was shooting at me. Immediately I lay down on the ground, too petrified to move. My heart was thumping like mad. After a while the shooting stopped. I didn't know what to do. The Germans must be quite near, I reckoned. I started to crawl, almost slithering like a grass snake. My dress, my knees and my hands were covered in dust. After several minutes I heard a cow mooing. A bullet had gone through her hind leg. Blood was pouring down and the poor beast was in agony. By then I was really scared. I got up and ran as fast as I could. When I got to the house, filthy and out of breath, Mama was furious with me. Before I had the chance to explain what had happened she spanked me. I went to my room and cried and cried. But then I remembered the poor injured cow. So I went to tell Grandpa about it. He praised me and said it was an act of God that I saw the incident, otherwise the cow, belonging to Anton's sister-in-law, might have bled to death. At once Anton went to the cow with his first-aid kit. Afterwards, when Mama helped me to change and wash, I think she was sorry for spanking me so hastily for she hugged and kissed me and said that it was a silly thing to do. Papa was quite worried when he learnt how near the Germans are. He went up to the attic to hide the wireless set. For the time being, Papa put it underneath a pile of dirty washing. After tea, Uncle Tadeusz went to the attic and knocked several bricks out of the chimney stack and built a handy hideout for the wireless on the side facing the roof. It was a removable panel and it is almost invisible. Uncle Tadeusz said it was all right so long as no-one lit the fire in the south side of the house.

21st September 1939

Our capital is on fire. At night we can see the sky stained with smoke and flame. The guns have died down. German troops have surrounded Warsaw almost completely. Papa says it's only a matter of days. We feel thoroughly dejected, forsaken by justice. Why, oh why, are the Nazis winning the war?

25th September 1939

Nothing but bad news. People are prepared for the worst to happen. A convoy of German troops on the main road to Warsaw has been reported by one villager. Grandpa is in a state of continuous anxiety. Mama is worried about his health. She's been brewing a herbal potion for his nerves. The odour of valerian pervaded the whole house and Papa said that anyone who can survive its wicked smell can survive anything. Mama made the brew in a jug and insisted that Grandpa should drink the lot. The effect was indisputable. Grandpa was flat out for the rest of the day. Mama got worried and wondered whether she'd cured him too much, and wanted to call the doctor. But Uncle Tadeusz said that, before getting better, it was quite natural for anyone to pass through a bad patch. Mama was not at all convinced, but she agreed that, at least, Grandpa's nerves were having a rest. After several hours, Grandpa was still passing through his bad patch. He remained in bed, sleeping it off, for two days. When the Germans came, Grandpa was beyond any fear, but the rest of us, quite literally, shivered in our boots. A full lorry-load of Gerries spilled out at our gate at the crack of dawn. They bashed on the front door, nearly knocking Uncle Tadeusz down, and rampaging through the house like a torrent of hoodlums. With their rifles at the ready, they poked and probed at anything and everything. Presumably, having found nothing they were looking for, they departed, leaving everybody alive, thank the Lord, but the house in a dreadful mess. After the visitation we all felt like a drop of Mama's valerian.

26th September 1939

Borowa-Góra is swarming with Gerries. There are at least two soldiers for every villager. Their uniforms are greenish-blue, and they are wearing black, knee-length boots. Some have helmets on their heads, others just forage caps, but all carry pistols hanging from their belts. The amazing part is that they feel quite at home in our village. They know exactly where to find food or water, how many men there are available for labour, and how many horses and carts there are at hand. They seem to know everything, though none, as far as I know, can speak Polish. Our German language is virtually non-existent. Uncle Tadeusz has a smattering of it and Aunt Aniela finds it not too difficult to guess what they say, German being somewhat similar to English. Though Papa feels it's useful to know *"nicht verstehen"*. So far, Herr Kommandant von Klein has only been wanting food, and he didn't ask for it, he just helped himself. Our cellar seems to have great fascination for Herr Kommandant. Fortunately, Mama and Aunt Stefa managed to smuggle out some of our precious preserves before they disappeared. Herr Kommandant set up his headquarters in the other house belonging to Grandpa which is usually let to holidaymakers, and which is situated near the main road to Warsaw. Thank goodness it's some distance from our house, and Papa still might be able to listen to an occasional news bulletin on his secret wireless.

28th September 1939

Warsaw surrendered yesterday. Mr Starzynski, the city mayor, has been shot by the Nazis. We feel appalled by this barbaric act. Grandpa took it very badly and asked for another dose of Mama's brew but she was somewhat reluctant to give it to him. Instead, Papa mixed him a vodka cocktail. Grandpa drank two glasses at once and a third one more leisurely. After that, he felt much better. So much so, that he went to see Herr Kommandant in his new headquarters and told him to clear out. Luckily for all of us, and even more so for Grandpa, Herr Kommandant had no idea what Grandpa was on about. Uncle Tadeusz, having learnt what Grandpa was up to, went to fetch him, explaining to the German commander that his father was suffering from mental aberration. Mama put Grandpa to bed and blamed Papa for everything. She said that vodka must have been invented by the devil himself, because it brings misery to so many. And pleasure to millions, pointed out Papa. Mama argued that all Papa does is to seek pleasure. To which Papa replied that he saw nothing wrong in enjoying himself. They argued for at least half-an-hour, by which time Grandpa got sober and Mama felt better for having made Papa miserable.

29th September 1939

Uncle Tadeusz has been trying to get to Warsaw but without any luck. The city is surrounded by German troops and no-one from the inside or the outside is allowed to cross the border. Apparently, the people of Warsaw are carrying on with their work as usual, in spite of the fact that many buildings have been completely destroyed, or burned down. Uncle is furious with the Gerries. He wants to know what has happened to his shops in Warsaw. The frontier between the city on the south side and the rest of the country is along the river Bug and the customs post, set up by the Germans, is at Zegrze. Uncle Tadeusz drove his Fiat as far as the bridge and there he was stopped. He had to show his credentials, the number of his car was taken, together with his name and address. At one stage, Uncle thought they would detain him. Luckily, he was released and lost no time driving back home as fast as he could. Gradually, we are learning to keep quiet and inconspicuous, but always hoping that tomorrow will bring a brighter outlook.

30th September 1939

Aunt Aniela has been summoned to cook dinners for Herr Kommandant at his headquarters in Grandpa's other house. Uncle Tadeusz tried to explain that his wife knew very little about cooking and suggested that Irka might suit him better. But the answer was no. Herr Kommandant knows exactly what he likes and Aunt Aniela was his choice. So she reported at his office just after six and was told to prepare pork chops, sauerkraut and potatoes for his supper. Aunt Aniela is as good at cooking as she is at digging, which amounts to very little. Not many people could produce a burnt glass of tea. Well, Aunt Aniela can, I know, because I've sampled it. Although we all felt sorry for her, Irka and I could not help giggling at the unlikely finesse of the cordon bleu meal prepared by Aunt Aniela. It serves Herr Kommandant right, and with a little bit of luck he might even choke.

3rd October 1939

A German soldier shot little Gabriel. We are sickened at this callous act of violence. The soldier came to tell us to report for potato picking next week. Gabriel doesn't like strangers and he could not resist nipping his leg. The soldier pulled out his revolver and shot Gabriel on the spot. The dog died instantly. Mama and Aunt Stefa are very upset. Uncle Tadeusz told Tadek to bury Gabriel somewhere in the garden. We wrapped him in a clean cloth and put him in a little coffin which Wojtek made from bits of wood. On the headstone, we inscribed the words: "Here lies little angel Gabriel who bit the big devil".

25th October 1939

I asked Father Jakob yesterday if it were a sin to be nasty to the Gerries. Father Jakob scratched his head and said that under normal circumstances it would be a sin. But, taking into consideration the fact that we are at war, or, to be more precise, the Germans are occupying our country, God probably would be prepared to give us some sort of dispensation. Then I asked him, even if I were to kill a German, would I not end up in Hell? Father Jakob said that in self-defence killing is permissible, but not premeditated killing. He wanted to know whether I followed him and I said that I did, which is a lie, because I didn't. In actual fact, the more

I think about the sin of killing the less I understand the whole business. To me, a killed man, for whatever reason, is a dead man, and to him surely it doesn't matter why he had died? His only worry is that he's dead and he can't do anything about it. Then I asked Papa if he would consider pinching spuds from the Gerries a sin. Papa said it was most certainly not. He explained it to me like this: suppose a burglar stole my doll and I pinched it back. That wouldn't be stealing because the doll belonged to me in the first place. The same with the Germans. They have no right to be here. It is they who are the thieves. They are taking our crops from our fields and, on top of this, they are forcing us to work for them. Papa said it was a triple sin. I can always understand Papa and I hope God will remember to give the Gerries three bad marks.

5th November 1939

The Gerries have declared that the city of Warsaw is to be called a Protectorate. Papa wants to know who is going to protect whom and against whom? The primary schools and the commercial colleges will be opened, but no higher education such as gymnasiums, lyceums and universities. They will remain closed. Papa said that a well-educated Polish population is against the interests of the Nazis. All they want of us is to labour for them. This is something that we all should try to resist. We can't refuse to work but we can work at a snail's pace, Papa said.

This afternoon we've been digging out carrots and storing them in dry sand. This is a nasty job and I could hardly wait till the last lot was brought in by Papa and Uncle Tadeusz. We put the carrots in layers in wooden boxes. Then Uncle covered them with sand, then another layer, and so on, ending up with a layer of sand. By the time we'd finished the job, I'd had enough of carrots to last me for a long time. But no. Mama had the bright idea of giving us some more carrots for supper. It would do us good, she said, plonking on the table a huge dish of stewed carrots with microscopic pieces of rabbit. Fortunately there was an apple charlotte to follow and it did soften the blow, for me at any rate. As I grumbled so much about the first course, Mama gave me two slices of cake to keep me quiet.

14th November 1939

Papa held a secret meeting with four other men. I have never seen them before, but they were not strangers to Papa. They called him by his Christian name. I think they must be papa's friends from Warsaw who are interested in politics because after they'd finished two rounds of vodka, they were listening to Papa's wireless or maybe they put a new set in the place of the old one. When they finished talking to Papa, they didn't go out through the front gate, but they went through a hole in the fence and disappeared into the fields and then nearby woodland. I wanted to ask Papa who they were, but one look at Papa's face told me it would have been no good. I expect they must be some sort of very secret agents.

26th November 1939

The Gerries have been deporting young men from our village to work on the farms in Germany. They need the labour. Mama is worried about the boys, but Uncle Tadeusz reckons they're still too young. Papa said that there is bad news from battles at sea. British and Polish liners have been sunk by German mines. Papa was so depressed that he went to bed early. Grandpa said that if the Gerries win the war it won't be worth living. If they win the war Poland will be lost forever, that's what Grandpa said, and it made me very sad.

14th December 1939

Papa says that the French and the British will attack the Germans in the spring. We must wait and hope and keep our fingers crossed. Meanwhile the people in the villages are devising new ways of hiding food away from the Gerries. Apparently, their army is like a swarm of locusts, people say. Uncle Tadeusz made a hide-out at the back of our barn. The barn has been partitioned and the entrance to the food-store has been camouflaged with bundles of straw. This is just in case our cellar gets raided by the Gerries. The longer we live with our enemies, the more we learn about their disregard for human lives and rights.

16th December 1939

When I got up this morning and looked out, I was dazed by the glistening glory. Ten centimetres of snow fell during the night and it seemed so fluffy and as light as duck's down. After a hasty breakfast I went outside to marvel at, and to touch, the snow. To me it is the eighth wonder of the world. Only snow has the cosmetic skill to turn an ugly eyesore into an object of sheer beauty. It also purifies the air. The sun has already climbed above the tops of the pines, eager to take a look at the new scene. The same lime trees which a while ago shivered in their trunks were standing so still, as if fearful of losing their newly acquired apparel. Every branch and every twig has been sprinkled with white. What a delight. I was reluctant to walk over this endless perfection. Almost afraid to spoil the vision of my sight's resurrection. There were tints of blue in the shade and the glow of pink where the sun stroked the snow. I stood amidst the wonderland hypnotised by its beauty, until Mama broke the spell. She said I'd catch my death without my winter coat.

19th December 1939

I am so stiff today that I can hardly move. Mama said it serves me right. Mama can be unfeeling at times. She could show me some sympathy at least. The frost has eased and there is a thaw on the way. Wojtek's made a snowman which looks very much like Hitler. He made the moustache from an old broom, the eyes from a broken beer bottle and he put a swastika on his left arm. His right arm was raised in the Nazi salute. On his head, he had Grandma's old chamber-pot. We all laughed so much. Our Wojtek is really quite clever. Uncle Tadeusz, however, told Wojtek to demolish it. He said it was too much like the Führer and it was too dangerous. He reminded us what happened to little Gabriel. So we armed ourselves with sticks and bottles and had a go at Hitler with unbelievable pleasure. First went his arm, then his head hurtled off. His rounded belly was speared with a broomstick, and finally he collapsed, reduced to a mere heap of snow. Wojtek stuck a little white and red flag on top of the rubble signifying our victory. The three of us stood to attention and sang the Polish national anthem.

Ephraim Shtenkler

POLAND ∞ 11 YEARS OLD

*E*phraim Shtenkler's account of how he was saved from the Nazis is extraordinary in every respect. He was no older than eleven when he wrote about being forced to live in a cupboard from age two to seven by a Polish woman who barely kept him alive. After this hideous solitary confinement, in a cabinet in which he was unable even to stand up, Ephraim's feet were twisted backwards. It took months of medical treatment before he was finally able to learn to walk at age seven.

After the liberation, he was sent from one orphanage to another and finally ended up in the children's village at Hadassim near Tel Aviv, Israel. One day Israeli Professor Edwin Samuel was touring the village in hopes of writing about it for the press when the headmistress told him about eleven-year-old Ephraim and the remarkable writing he had done. Samuel decided that nothing he could write about the children's village would be as powerful as Ephraim's work, which the boy had entitled "What Happened to Me in My

Childhood." Edwin Samuel translated Ephraim's story into English from the archaic Biblical Hebrew in which it was written and had it published in the Jewish magazine Commentary *in May of 1950.*

In Bialisk my family was rich and we also had a shop and life was pleasant. But when the Germans came, they took away the shop and drove us from town to town, as they did the other Jews of the Diaspora, until we came to Zvirdje. And in Zvirdje, they took a part for slaughter and a part they kept alive. Although my father, my mother, and I were in the part that was kept alive, my aunt was in the part that was due to be taken to slaughter. But she was saved, as we had a German acquaintance and my father asked him to arrange for my aunt to be transferred to our part and he spoke with the officer and they transferred my aunt to the part where we ourselves were. And the part that was taken for slaughter died and the part that they kept alive was given places in which to live and my father began to work again and we earned our bread. After some months the Germans came and made a ghetto: then my mother fell ill with a serious illness.

One day we heard that the Germans were coming and we broke through the walls of the ghetto and some escaped. And my father heard that they had broken through the walls of the ghetto and he took me and gave me to a certain Polish woman and said to her, "After the war I'll come back and fetch my son." And the Germans came to our house and my mother lay in bed and they said to her, "Get up!" And she said "How can I get up? I haven't any strength left." And they killed her in her bed and the neighbors heard of this and told my father and my father told it to the Polish woman, and the Polish woman, when she sent me away, told it to me.

And, meanwhile, when my father went with me to the Polish woman, he was delayed among our neighbors and I went by myself to the Polish woman. I don't know what was said between my father and his friends, but the next day my father came and told me that they had killed my mother and murdered women and babies and that now the Germans were seizing those children that remained and were putting them into tarpaulin bags and putting them on the train in a closed wagon and there they were stifled. And my father said "It's good that my only son doesn't suffer as the other children suffer; but it's bad that all the Jews suffer; for why are the Jews to blame?" The Polish woman kept silent, but nevertheless she didn't like Jews and when my father had left she said "Damned Jew! When will you get out of here?" and she knelt before the Virgin Mary.

On the day after I was hidden in the cupboard my father came again. He didn't talk much. He only said "I'll come every day at noon," but those were the nicest words he spoke. And he really did come. Once he brought me a pocket knife and once he brought me a ball. And the Polish woman used to take all these things away from me and give them to her two daughters, one of whom was twelve and the other about sixteen. And my father used to come in silence every day.

One day my father didn't come and on that day the Polish woman wanted to send me away, for she said "The child's father doesn't give me any money, so I'll take him and hide him until he gets sick of it." And she put me under the bed. Suddenly we heard a voice, steps, and a ring at the door. The Polish woman was pleased and opened the door and saw there a friend of my father's and when she asked him, "Have you brought any news?" he said "I have," and she said "Speak," and he began to talk and said "That child of Shtenkler's, I don't know where he is." And when I heard my family name, I peeped out and saw the Polish woman's face was pale. So I understood that she was frightened, for she said "Is there anything else the matter?" as she wanted to change the subject. And he said, "There is," and her face paled and she said "Speak," and he said "Another damned Jew is dead." So she asked "Who?" And he said "Mr. Shtenkler." The Polish woman gaped. She didn't close her mouth: She only closed the door in the man's face and took me and flogged me with her husband's belt, saying "I'll drown you in the well this very day."

In the end she saw that the Germans weren't clearing out, so she was afraid that they might catch me and ask me where I'd been. She knew that then I'd say that it was she herself who had kept me and then they'd hang her and me. So she wanted me to break my heart so that I'd die and she could then tell the Germans that she had found me dead. But, to my luck, she didn't succeed, for I was then a mere child and couldn't understand what death was, so I wasn't afraid of it.

Weeks and months and years passed and nothing happened. And I lay either in the cupboard or under the bed. One day, the elder daughter of the Polish woman came in in a panic and entered with a rush and threw open the door and said "Mother!" And the Polish woman, who was cooking, asked "What's the matter?" "Mother! Mother!" shouted her daughter, "I saw a Hebrew mother and child who were walking hand in hand and a German told the child to let go of his mother's hand and get into the bag. The mother began to plead with him and the fine German shot at the two interlocked hands and took the child and put him in the bag and put him in a wagon and the mother . . ." And the girl stopped speaking. And the mother said "Why don't you go on?" And she said, "I'm afraid that's what'll happen to you, Mother. In the name of the Virgin Mary and Jesus her son, won't they punish us?" And she continued by saying, "And the mother he stabbed." I was terrified. I was then already six years old and understood a good many things and thought that perhaps that's what they did to my mother and I became as white as chalk. After the elder daughter had gone to play outside I wanted to cry, for I envied her. It was already three to four years that I hadn't gone out of doors.

And so the years passed and nothing happened and I was already seven years old, but I didn't know how to walk. And one day, when the war was nearly over, the Polish woman invited in a certain Jew who used to make woolen things—stockings, trousers, sweaters and so on. She thought that he would make her many sweaters, so she invited him in. And when I heard that someone had come I peeped out and in so doing shifted the bottles in the cupboard. He asked "What's that?" I was terrified: I thought it was some German. And the Polish woman, who by this time really wanted to drown me in the well, said, "It's a mouse!" Then he heard the noise again and asked again and she replied "A mouse" until eventually I peered out and he saw me. Then he got furious with her and said, "Why, that's the son of my friend Mr. Shtenkler!" The Polish woman grew pale. And he took me to his house in the next street and asked me what I wanted to wear and I said "Clothes." He laughed and said "Good!" He took out some stockings and a few sweaters and went to the market. I waited for him in his house. Eventually he came with a parcel in his hand. He took off my rags and dressed me in the sort of clothes one wears in this world.

After a day the acquaintance decided to look for a doctor who would treat me so that I could walk. So we got on the train and went to Katowitz. But all of a sudden a man came and spoke to him. In accordance with what he said, I was taken in another train and, like an arrow from the bow, the train flew along, straight to a children's home. There they told him to wait a little. He waited patiently and in the end went into the office and telephoned and after a brief hour a doctor appeared, the one who actually did treat me.

Month after month passed until I learned to walk. It was hard for the doctor to treat me and for me to walk. After I knew how to walk not so badly, they took me to a place in the high mountains and taught me and some other children how to walk. The other children taunted me because I didn't know how to walk properly. I used to walk with crooked legs: my feet were twisted backwards. The children hit me and did what they liked with me. The teachers didn't protect me, so they taunted me.

So passed a whole month. One day they heard a ring on the telephone. This was a woman who had known my father. She wanted to take me away to her house; but this was not allowed as they were afraid that something might happen to my legs. Only after some time did they send me there. She was already waiting for me. She was pleased at my arrival—hale and well—and she took me to her house. There I spent some time. And on one occasion my father's best friend came and took me to *his* house and, later, he took me to a children's home. There I had a good time. Once, three acquaintances of my father's came and told me things and gave candy to the children who were in the room. They told me that I was already a big boy and that I couldn't stay any longer in this [children's] home. And the three men took me and put me in the [youth] movement and I was there for a number of months. And the friend who was in the Polish Army thought of taking me away from there and took me for a day. And when he saw that there wasn't any other place, he went with me to one of the nearby places and said to me, "Go and tell the headmistress that I'll come back in the afternoon and talk with her." And I went and told her that, and the headmistress said "Get out of here!" and chased me away with insolence. So I went to the market. There I met my acquaintance and told him about it. And he said, "Well then, come now," and we went.

When we came she didn't want to receive him and didn't open the gate. So he told her that he'd put me into a rival [youth] movement. She screamed and shouted but nothing was of any use. For we had already got into a train; so we traveled along and came to the railway station. There we found a certain woman who was traveling to one of the places from which it was possible to go where I had to go. This was a children's village in Poland. The place was lovely.

There were woods and hills nearby: on one hill was a cemetery. And the time passed pleasantly.

I was there a long time. There the children didn't tease me as they used to in the previous children's home. Now I already knew how to walk. One day they asked which were the orphan children. I was among those children. Everyone wanted to know why they asked us this. Eventually we learned that we were going to be the first to go to Palestine. We were extremely glad. The children danced and sang. The next day all us orphan children got into a car and we rode to the railway station. We traveled in two groups to one of the places in Poland. Here something strange happened. We waited all night and the car didn't turn up. Next day, everyone was in a state of confusion. The day after that, they fetched the group that had traveled with us and told us to wait another couple of days. At the end of these two days a car came and fetched us. We traveled for many hours; and meanwhile I slept. Eventually we arrived. I heard shouts. There a small ship awaited us—I should rather say a large boat—and they put us all into it and we started off. And the boat rocked on the surface of the quiet waves. All of a sudden the boat heeled over to one side. All the things on the top fell off but by a miracle we were saved. There was a certain soldier there from the Russian Army. He knew what to do in moments like this. And the day passed and it grew darker, until night fell. We were sleeping and the soldier couldn't sleep and went up on top and suddenly he saw something shining in the water. He pulled out his revolver and took his torch and looked and saw and behold there were mines in an enormous line! In that instant he let out a yell. At the sound of that shout we all woke up. The pilot wanted to take the boat on a detour around Berlin and thus was about to run into the mines. But the man with his revolver in his hand leapt straight down into the engine room. He broke through the hatch and jumped on top of the pilot. The pilot started back and thought—bandits! He sat himself down in front of the soldier and steered the boat over many, many kilometers to Berlin.

We were unhappy. I and several other of the children had some disease. We had to be in the hospital. The remaining children went to a school, played and jumped for joy and we stayed all the time in hospital for many days. This continued, and after these sad days we left the hospital. At that time all the children had gone to school, and when they came back we weren't allowed to go into their rooms: not only that, we were shut up in a special room. After three to four days we were allowed out with the other children. What a lot of games there were there! Endless! Many political parties too! There we used to go almost always to the movies. And during the performances, the Jews all used to cry. Even the grown-ups used to hide their faces in their coats.

It was clear that each youth movement hated the other. Occasionally a fight broke out with knives and sticks. They used to hand out terrible punishments there: for example, spending the whole night out on the balcony. After days of punishments and beatings for every little thing we left Berlin and came to a terrible place where every blow ended in a battle with knives and sticks as if they were gloves. In the end, when they saw that our movement was the quietest of the lot, they gave us a place that really took the prize for beauty—woods where there were terrible wild beasts. There each group was in its own house and they used to beat us for every stupid little attack on the other groups. The names of the groups were Trumpeldor, Nitzanim, Bar Kochba, Nishrim, Ariye. I was in the Trumpeldor group.

One fine day all us orphans set out for Palestine. They told us many tales then—endlessly. They woke us up at midnight and the car came in the morning. The car was like the chrysalis of a butterfly. Eventually we arrived at one of the camps. The next day we traveled and went on and on without end. But I remember that finally we came by train to France. I don't remember the journey. It was for three days and three nights. And from France we went on board a ship and on the ship no one suffered from seasickness. And when we came to Palestine we were obliged every one of us to hold on to all the bits of paper, even to the numbers of our rooms. One of our group was a boy—Isaiah Zelik—and he put all his papers on one of the benches, and if it hadn't been for one of our teachers, Moshe, he would have gone back to Germany.

How excited we were when at last we were assembled on parade and disembarked from the ship! And we came to Ahuza—the children's village on Mount Carmel and from there to the children's village at Hadassim. And after some time more children arrived.

One day I received a letter from one of the women in Canada:

Dear Ephraim,
    I found your name in the Jewish Emigration Department

and I want to know who you are. You bear the same family name as I do. Where do you come from and who were your parents? Write everything that you can remember and thus we can prove whether you are of my family. Do you remember the name of your grandfather? Write to me all you can remember. If you are one of my relatives, I will write to you about myself. Write quickly.

Yours, Sarah.

At that time, I was given a piece of paper and this was written on it:

Women's International Zionist Organization, Children's Village, Hadassim. 21st. January 1949

To the Director General of the American Jewish Joint Distribution Committee
P.O.B. 640, Jerusalem
Subject: The Child Ephraim Shtenkler

Sir,

In reply to your letter No. 18871/40/1 of 22/12/18 we have to give you particulars of the above-mentioned child and of his family. The child's name is Ephraim Shtenkler, born in Bialisk. Father's name Jacob: mother's name Bilha. Only child. The child is ten and a half years old. He was in the hands of Poles in Zvirdje from the age of two to the age of seven. After the Russian occupation, a certain Jew came and took him and put him in a children's home. The name of his father and mother he learned from a friend of his father's in the Polish Army. These are the details known to the child. We shall be very grateful if you will be good enough to inform us if nevertheless any of the child's relatives are traced.

Yours faithfully
The Secretariat
The Children's Village.

About a month after that letter came, I found my uncle. How delighted the whole village was!

But everyone tells the story differently. One says that my uncle came to me and inquired.

Once I told several of the children all this and it was they who suggested that I should write all this down.

Dirk Van der Heide
(pseudonym)

HOLLAND ⎄ 12 YEARS OLD

*D*irk Van der Heide, a twelve-year-old blue-eyed Dutch boy with taffy-colored hair, was living in Rotterdam with his mother, father, and little sister Keetje when the blitzkrieg of 1940 began. Encouraged by his mother, he began a diary of the terror he and his sister were living through.

Shortly after the German bombardment started, Dirk's father went off to fight the Nazis in another part of Holland. Then his mother was killed in an air raid. The children's Uncle Pieter made the decision to try to transport Dirk and Keetje to safety in England. Despite tremendous odds, he was able to drive them from Rotterdam to the coast of Holland, where he secured passage for all of them on a boat to England.

The safety they gained by risking their lives at sea was all too brief. The bombing of London began just as they arrived *there and the children had to be evacuated once again. Dodging German submarines and mine fields, a "children's ship" took them to America.*

Dirk used the time on the boat to rewrite and add to the diary he had kept of the nightmare he and his sister had experienced in Holland. It was translated and published in London and New York, in 1941, when Dirk was only thirteen years old. All of the names in the book, including the author's, were changed, presumably because the war was not over and the risk of Nazi persecution continued.

Friday, May 10, 1940
Something terrible happened last night. War began!!! Uncle Pieter was *right*. The city has been *bombed* all day. Am writing this in the Baron's air-raid shelter. There are not many air-raid shelters here but the Baron and Father and Mevrouw Klaes had this one built for us and all our neighbors said it was a waste of money. This has been a terrible day and everything is upset and people are very sad and excited. This is what happened. Before daylight I woke up and for several minutes did not know what had happened. I could hear explosions and people were shouting under our windows. Mother came running in in her nightie and dressing gown and told me to get my coat on and come quickly. On the way downstairs she told me there was bombing going on but no one knew yet what it meant but she supposed it was war all right. The noise seemed very near. Father had Keetje in his arms and we hurried across the street to the Baron's and went down into his air-raid shelter.

Father pointed toward the city and Mother nodded. There were great flames shooting up into the sky and beams of light from the searchlights and the sirens were going very loud. They are on the tops of buildings and have things on them to make them very loud. We could see bullets going up from our guns. The Baron's air-raid shelter was full of people, all our neighbors and some people I didn't know. They were all talking loudly and no one was dressed, just coats over their nightclothes. Keetje began to cry and Father whispered something to her and kissed her and she stopped. Finally she went to sleep in his arms. We waited about two hours. At first most people thought the noise was only practice. All the time people kept running outside and coming back with news. It was war all right and the radio was giving the alarm and calling all the time for all men in the reserves to report for duty at the nearest place. The radio said this over and over. It was very exciting. The bombing kept on all the time, boom—boom-boom, and everyone said they were falling on Waalhaven, the air-port, which is only about five miles away. The Baron went upstairs and began telephoning. The voices on the radio sounded strange and terribly excited. Father put Keetje into Mother's arms and went away. A few minutes later he came back dressed and carrying a gas mask and a knapsack. He kissed Mother and Keetje and me very hard and then hurried out. He shouted back something about taking care of his animals and Mother nodded and told him to be careful, *please.*

All afternoon we waited around not doing much but listening to the grown-ups talk and listening to the radio. People are all very kind to each other and friendly, even the ones who don't speak to each other usually. By five o'clock half of the fifty people at the Baron's house had gone home or run away in their cars to the country or somewhere. Anyway they were not around.

We got up a game with several other children playing soldiers and bombers. We took turns jumping off the high back steps holding umbrellas and pretending we were parachutists but we had to quit this because the grown-ups said it made them nervous. Just as it was getting dark the bombing started again. Mother came home on a bicycle which was not hers. She had taken the car in the morning but she said the roads were being barricaded and it was quicker to come by bicycle. We asked her many questions but she didn't talk much. She looked tired and white faced when she came into the air-shelter. The Baron and neighbors have brought in many cots and mattresses and a small electric stove on which coffee urns stand. It is damp and uncomfortable in the small shelter with so many people. It was all right this morning but it is not pleasant as time goes by. There are four old sick people near the stove but I don't know any of them. The old sick people keep their eyes closed most of the time. Once in a while someone speaks to them and pulls the blankets up when they slip down. They are very silent and tired and dead looking.

LATER

The air-raid that came this time lasted 30 minutes. It was no better than the others but no worse. The Baron brought down a Victrola and turned it on full blast to try to shut out the noise outside. Some of the music was German music, Mother said. How could it be from the same race who were attacking us she asked. The radio was off during the raid but it started up soon afterwards. The Premier of Holland, Dirk Jan de Geer, spoke and said for us to be confident because the Allies would help us and that hundreds of troops had been landed at Hoogezwaluwe, the big bridge which is between north and south Holland. When he finished, the radio said the landing field at Schiphol airdrome had been destroyed. Everyone was sad about this for it is our largest field. Had supper at the Baron's and settled down for the evening. All the lights have gone out upstairs and we are burning candles and lanterns down in the air-shelter.

Mother called the hospital after the last raid and Uncle Pieter but Uncle Pieter's hotel didn't answer. It is very hard to get anyone on the telephone. Everyone is calling everyone else after the raids are over to see if they are safe. The telephones are off during the raids. I hope Uncle Pieter is safe and Father too. Mother thinks Father has gone east to Maastricht and that's where the fighting is thickest the radio says though the bombing is bad everywhere.

Saturday, May 11, 1940

The worst air-raid of all has just come. About half the houses on our street are gone. One bomb landed on the lawn by our air-shelter and one side of the shelter is caved in but the Baron and others are repairing it now. Mevrouw Hartog broke down and cried during the air-raid and got everyone very nervous when she yelled. I think she almost went crazy.

Heintje Klaes was killed! He went outside to see the light from the big flares and incendiary bombs and didn't come back. He slipped out. Heintje was not afraid of anything but the bombs got him. The whole house rocked when the bombs came close. We put our fingers in our ears but it didn't help much. The fire wagons are working outside now and half the people in the air-shelter including Uncle Pieter have gone out. I went out for a while and they were taking dead people out of the bombed houses. Uncle Pieter sent me back to stay with Keetje. There is a funny smell in the air like burnt meat and a funny yellow light all over the country from the incendiary bombs. Three men were killed trying to get a bomb away that hadn't gone off yet. One of the men was our postmaster and I loved him very much. He gave me my first bicycle ride. It is awful to watch the people standing by their bombed houses. They don't do much. They just walk around and look at them and look sad and tired. I guess there isn't anything else they can do, but it seems awful.

Our house wasn't hit but the street in front of it between our house and the Baron's is just a great big hole and all the cobblestones are thrown up on our lawn and the Baron's until it doesn't look as if there ever was a street there. Mother is going to be surprised when she sees it. The street was just made over last year and was very smooth and nice.

At the end of our street the water is coming in where the canal locks were hit and I guess it will just keep running over the land until it is fixed. No one does anything about it because there are too many people to be helped and fires to fight. Twelve people on our street were killed and I knew every one of them but I knew Heintje best. Mevrouw Klaes has been crying ever since the bombing. Some people prayed all the time and some sang the national anthem and some just sat and stared. A woman who is very sick with a bad heart looked as if she might die. She was very pale when she came and still is.

I said a prayer to myself for Father and I hope God heard

it in spite of all the noise. I told Uncle Pieter I had prayed
but he didn't say anything, just laid his hand on my shoulder. Uncle Pieter has gone off to the hospital to try to find
Mother. It is getting late and he is worried I think. I know
he will find her. Keetje has gone to sleep again but she talks
in her sleep and wakes up all the time, asking if the war is
over and things like that. Poor Keetje, she is so little and
doesn't know what is happening. I think I do and it is worse
than anything I ever heard about and worse than the worst
fight in the cinema. The ambulances coming and going and
so many dead people make it hard for me not to cry. I did
cry some while the bombing was going on but so many other
little children were that no one noticed me I think. I just got
into bed with Keetje and hid my face. I was really frightened
this time.

LATER

Uncle Pieter came back. He didn't find Mother because
she is dead. I can't believe it but Uncle Pieter wouldn't lie.
We aren't going to tell Keetje yet. The ambulances are still
screaming. I can't sleep or write any more now or anything.

Sunday, May 12, 1940

I am writing this in the morning as Keetje and I wait for
Uncle Pieter. He is taking us to Dordrecht and then to Zeeland if we can get there. I can't believe Mother is dead and
that we will never see her again. Mother was killed when
the hospital was bombed. I cried almost all night and I am
ashamed of what I did in front of everybody. I tried to run
away from Uncle Pieter after he told me about Mother getting killed. I tried to get out in the street to fight the Germans.

I don't know what all I did. I was crazy. I was all right until the bombs started to fall around midnight and then I couldn't stand it. I know I yelled and kicked and bit Uncle Pieter in the hand but I don't know why. I think I was crazy. I went to sleep later but I don't know what time it was.

Today I am tired but everyone is so kind.

Monday, May 13, 1940

The fires on the street are not all out yet. The air is still full of smoke and now the house is smoky inside. No one is talking very much today. Two of the old people died last night during the bombing. They were not hit by bombs. They just died. I heard the Baron say it's just as well. The Baron is sad today and his face, which is usually red and jolly, looks white and he has great dark circles under his eyes. The radio this morning says the Germans have come far into Holland and they are getting most of the bridges that aren't blown up. I don't know how Uncle Pieter expects us to get to Zeeland. No one understands why Holland is losing the war so easily. The first day people said we could hold out until the French and English would come. The Germans are using many new tricks, I think. A man came in this morning and said the Germans had taken one of our forts in the east by using a new kind of gas that makes the Dutch soldiers numb. Someone else said, Mijnheer van Helst, I think, that the Germans have a bomb so big that it tears up a whole city block at one time. He said the Germans have a fire thrower now that shoots out a long line of fire for a great distance. Almost everyone seems to think that the new kinds of guns and things the Germans have are the cause of all the trouble, but Uncle Pieter doesn't think so. He says they just have more of everything, that's all. Our defenses are fine he says except we didn't have enough anti-aircraft guns or planes. We are like every other country the Germans have beaten he says. We weren't expecting the war from the air or parachutists or tricks like that. Brenda has just come in with our traveling bags. We have to wait for Uncle Pieter. Brenda brought Dopfer, Keetje's big doll. Dopfer is very big and Keetje shouldn't try to take him but she wants to. She has been asking Brenda when Mother is coming, and is Mother going with us.

About three o'clock some German planes came over. They were seaplanes going toward Dordrecht. They dropped no bombs but five of them dived down toward the road until we thought they were falling and then they shot at us with machine guns. We all got under the car and many people crawled in beside us. Other people threw themselves on the ground and dived into the roadside ditches for protection. The soldiers tried to shoot the pilots with their rifles. The planes kept going back and forth above us very low and loud and then suddenly they went away south. There was great confusion after they left. Several people were hit. One woman in front of us, a young woman, sat by the roadside holding her head and groaning. There was blood coming out of her head and a hole in the side. It made me sick. About fifty people were wounded and many were killed. Uncle Pieter helped the wounded all he could and then we hurried away. All the way down the road we saw wounded people and people just lying still in the road.

Once Uncle Pieter had to get out and move three bodies to the side to get by. It was awful. Many children were crying. People were trying to be brave and pretend nothing had happened but they were all very sad and angry. The Germans are cowards to shoot people who have no guns. When they drop bombs they don't know where they go but they just came down on the road and shot at us today. I hope those Germans in those planes fall out of the sky and never get home and are killed. There are no towns along the Dordrecht-Rotterdam highway for the poor wounded people to get to. Nothing more happened until we got near Dordrecht and then we heard firing again. We were stopped and had our papers looked at and told not to go into the city but to go around it as there was fighting in the center of the city because of the Dordrecht bridges and the parachutists who were there.

Tuesday, May 14, 1940

Uncle Pieter must have been very clever to get us on the boat with so many trying to get on. We have been on the boat an hour but it hasn't left yet. It is late at night. There are no lights on the outside of the boat but inside there is some light but the portholes are covered. The boat has started and I wish I could go out on deck. But this is not permitted.

LATER

The boat slipped along in the darkness and we could hardly see a thing through the cabin windows. There is not a single light in Vlissingen because of the bombers. I wonder if the little boy and girl we left at the café in Dordrecht are all right now. I hope so. I feel very sorry for them. There are many people on the boat. No one talks, for it is against the rules. There are no beds for us and we have to sit up but

Uncle Pieter has taken Keetje up in his arms and she is asleep now.

LATER

I've been asleep for several hours. I woke up a little while ago. I had a terrible nightmare about bombing and I thought a bomber was chasing me and Keetje around and around the canals and we were on ice-skates and kept slipping and falling and couldn't get away. The nightmare was terrible. I was cold when I woke up and Uncle Pieter wrapped his big coat around me. We are sailing on.

LATER

The boat has been tossing around a great deal. I asked Uncle Pieter how long it will take to get to England. He says a good while because we have to go back and forth zigzag to get through the mine fields in the water. I am scared we might hit one and sink. I can't swim very well and Keetje can't swim more than ten strokes without puffing. Uncle Pieter says not to think about it. I try not to but I keep thinking about it. I was very frightened when I heard a loud explosion ahead of us some time later. Our boat slowed down after that. I thought the bombers had come again but there was nothing in the sky. The boat's searchlights went on for a few seconds but I couldn't see what had happened. We found out a few minutes later. The boat ahead of us had struck a mine and been blown up. Our boat tried to pick up a few people from the water and did pick up some but not many. The Captain of the boat tried to find the others but he couldn't find many because he didn't want to have the lights on. I hate to think of all the people out there swimming

43

in the cold sea while we are going on to England. I hope they don't all drown. This war is terrible. It kills just about everybody. I'm glad we're going to England where it will be quiet. I hope the Germans don't come there the way they did in Holland. I don't feel very well tonight. I have a bad headache and my stomach feels funny. Maybe I am going to be seasick but I think it's just from the bombing and everything. I forgot to say how nice Keetje was before we left Dordrecht. She gave her big doll, Dopfer, to the little girl. Keetje was nice to do this. She is often very selfish but she was good to do this. It seems funny to be out here on our way to England. I have always wanted to go to England but I never thought I would go so soon. I pray God will keep our Father safe. We could not bear to lose Father after what happened to Mother. Uncle Pieter is very good to take care of us while Father is away fighting the Germans.

Wednesday, May 15, 1940

We have been in England all morning. It was daylight almost when our boat got in. We landed at a place called Harwich. Everyone cheered and sang when we came into the harbor safely. We took the train to London, which took about three hours, and went to a place in the station where refugees have to go. There were many English people there to give us breakfast and to help us. They were all very cheerful and smiling.

Some of the refugees looked ill and very unhappy and lost. There were children there without any parents or relatives or friends. Some of the children were French and Belgian. There were several English doctors there and some of them spoke Dutch. They were helping to fix wounded people. Uncle Pieter has taken us to a hotel near the station. I am writing this in the hotel. Uncle Pieter says most of the Dutch and Belgian and French refugees are going to the country away from London so that if the bombs come again they will be safe. They will go to Ireland and Yorkshire and the Isle of Man and places like that where I have never been.

LATER

Uncle Pieter has just come back with terrible news. Holland has surrendered to the Germans. It is all in the newspapers. Uncle Pieter is almost crying. Ever since he came in he has been drinking and smoking and walking up and down. He says the fall of Holland threatens England and we must go to America if we can get a boat. Queen Wilhelmina, the paper says, is going to speak over the radio but we have no radio and cannot hear her. Uncle Pieter says maybe he won't be able to get back to Holland or find out any news of anything. I wonder where Father is. I hope he is all right and safe and can go back to doctoring his animals. I just asked Uncle Pieter if we couldn't go back now that the war is over and he said never, never could we go back there while the Germans were there. He says it is worse than death for Hollanders to live as slaves. I hope the Germans don't make a slave out of Father. I don't think they could. Father gets very angry and he would not stand for it.

Keetje is feeling very tired and ill. Uncle Pieter is having some food sent up to her, some warm milk and toast and eggs. I am having roast beef and pudding here with Keetje and Uncle Pieter is going to eat later. We haven't seen much of London yet and we have to stay inside tomorrow and rest. This is a very large room with high ceilings. Keetje and I stay in here and Uncle Pieter stays beyond the double doors. We have a private bath and it is very nice and quiet. The windows are all covered with thick cloth because it is after dark and no light must be shown because of the Germans. Keetje says she hopes there won't be any noise tonight and that the Germans had better not come to London.

Monday, July 1, 1940

We have been in England many weeks. Now we are in Liverpool waiting for a boat to America. Uncle Pieter has heard from Uncle Klaas in America and he wants Keetje and me to come. Uncle Klaas had to cable the American Consul and his bankers in America had to do the same thing. Uncle Pieter had to get visas and things and all kinds of papers and pay a great deal of money, I think. A great fuss. We are having much fun in England but we miss Holland. Keetje was ill for a week in the hotel in London. A doctor came to see her and said she was nervous. He gave her some medicine. He was very kind. He wouldn't let Uncle Pieter pay him anything. He said it was his pleasure and his gift to gallant Holland. Uncle Pieter argued with him but the kind doctor said no. Uncle Pieter says the English are just that way and good enough people when you know them.

Dear Uncle Pieter. He is so sad about Holland and so good to us. We have done so many things. In London he took us everywhere. The policemen—*bobbies* they are called!—are very funny and big and polite. We asked them many questions on walks when we got lost. We used to take taxis everywhere but now we use the little trams. All over London there are many things for war. Sand-bags everywhere. They were banked around the British Museum the day we went. The

Museum has big pillars outside and many heavy doors before you get inside. Uncle Pieter was surprised to see so many people inside reading while there is a war on. There are many trenches everywhere and sand-bags at St. Paul's, a big church. In the gardens at Kensington there were many flowers but trenches too.

There are big black and white posters everywhere with ARP printed on them. This means Air Raid Precautions. People all carry gas-masks and we have them now. They were fitted on us by a nice woman in London. The gas masks have long snouts and look as funny as the Dutch ones. They have straps to hold them on. We must never carry them by the straps because they stretch and might let the gas in. That's what the woman said who gave them to us. Uncle Pieter put his on yesterday for the first time and looked at himself. He said he looked no better at all with it than without it. I laughed and he laughed too. I was glad to see him laugh for he has been so sad since he found out that one-fourth of our army was killed. When he reads the newspapers about the war he gets sadder and sadder. We haven't heard from Father.

When Belgium fell Uncle Pieter was almost sick. I saw a funny dog today. It was an English sheepdog, Uncle Pieter said. Keetje thought it was a bear that had escaped from the zoo. Keetje asked if the animals had gas masks too and Uncle Pieter said no. It is a shame they don't have. We had tea at the zoo with bread and butter and strawberry jam. I tasted Keetje's milk and it was good but not so good as the milk from the Baron's cows.

There are no street lights in England after dark. We are getting very tired of the dark but not as tired as we were.

We have only been out once late at night. We were in a taxi with Uncle Pieter coming home from the Mickey Mouse cinema. There are no crossing lights except little shaded crosses no bigger than a button. It is very exciting going along in the dark. In the daylight we have gone into the country. The roads are all fixed to stop the Germans. There are many barricades and trenches and tank traps. We have seen many lorries in the streets with big searchlights and guns and soldiers.

Uncle Pieter has just come in with news. He says I must stop writing now. He has just had news from the ticket office that we have a passage and will leave sometime soon. He says he cannot go to see us off as it is against the rules because of the war. The ticket man is sending someone for us. I asked him the name of the boat and he said he didn't know that either because the ticket office couldn't let any secrets out because of the Germans. I must stop and help Keetje and Uncle Pieter pack. I hate to leave England. I have had a good time here and I hope the Germans never do to England what they did to Holland. Good-by, England. We have to leave you just as we were beginning to love you. I suppose we will have to get used to having new homes since we can't go back to our own dear home in Holland.

Wednesday, July 3, 1940

We are on the boat now. We sailed yesterday sometime after dark. We had to wait many hours on the dock with the ticket man who told us animal stories. It was hard to leave Uncle Pieter. He kissed us many times and hugged us hard. He is going to let us know about Father if he gets back to Holland. Uncle Klaas will meet us in New York. We are on a big boat and there are many other children going to America. There are so many people going away because of the war that some of them have to sleep in bunks in the smoking rooms and halls. Everything is very strict on this English boat. Before we sailed a sailor told us what we could do and what we couldn't. We are not allowed on deck after the trumpet sounds in the evening. All the portholes are fastened tight and can't be opened. They are covered with thick cloths to blot out the light. The ship doesn't even have lights on it to see by at night because of the submarines. The English sailor said no one could smoke on deck at night. A lighted cigarette can be seen two miles at sea, he says. If anyone disobeys he will be severely punished and put in a room and locked up for the rest of the trip.

There are double doors at the dining salon and we go in on the side so the lights don't show. There are many ships sailing beside us. We counted twenty. Six carry passengers and the rest are going along to keep the submarines away. There are torpedo boats, warships, and one airplane carrier. They keep very near us all the time and we wave back and forth. The boats are all painted gray so they will be hard to see in the water. Everyone is afraid of the German submarines. The English Captain says for me not to worry because anyone who was born around as much water as we have in Holland just couldn't be drowned. He is a nice man and is always making jokes. There are two other Dutch children on the boat. They came from The Hague. Their father is working for the government. We speak Dutch together just to rest our tongues. We practice *J*'s and *th*'s on each other. Keetje has been seasick ever since we left but the Captain says she will be better when we get away from Ireland. He says he will be too because most of the submarines stay around here.

I have never been on such a big boat. I have been on many boats on canals but this one is like the Adelphi Hotel in Liverpool only it wobbles. A man was caught smoking a cigarette today and put into a room and locked up just as the sailor said he would be. Many boys in Holland smoke at my age but I do not. There goes the bell for dinner and I am very hungry, and Keetje is pulling at my sleeve. She feels like eating tonight.

Saturday, September 28, 1940

I have not written in my diary for so long. Not since I got to America. Uncle Klaas and Aunt Helen met us. Aunt Helen is an American with long red fingernails and a very pretty face. Our boat came in to New York at night on the tenth day after we left England. We came slowly because our boat had to take a longer way because of the war. We stayed all night in the harbor. We thought New York looked very exciting in the distance. There were so many lights and they were all on. All during the time we were in England there had never been any lights at night in the streets. It looked fine to see so many all going at once with so many colors. Uncle Klaas took us off the boat the next morning without waiting. Some of the children who were ill had to be taken off the boat somewhere else and some had gone to a place called Ellis Island.

When we got through the customs we drove to Uncle Klaas's apartment on Morningside Heights. The streets were very exciting. I remember particularly when we crossed one and Uncle Klaas said this is Broadway. I came over here just to show you, he said. Aunt Helen said it is prettier at night. Uncle Klaas has a beautiful apartment that is very near the river. Maybe he took it because he is Dutch and always wants to be near some water.

We have been in America several weeks now. Keetje and I go to a private school. We like it very much although it was strange at first. There were many new words and studies, but not so many languages to learn as in Holland. I am learning to play football and other sports. Keetje likes the movies and the drugstore sodas best. Keetje seems very happy. Sometimes I think she has forgotten about Mother entirely. But I haven't. Everyone is very kind to us and I have been made a monitor at school. School hours are shorter in America. My English has improved and I have learned many new words that I never heard in England and some not in my dictionary.

Several letters have come from England from Uncle Pieter. He has not been able to get back to Holland. He is working for the English now and is a volunteer fire warden. Uncle Pieter says he misses us. He has had one letter from Father and we have had one. Father is safe and back in Rotterdam. The letter we got from him had a Swiss stamp. It must not have been seen by the Germans, Uncle Klaas says. Father tells about what Holland is like now. There is not much food and many things like coffee and cocoa cannot be bought. The Germans have done many things. They have changed the names of the Royal Museum and anything with the word "royal" in it to National. No taxis are running. None of the Dutch can listen on the radio to anything but Spanish, Italian and German programs without being fined 10,000 guilders and two years in prison. People have to stay home after 10 o'clock at night. The food is getting worse and worse. Father said not to worry, he would pull through. He wants to come to America. I wish he could and so does Keetje. We write to him often but we don't know whether he gets our letters. I will be so glad when the war is over.

Keetje and I are happy here and everything would be perfect if Father and Grandfather and Grandmother were here and of course Uncle Pieter. I haven't had very good marks at school. The doctor says I am nervous and can't concentrate very well yet because of the bombing but that I will be all right later. The American doctor was just like the English one Uncle Pieter had for Keetje. He wouldn't charge any money for taking care of me. He said, *this is on me,* which is slang but very kind. I think he is a good doctor for I know I *am* nervous sometimes.

Sometimes when airplanes go over I want to run and hide. One night when it was raining I woke up and heard the rain on the glass and was frightened. I thought I was back in Holland and that what was striking the windows were pieces of bombs. That is why Uncle Klaas doesn't like it when people ask me about the war. When he saw the theme I was trying to write in English for my English class about the war in Holland he was angry. I heard him tell Aunt Helen that he thought it was dreadful and that he wanted Keetje and me to forget about the war. But I know I'll never forget about it anyway, or forget the Germans and how Mother died. I won't forget America either. It is a good country that has made us feel welcome. Keetje is looking over my shoulder as I write this and says why don't you say it's "swell," that's an American word.

I know one reason why I'll always love America. It's because of something that happened on the boat trip here.

When we were one day away from New York all the battle-ships and boats that had brought us over so safely turned around and went back toward England. We were all alone and very frightened. I was frightened because I don't swim very well and Keetje can only do ten strokes and they don't get her very far. When the boats all turned back we could see how frightened everyone was. That's what made us frightened. We weren't frightened before. But then someone started yelling and pointing at the sky. There was a big zep-pelin over us. It said United States Naval Patrol Number 14 in big letters. We all yelled and cheered. I won't ever forget that number 14, and the nice safe way it made us feel. The zeppelin followed us and watched over us all the rest of the way to America. And people have been watching over us ever since and there haven't been any bombings. Not one. And that is why Keetje and I are happy now.

Werner Galnik

GERMANY ∞ 12 YEARS OLD

Werner Galnik was eight years old when he and his family were deported from Germany to the Riga Ghetto, in Latvia, in 1941. His account of what happened to him there, and then later in two concentration camps near Danzig, is not, strictly speaking, a diary. There are no individually dated entries and it appears that he waited until his liberation from the Nazis, in 1945, to write about the horrors he had endured in the ghetto and the camps. Of all his family, only he and his brother are known to have survived. His mother was never accounted for.

What follows is the entire, unedited English translation of Werner's writing as it appeared in the magazine Jewish Life in April of 1947.

I came to the Riga ghetto on December 12, 1941. Our family was made up of five persons: my father, my mother, my brother and I, and my sister.

My father, Schmuel, is 48 years old, his trade is tailor. My mother, Irma—39 years, by trade a saleslady. My brother Horst, 11 years, is a student, and I, Werner, 8 years old—a student; my sister, Vera, is four years old.

We had lived in seven rooms: the tailor shop, fitting room, office, kitchen, bedroom, dining room and maid's room. Suddenly we received notice from the Jewish community in Cassell that we must appear on December 8, 1941 at the depot where thousands of Jews had already collected, men, women and children.

My aunt, Bertha Klurman, thirty-four years old—she was a milliner—my cousin, nine years old, a student, were also at the depot. There were also my playmates, boys and girls of my age.

I had already heard about a ghetto in Lodz several months before. I thought that we would also have to go into such a ghetto where there are barracks and where we would have to work.

I figured this way: Hitler loves only the Germans, but no other people, and particularly not us Jews. Does it follow that because we are Jews we must be prisoners? Did my father perhaps steal or murder that he should be arrested?

And what had my dear mother done? And what did we children do?

On December 9, when we went to the railroad station under guard, I was very despondent. We were crowded together. Many Jews wept, especially those who had left their sick relatives in Cassell. I also cried: Why should not the old people go along with their near ones?

On the trip to Riga there was very little water. We were very thirsty. When we stopped at a station all the Jews ran to bring some water. But the German police came and beat and drove us back.

When we arrived in Riga we were told that whoever had money or gold must give them up. Otherwise they would be shot. The money and the gold was given up. The heavy baggage, in the baggage cars, was also taken away. Only the light baggage we had with us we could take along to the ghetto.

We arrived in the ghetto under guard.

We had one room—filthy, and the kitchen was also—filthy. They had been left by Jews who had gone in a German roundup. We cleaned the two rooms and lived there.

My father went to work every day and I went to school every day. My little sister went to a kindergarten in the ghetto, and my brother studied barbering in the ghetto.

The Latvian Jews told us that there had already been a roundup in the ghetto. But I could not believe it until I lived through it myself.

The SS often beat or shot any one who brought bread, butter or other food home from work. If it was discovered, the person was either shot, placed in confinement or punished with blows.

When we were freed, I also saw the Hanover, and Vienna bunkers.

If anyone exchanged something at work or ran away from the ghetto, he was either hung or shot. One Jew was hung because he ran away from the concentration camp in the ghetto to his relatives. He hung for three days, and every Jew in the ghetto had to look at him. He was hung under the supervision of SS Officer Kreuze, and his dog also was around. The Jew was big, his hair black, his hands bound behind his back, his tongue hanging out, his head on a side. In this way he hung for three days, beginning to stink. In the evening when Jews came from work, they had to march by the hanging man, and the commandant pointed to him and said, "This is what will happen to every Jew who tries to run away from us."

On November 2, 1943, my father started to go to work. But he returned home and said, "The air is very heavy in the ghetto today. There are many autos and SS higher-ups near the commandant. I'm afraid there's going to be a roundup in the ghetto. . . ."

My sister and mother hid in the cellar. My father, I and my brother waited near the door of our house. Suddenly five autos with SS troopers arrived. They went around the ghetto chasing every Jew. At the assembly point the commandant stood by. Every Jew, man, woman and child, passed him. Every Jew was studied: the old, the weak and the children went in the roundup. My aunt and her child also went in the roundup. Young people, who did not go in the roundup, went to the central work room and after that were sent home. My father and I and my brother, when we saw the SS come, hid in the cellar. My brother was found by an SS trooper and was taken to the assembly. He came before the commandant and said, "I am eighteen years old."

"What do you do?" the commandant asked.

"I am a barber."

The commandant said, "Right, with those able to work."

My father, I, my sister and my mother were in the cellar a day and a night. It was very dark. We heard in the cellar, how the SS cried, "Get out, you Jews. Out to the assembly!"

I lay on the straw and wanted to fall asleep, so that I would not hear the commotion. But I was afraid. This was the first night in my life that I could not sleep. The night dragged on so that I thought it would never end.

My brother returned home and said, "Come out, the roundup is over." I thought: the roundup is really ended. But the night I had just lived through was not over. I cannot forget that Jews were shot for nothing. . . . They went under guard to the cemetery and there were forced to stand, face to the wall, and from a distance of ten feet the commandant shot—that I will never forget.

In February 1942, there was another roundup in the ghetto. The Jews were told that volunteers would be sent to the fish works in Dinamunde. But they were not sent to the fish works. They were shot. It was very terrible, because no one knew whether to volunteer to go, or remain.

The ghetto was liquidated in November 1943, and we were sent to the Obea work camp. There my father worked on the docks and my mother in a laundry. And I and my brother dragged wheelbarrows. The work of us children was very hard. Our marking in the camp was a star of David and convict number 13,228.

On April 22, 1944 all the small children under ten, who

could not work, were taken away in an auto and were sent to Auschwitz. There they were gassed and burned.

I came home from work and looked for my sister, but she was no longer there. My father and I and my brother and mother cried for days.

I thought: why shouldn't my little sister live? My little sister was seven years old when she went away in the children's roundup. My little sister was a beautiful little girl. She had beautiful blond hair. It is a pity that I no longer have a picture of my little sister. All the pictures of my father and mother were taken away.

If someone brought food—butter or bread—from the work gang, and the camp leader, non-com Miller, got wind of it, that person would receive 25 blows with a rubber hose, on his buttocks and was obliged, in addition, to work hard and sleep that night in the cellar. People were punished for nothing. The body of the one who was punished was black and blue.

One day, August 5, 1944, when all the people returned from work, he ordered all men to present themselves. That meant another roundup was taking place. The roundup was ordered by SS Leader Dr. Krebsbach.

All the men had to undress completely and he examined each one of them thoroughly. Old people, sick Jews with ruptures, and those who wore glasses, were taken away in the roundup.

At the moment when he examined me I was very frightened. I thought he would say: into the roundup! But I was strongly built, and he let me and my brother alone. When he was through with the men, he ordered the women to present themselves. The women also had to undress, and he examined every one of them. He wrote down the numbers of those who were sent away in the roundup. I was freed and so was my brother. But my mother was not yet examined. She was in the court where the examination of the strong mothers took place. The weak and older mothers were taken away in the roundup. I worried very much about my mother who was not built very strongly. It took a long time before my mother came home because she was among the last women at the roundup. But my mother presented herself with firm posture and the storm-troop leader let her go. I was very happy when I saw my mother return free from the roundup. A boy I knew, Wolfgang Katz, 14 years old, whose mother was taken in the roundup—his mother was 55 years old—wept bitterly because his mother perished, as well as his brothers and sisters.

His mother worked and always brought him something to eat from her place of work. Now he remained quite alone. A Jew, Joseph Strauss from Cassell, took care of him, and always gave him something to eat in addition to his ration.

My father was caught with a little bread and butter on the docks in December 1943; he was taken away from us and was sent to the Kaiserwald concentration camp, where he worked very hard, and we remained without our father. We wept very much because our father was no longer with us. When my father was with us no longer, my mother had to work even more, in order to be able to feed us a little—my father had done this before. After she came from work, my mother always washed clothing in the evening in order to earn an additional bit of food.

On September 25, 1944, when the Red Army was not far from Riga, the Germans sent us Jews to the Stutthof concentration camp near Danzig. On the way, on the Baltic Sea, Russian flyers came and bombed three ships: one ship with ammunition, one with supplies, and one with German soldiers. The three ships were sunk. Fortunately, they did not bomb the ship in which we Jews were.

It was very crowded on the ship. There were more than 3,000 Jews packed into the space, and there was very little air. No toilets were available. The majority of the Jews became seasick. There was an epidemic of coughing. Thirst was so great that you could choke. And if anyone wanted to get a little water for himself, he was hit over the head with a rifle butt.

When we arrived in Danzig, we were guarded at bayonet-point. Here we took a small ship to Stutthof. One hundred and fifty people were on a ship that could hold only fifty. For two days we got nothing to eat. But that was not the worst. The worst was that we all wanted water and there was nothing to drink.

Everything was taken away from us at Stutthof. We were allowed only the prison clothes we had on our backs. We had to come to assembly and be counted. Then we were shown our sleeping quarters. Four people had to sleep on a cot six feet long and 20 inches wide. I was here only with my brother. My mother was in the women's camp, and I was in the men's camp. I could see my mother only through a fence.

When I got a piece of bread for a present because I was small, I would carefully throw a piece of bread to my mother over the barbed wire. When a woman guard saw it, my mother would be hit with a belt. Once, a woman guard saw that I gave my mother a little piece of bread. My mother was terribly punished. I begged them not to hit my mother, but they hit her even more.

I did not want to part from my mother. I succeeded in becoming a furnace stoker in the same place where my mother worked in the tailor shop. The work was hard, but I was nevertheless happy because I could give my mother bread without fear of her being beaten.

Every day when I came from work tired, I still had to attend assembly for three hours. And when the assembly ended, I still had to run around to try to earn an extra piece of bread. You could not live on the ration. For a whole day you got barely two hundred grams of bread and a quart of watery soup.

We were infested with lice and many became sick with typhus from it, and the majority died. There were so many sick and dead, that no one worried about them. The sick received only half rations so that they would die sooner. So many dead were lying about that no one even bothered with them.

Late in the evening, we had to bathe under a cold shower. Here also you had to dip your clothing in disinfectant, put them on while still wet and go to work. Many became sick from this. Every day we had to get up at half past four and slave the whole day.

When the Red Army was not far from Stutthof, the Germans moved us again. My brother and I were very weak, because we had not yet recovered from the illness we had contracted. But we didn't tell anyone that we were weak. Otherwise we would have been forced to remain in Stutthof and they would have burned us.

We marched but where we did not know. I had marched

30 miles when I became weak and I remained lying at a farm. I was frozen. At the peasant's place there were British prisoners of war. They massaged me to get my hands and feet to work again.

On this march, my brother had all his fingers frostbitten.

I have never again seen my mother, because she was also taken away from Stutthof.

Then a horse and wagon were brought, and the sick and weak were taken to the camp to which we should have gone, Proist, near Danzig.

We were 14 Jewish boys of the 580 who had remained; the rest were all sent to Osweicz in October 1944. There they were gassed and cremated. We fourteen had saved ourselves because we ran into the labor colony and hid ourselves there by working. The Germans told us young boys that we were going to the fish works to clean fish. But I told myself I would rather remain here and not clean fish. This was not to clean fish. This was to burn.

Later, when all the boys had left, the commandant asked me why I did not go with the rest of the boys to clean fish in the fish works. I told him that I worked at the camp. He said to me, "Here there is work only for grown-ups." I answered him on that: "I am fifteen years old already and I am already able to work among grown-ups."

On the first day, when this happened to the boys, I was very frightened at work.

At Camp Proist near Danzig things were very bad. For a long time we did not get any bread, only soup twice a day. There was an epidemic of typhus. Many people died. Many people froze parts of their bodies at work. Jews who froze any parts of their bodies were taken in a car to Stutthof and killed there. When the Red Army encircled Danzig, the Germans could not send us away. You could hear firing very close by.

One morning when we awoke, we could not find a single SS man. We looked and we looked—but it was true. There was not a single SS man. The firing became very loud. We went down into the cellar.

On March 23, 1945 I came out of the cellar, and saw the first two Russians. I was very happy. I became a free person. I ran back and cried to the Jews, "Come, come, the Russians are here, we are free people." They all ran to the Russian soldiers and kissed them in joy.

Then we fourteen boys went to a German village. There we dressed in German clothes and took pigs and cows to eat. Then we kicked the Germans out of the court, and we boys lived there. We lived there for fourteen days. Then we left for Danzig and for a hospital, where we were cleaned and disinfected so that the sicknesses we had in camp would not spread through the hospital, where I remained for three weeks. Then I went by auto to the discharge center at Grodenz. Here I stayed for six weeks. Then I went to Riga with some Jews I knew, Glazer, Sverdlov, Gutkin and Bloch.

Now I would like to have my parents, and would like to live again like we lived before with my parents. I hope very much that my mother still lives, and that I will meet her again.

RIGA, AUGUST 26, 1945.

Janina Heshele

*J*anina Heshele was almost twelve when she began writing her diary on the day the Germans took over Lvov, the Polish city in which she lived. Soon after, her father was taken by the Nazis and never seen again. She and her mother changed their names and tried to hide from the Gestapo but they were eventually discovered and imprisoned in the Janowska death camp. Knowing the horrors that awaited her, Janina begged her mother to let her take a cyanide capsule and die. But her mother steadfastly refused to allow her to commit suicide.

Janina endured terrible conditions in Janowska, but then a miracle occurred in 1943. A group of prisoners who were extremely impressed by her writing, particularly her poetry, determined that her talent was so great that they could not allow it to be consumed in the Nazi ovens. By pooling their efforts, they were able to help her escape to the Aryan side of Cracow, where she survived the war and lived to see her diary published.

What follows are excerpts translated by Azriel Eisenberg (from a Hebrew translation of a part of Janina's diary), which appeared in his book The Lost Generation: Children in the Holocaust. *Janina's diary was originally published in Polish by one of her rescuers, Maria Hochberg Marianska, but it is so rare today that no library in the world reports having it.*

1941–1943 [Dates unknown]

On the second day of the invasion, Father and I went out to view Lvov after the enemy's bombing. The city was unrecognizable; the stores had been destroyed and plundered by the populace. The houses were decorated with blue-and-yellow flags. Automobiles and cycles ornamented with flowers rolled through the streets, their drivers and fellow travelers jubilant.

Father, sensing he was in grave danger, kissed me and said, "Yanya, you are a grown person and from now on you have to be independent, fully on your own. Do not pay attention to what others say or do. Be strong and of good courage." He kissed me again and was about to part from me when I began to grasp what would happen and started to cry. But Father declared sternly, "If you love me, leave me. Be brave. Never cry. Crying is degrading. Return home immediately and leave me here." I gave Father a last kiss. At the street corner I looked back and I saw him returning a flying kiss to me.

[Janina's father is caught in the dragnet of the doomed and

is never seen again. Janina goes underground and assumes a Polish name.]

One day a strange woman came to see me. I thought she had a message from Yadjah [a Christian friend], but she did not. She said to me, "I serve in the Gestapo. Your name is Janina Heshele but you pass as Lydia Wirischinska. If you don't bring me 5000 gulden by four o'clock, you will be sent to death at Camp Janowska." I ran to inform my uncle, and he transmitted the message to Mother. At four the woman showed up, and so did Mother. Mother knew intuitively that she was an extortionist. After a little haggling, the "lady" left with 100 gulden. [Janina and her mother go into hiding but are caught.]

We were brought to prison and pushed into a small, crowded cell where we found sixty people squatting on the floor, one on top of another. When we were thrust in, someone growled, "Oh, another herring!" Another replied, "Two in one." Mother did not let me lie on the floor, and we stood upright a full day and night.

In the morning, coffee and bread were brought in. Everyone had to pay for the food and drink. But Mother and I could not swallow our food. Even though it was the month of February, the cell was hot and stank. In the corner was a broken bucket where women and men attended to their physical needs. I had no strength to stand on my feet any longer, but Mother would not let me lie down for fear of my becoming infected with lice. I argued with her, asserting that I wished to catch typhus, for I couldn't bear to live any longer. I lay down on the floor. Mother did too, but since there was no room for both of us, she had me lie on top of her.

The day for deportation arrived. We knew our end was near. The anticipation was unbearable. We wished it were over. We knew we were doomed. I lost all control of myself and wept without stopping. I did not fear my own death so much, or even the shooting of the children, but the terror of seeing children buried alive was too great. Some prayed and chanted in Hebrew. A number of us prayed to be shot immediately. Mother calmed me down and promised that she would blindfold me when the shooting began. My panic subsided and I joined in chanting with the other victims.

About three in the morning a policeman came and asked Mother to come out with him. He inquired if there was a child with her. We both went out into the corridor and were taken to another cubicle. Here we were prohibited from loud talk and not allowed even to sneeze. On Saturday, at seven in the morning an automobile arrived to remove those condemned to die. . . . Periodically, five of us were taken to the basement, where we heard shots. We were saved. When they led us outside and I breathed the fresh air, I fell to the ground like one intoxicated.

[Janina falls ill with typhus and is taken to the hospital where her mother works.]

Mother, who was deathly pale, lay in bed. I lay down near her and asked her "Why are you so crushed? I am still alive." She replied, "I do not care what happens to me. I have a poison tablet which will bring instant death. But what will happen to you?" She broke out in loud sobs and implored me, "Anula, save me from further anguish. Go away. I don't want you near me. I don't want to see what will happen to you.

But I refused, saying, "What have I to live for? Without

documents I cannot exist on my own. Mother, do you want to prolong my agonies? Isn't it better to make an end to my life once and for all? Let us die together, with me in your arms. Why live on?" Mother implored me, "You must go on! You must live to vindicate Father's death and mine."

My struggle with Mother robbed me of my strength. I could not glance at Mother's face because overnight it had become a network of wrinkles. She looked like my grandmother. I could hear her loud heartbeats. I gave in on condition that she give me a pill of potassium cyanide, but she refused. She gave me 2700 gulden, accompanied me to the exit, kissed me, and whispered to me, "Bear up for Mother's sake."

I begin to understand why my fellow victims go to their deaths without resistance. I have lost the desire to exist and feel a deep disgust for living. . . .

A day before the Jewish New Year all the sick patients were sent to the death chamber. Urland, the Jewish police officer, greeted us loudly, "I bless all of you with a New Year of Freedom." All of us, including Urland, wept. . . .

At the table sat Mrs. Jacobowitz, who had lit two candles which stood before her. Around her women crowded, exchanging New Year's blessings with one another and crying loudly. With composure, Mrs. Jacobowitz returned the blessings to each one. I could not bear to witness the scene and walked out.

A day before the great fast [Day of Atonement], we arranged a party with singing and constrained dancing. Urland prepared for each of us a repast of soup, two slices of bread, and an apple.

When we returned to our dormitories, night had fallen. The women lit candles and ushered in Yom Kippur with the appropriate blessings, accompanied by copious tears. I looked closely at the candles, at the halos ringing the burning wicks, and suddenly I felt a deep intuition that, despite it all, God is still with us. He sees how we give Him thanks for living, in spite of the horrors around us. I believed that ultimately He would not let the few remnants of Israel be wiped out.

I lay down on my bunk and asked myself, "Shall I fast?" I was uncertain. Fasting was a Jewish religious ritual, and I *am* a Jewess. I did not want to ponder long and deep, because I felt that if I did so, I would reaffirm my disbelief in God. I was persuaded that faith in God bears with it the hope to live. I decided to fast. . . .

From the showers the prisoners go to eat. On the tables are pots of soup, but no one tastes a spoonful. Ten men [a religious quorum for prayer] enter. Urland locks the door, and the Jews begin the prayer service. A few women draw forth paper leaves—remnants of prayerbooks—and recite the Yizkor [Memorial Service for the Dead]. Others repeat after them, and all weep in unison. But as for me—my doubts reawake and reassail me. Why should I fast? Does God really exist? My former doubts return and shatter my erstwhile faith.

Winter is upon us, savage and murderous. I am cold as ice and can't sleep. My benefactors give me strength to persevere and console me that I will yet find safety on the Aryan side of Cracow. I cannot persuade myself to believe them. All mankind is egotistic. They think first of themselves and of their own welfare. I have no strength to hold up, to hope, to live. But in my ears there still echo the last words of my mother. "Carry on, do not despair, for your mother's sake!" Only these words keep the spark of life aglow within me.

Helga Weissova-Hoskova

CZECHOSLOVAKIA ∞ 12 YEARS OLD

*I*n 1939, twelve-year-old Helga Weissova-Hoskova was *deported to the Terezín Transport Camp near her home in Prague. She lived there in a bunkhouse with other boys and girls, all of whom had been separated from their parents. The children were ruled with an iron fist and fed only enough to keep them alive. The Nazi guards enforced their discipline with weeks of confinement to the barracks* (kasernensperre) *and no lights at night* (lichtsperre).

After three years in Terezín, Helga was sent on to three other camps, all of which she survived. Then, soon after liberation, she went to art school and devoted herself to painting. She married, had two children, and became an artist of international acclaim.

This excerpt was published in English in the book Terezín *by the Council of Jewish Communities in the Czech Lands, in 1965.*

———

73

1939 [Dates unknown]

Three young boys ran away. For that we have already had a week of "Kasernensperre" and "Lichtsperre." We walk only in columns to work, and after six o'clock in the evening, no one is allowed on the street. We come home from work in the dark and in the morning we go to work in the dark. We dress and undress by the touch system. Our windows must be darkened and it is forbidden to have any sort of light. Tomorrow I'm going to the Hamburg barracks for bread and perhaps I'll manage to see Mom.

... "Kasernensperre" has been cancelled, but "Lichtsperre" continues, evidently for the whole winter. We have to save on electricity. Each of the different blocks gets it every third day in turn. We may use candles for light, but they don't last long. Supplies from home are being used up and we can't manage to get more. It is terribly stupid, we can't even read in the evening. Without light everything is so sad and gloomy. I am awfully homesick for Prague. Evening after evening Francka and I recall things in Prague far into the night and often we dream of it in our sleep.

... Last night I had a beautiful dream. I dreamed that I was at home, I saw quite clearly our flat and street. Now I am disappointed and out of sorts, because I awoke in the bunk instead of my own bed. But maybe this was some sort of omen of an early end. Then there should be permanent "Lichtsperre" all over Germany. . . . This isn't a Home any more, it's a regular hospital. Everyone avoids us, half the children are sick in bed. The thermometers don't go below 40 degrees. The number of sick goes up every day. The rooms are full of patients and the doctor does not know what to do. I feel rather bad myself. I'd better lie down, after all I have to keep up with them. I've had every illness that has occurred here. "Girls, who's going to Hamburg barracks? Tell mama I shan't come today. I have 40 degrees."

They put Zorka in sick bay yesterday. She's in very bad shape. The doctor doesn't give much hope. It's probably typhoid. They want to put us in quarantine. Everyone is suspicious here. It looks bad. Not a single room has more than three who are well.

. . . Yesterday I had 40.3°. I had a nosebleed. I felt terrible. They could not stop the bleeding until the doctor came. I thought I'd die, I felt so bad. Today I'm better. If only my fever does not go up . . .

. . . I was lucky. My fever went down exactly on the day when everyone whose fever went over 38 had to go to the sick bay. It's typhoid. I don't know, maybe I had it, maybe not. In any case my fever did not go up and they did not put me in the sick bay.

. . . Typhoid has raged throughout Terezín. The hospitals and infirmaries are crowded. They have cleared out a whole house and made a typhoid ward of it. Everywhere you see the sign "Achtung, Tyfus." At every water faucet and pump,

"Don't forget to wash your hands"—but, anyway, the water hardly ever runs.

And a transport again ... they say it didn't go to Poland, that the front lines are there already and the transport went to some new camp on the Polish border. Somewhere near Bohumín. It probably is the same everywhere.

... Old people's transport. Ten thousand sick, crippled, dying, all of them over 65 years old.

It's horrible everywhere. The rays of sun fall exactly on my bunk and reach on farther, I try in vain to get away from them into the shade. Today I shan't go and report for "Hilfsdienst." I haven't left out a day yet, but I am too exhausted to stand the sight of misery and suffering again. The old people's transport, the young people cannot volunteer. Children have to let their old parents go off and can't help them. Why do they want to send these defenceless people away? If they want to get rid of us young people, I can understand that, maybe they are afraid of us, don't want us to give birth to any more Jewish children. But how can these old people be dangerous? If they had to come here to Terezín, isn't that enough, can't they let them die in peace here? After all, these old people can't hope for anything else. Half of them will die in the "šlojsky" and in the train.

Under the window the Gestapo are shouting and beating people, closing the street. Another group is going. There they are, carrying stretchers, two-wheeled carts with corpses, baggage and the "corpse cart." The street that had blossomed in the August heat was wrapped in heavy, filthy dust. Baggage, stretchers, corpses. That's the way it's been going on for a week. The dead on two-wheeled carts and the living in hearses. Everything is transported in hearses here: dirty linen, bread—we have one, ourselves, in the Home, standing in the courtyard. It has a sign on it, "Youth Care." What's the difference, one cart is like another, and so far no one seems to wonder at it, but to transport people in them, that's a little too much. Again a cart is rattling under the window. In front there are two transport leaders, then the load, and behind are some "Sick people's bearers," and the "Hilfsdienst." And that among the baggage, is that corpses? No, one is moving, through the cloud of dust whirling around the cart a yellow armband shines through. Who could forget that! We met them daily in the kitchen, on crutches, blind, with a little bowl in hand, begging a little coffee, soup, scraping out the unwashed troughs and kettles that had food, or else raking through piles of rotting potatoes, peelings and garbage. Yes, that's who it is, skinny, hungry, miserable, there they are, alive in hearses. How many of them will arrive at their destination, how many will return? All the hearses are in operation. For the first time they have a load of the living, and yet this is more fitting than anything else. Where will these human wrecks land, where will their bodies be laid down? No one will weep over them, no one pities them. Some day perhaps there will be a mention of them in readers, and then the only title that would do them justice would be: Buried Alive.

... The barracks by the physical culture hall must be cleared out, a special dinner is being cooked, and the reception centre is getting ready. They say some Polish children are coming.

This is all incomprehensible. Why, and how does it happen that they are brought here from Poland?

They came yesterday at 5:00 o'clock. No one is allowed near them. In the night they called some nurses, house representatives and doctors. Besides these no one is allowed near their barracks. We managed to get some news from the barracks. None of the children can speak Czech, we don't even know if they are Jewish children or Polish or what. You can see them a little from the fortress wall, and then they went in the morning to the reception centre. They look awful. You can't guess how old they are, they all have old, strained faces and tiny bodies. They are all barelegged and only a very few have shoes. They returned from the reception centre with their heads shaved, they have lice. They all have such frightened eyes.

... Yesterday they were taken off, doctors, nurses and house representatives with them. All during quarantine their food was cooked separately and clothes and shoes were collected for them. The only one who came in contact with them was Fredi Hirsch, who is now sitting in a bunker in the camp command for it.

Where they came from we never found out, nor where they were taken either. Rumours were circulating about deportation to Palestine, but no one believes this. They have gone. All that is left is a few lines scribbled on the wall of the barracks, that hardly anyone can figure out.

Dawid Rubinowicz

POLAND ∞ 12 YEARS OLD

Prompted by the beginning of the Nazi occupation of Poland, Dawid began his diary when he was twelve years old. After the Nazis overran all of the country, he and his family were forced to move into Bieliny, a ghetto where thousands of Jews were murdered. From there, his father was taken away and forced into slave labor.

Dawid's diary breaks off abruptly in mid-sentence, and although his father did return from slavery, we are left without an explanation of what happened to Dawid and his family thereafter.

After the war was over, the diary was found in the rubble of the ghetto. It is almost certain that Dawid and his family were sent to the Treblinka death camp and executed.

Dawid's diary was first published in Polish, in 1960. It was translated into English and published in Edinburgh, Scotland, in 1981. The book remains in print from Laing Communications/Laing Research Services, Redmond, Washington, original packagers of the 1982 American edition by Creative Options Publishing.

———

79

12 August [1940]

All through the war I've been studying at home by myself. When I think of how I used to go to school I feel like bursting into tears, and today I must stay at home and can't go anywhere. And when I think of how many wars there are going on in the world, how many men are daily dying by bullets, by gassing, by bombs, by epidemics and other enemies of man, then I feel fit for nothing.

1 September

Today's the first anniversary of the outbreak of war. I remember what we've already gone through in this short time, how much suffering we've already experienced. Before the war everyone had some kind of occupation, hardly anyone was out of work. But in present-day wars 90% are unemployed, and only 10% have a job. Take us, we used to have a dairy and now we're utterly unemployed. There's only very little stock left from before the war; we're still using it up, but it's already running out, and then we don't know what we'll do.

22 June [1941]

It was still dark when Father woke us all up and told us to listen to that terrible din coming from the north-east. It was such a din the earth quaked. The whole day thundering could be heard. Toward evening Jews dropped in from Kielce and said Soviet Russia was at war with the Germans, and only then did it dawn on me why there'd been that din all day.

1 November

Today notices were put up in Kielce that anyone who goes in and out of the 'Jewish Quarter' will receive the death-penalty. Up till now people could go in and out of the Quarter. This news made me very sad, not only myself but every Israelite who heard it. These notices were not only put up in Kielce but in all towns under the 'Generalgouvernement' (that's the name of the area which used to be Poland).

19 January [1942]

After breakfast I went with my brother to grind some rye. On returning, I saw Jews standing in a circle in the snow by our house, with the village constable in charge. The village constable ordered us to go and shovel snow right away. He gave the order to work until the mayor returned from the local authority offices, because he'd gone there that morning. He returned at 4 o'clock, drew up, entered the shop, the constable following right behind. When the constable emerged, he ordered us to line up in twos and march up the street with our shovels on our shoulders. He said the mayor had given him this order and he had to obey. He took us right up the hill where the worst frost and driving snow was, and we had to work until sunset. We were weeping with cold; everyone had to stay till sunset. Then he returned and made us line up in twos, and we had to march. When we arrived outside the shop the mayor was still inside. It was already evening, but he still didn't allow us to go indoors. Not until it was evening did he release us, saying we had to report for work next morning.

24 January

The village-crier came to our house, saying we had to work in the snow, and we went right away. Other Jews had come too, and we cleared the highway as neatly as a street. The police went by—they *were* pleased.

9 February

Today they were in another village, making a house-to-house search. We were very frightened as they stopped outside our shop, and we thought they were coming in, even though they'd never have found a thing. While I was eating my dinner, the village constable came and said I'd have to go and shovel snow at the back of the school, so I went right away. On the way I called in at another Jew's to see if they were going to shovel snow too. Just as I was going there the German came out with the committee. When I entered the house it couldn't be recognized—they'd turned the place upside down. Everyone there had been beaten up; so much was obvious. The head of the house wasn't present, he was shovelling snow, so they went after him and beat him up dreadfully and cut off his beard. We had to shovel snow till evening. Father came from Kielce just as the German and the committee entered our house. They didn't make such an exact search of the house. As they were leaving they demanded two chickens and a bottle of vodka for supper. We had to hand them over a chicken and a bottle of vodka. So one day follows another—always expense and fear.

12 February

After breakfast we went out to shovel snow, even though no one had ordered us to, but the highway had got covered with snow during the night. I recognized the village constable and asked him where he was going. He said he was going to the mayor with notices. About two hours later the village constable came up and began putting up a notice. It wasn't a notice but a caricature of the Jews. On it a Jew is shown, mincing meat and putting a rat into the mincer. Another is pouring water from a bucket into milk. In the third picture a Jew is shown stamping dough with his feet, and worms are crawling over him and the dough. The heading of the notice reads: 'The Jew is a Cheat, Your only Enemy.' And the inscription ran as follows:

Dear reader, before your very eyes,
Are Jews deceiving you with lies.
If you buy your milk from them, beware,
Dirty water they've poured in there.
Into the mincer dead rats they throw,
Then as mincemeat it's put on show.
Worms infest their home-made bread,
Because the dough with feet they tread.

When the village constable had put it up, some people came along, and their laughter gave me a headache from the shame that the Jews suffer nowadays. God give that this shame may soon cease.

8 March

The chairman of the Elders' Council sent a card, saying Father and some others had to go to Bieliny where dwellings had been allotted to the Jews. Father and some others went. They were all back toward evening.

10 March

Early in the morning I went to order a cart. I arranged with a peasant for him to fetch some things from our house and transport them tomorrow. When I got back home, I met my cousin at our place who'd just come from Bodzentyn. I then intended fetching an iron stove as well which had been lent out, because if we are going away, we may need it. There's hardly anyone in our village who's not sorry for us. Many don't even want to come and see us—they say they don't want to witness other people's misfortune. My cousin asked me to go with him after a machine. I went by sledge in the early evening. He loaded the work-bench and ½ cwt of potatoes onto the sledge. I went home and he stayed behind. I was supposed to go back. When I got home supper was already prepared. I didn't go, instead my brother went. After supper many peasants came to our house, wanting to visit us since we soon won't be here any more. Thinking of how we had to leave here, I had to go out into the yard. I cried so much that I stood there sobbing more than ½ hour. When I'd quietened down a bit, I went back into the house. The peasants had already gone. Only two who wanted to buy the cowshed remained behind. One came to an agreement with Father, and he's coming tomorrow to dismantle the cowshed.

16 March

At home everything was different from here. There was always something to occupy you. Here I go out into the street, but in no time at all I'm back—what's there for me to do in the street? Someone at home said that in Krajno 4 Jewish persons had been shot while walking in the direction of Kielce. Two persons had only been wounded with bayonets, and two, a mother and son, were dead. When you hear endlessly of such atrocities how can you live calmly, without fear? When you hear such things you really do get very frightened. The militia came today, but everything was quiet. Acquaintances came from Krajno today. They came because they were afraid to stay there, because a punitive expedition had gone there for requisition purposes. They take away every scrap of corn, and if they don't find anything they lay about them cruelly, beating up men and women indiscriminately. Father went to Krajno today, he's staying there overnight and tomorrow he's going to Kielce.

10 April

They've taken away a man and a woman from over the road, and two children are left behind. Again it's rumoured that the father of these children has been shot two days ago in the evening. The woman, very ill, was transported to Kielce. The militia was in Slupia and arrested three Jews. They finished them off in Bieliny (they were certainly shot). Already a lot of Jewish blood has flowed in this Bieliny, in fact a whole Jewish cemetery has already grown up there. When will this terrible bloodshed finally end? If it goes on much longer then people will drop like flies out of sheer horror. A peasant from Krajno came to tell us our former neighbour's daughter had been shot because she'd gone out after 7 o'clock. I can scarcely believe it, but everything's possible. A girl as pretty as a picture—if *she* could be shot, then the end of the world will soon be here. If only you could have one quiet day. My nerves are utterly exhausted; whenever I hear of anyone's distress, I burst into tears, my head starts aching and I'm exhausted, as if I'd been doing the hardest possible work. It's not only me, everyone feels the same. Not enough that in the previous war the Cossacks shot Papa's father, and he was a witness, and only 11 years old at the time. That's why nowadays he only needs to see a German and he's so scared he starts shivering in his shoes.

18 April

There hasn't been such weather as today for a long time. If only there were freedom then everything would be fine. But we're not even allowed to leave the town. We're now tied up like dogs on a chain. They've taken away the parents from across the road, leaving two little children on their own. Next door they've again taken the husband away; if you look into their window you can see the sadness there. You can forget other people's troubles until a fresh worry comes along. Wherever you go, whether to a flat or to a café or elsewhere, everywhere people are talking about how much they've taken away from this man, how much from that etc., etc. While we were sitting quietly over our dinner, the policeman came to remind us we still had to pay the 150 zloty from Krajno for the corn we'd ground. We must pay up right away; if we don't hand over the money, it'll mean 18 days immediate detention. Mother went to the police station immediately, and the commandant said it must be paid by Monday at the latest. Of course we didn't think we'd get out of it, but nowadays in these hard times it's so difficult to pay 150 zloty.

6 May

A terrible day! About 3 o'clock I was awoken by knocking. It was the police already making a raid. I wasn't afraid. After all Father and my cousin were in Krajno and knew what was going on. The other cousins had hidden. After a few minutes I heard more knocking on the door and Uncle opened up right away. A Jewish and a Polish policeman entered. Immediately they began making a search; one of them eyed me and ordered me to get dressed. The other asked how old I was, I answered 14, he then left me alone. They rummaged about a bit, found no one, however, only they took the two from Plock. I wasn't afraid, even so I was trembling as if I had a fit of the shivers. As soon as they were gone I fell asleep. In the morning my cousin woke me—Father had arrived with the cart. I dressed quickly and went out, but Father was already no longer there—he'd run away before the police patrol arrived. The merchandise had already been unloaded from the cart, and then I saw a policeman come and turn into our yard. I ran away, but heard the policeman shouting: 'Where are the potatoes? Hand over the rest!' And he shouted other things, but I didn't understand what they were. Now we're finished, I thought, they've loaded everything onto the cart and driven to the police-station. And Father's not here. What can I do?—Mother and Auntie went to the police-station. I was utterly confused. Everything we had has been taken away, now we're forced to hanker after a crust of bread. Anciel came, saying Father and my cousin had been caught as well. Only then did I start crying. They've taken Father from us, they've taken our property, and now I felt such a yearning for Father. We soon forgot the merchandise. Mother went to the Jews' Council to ask for Father's release. After all he's ill, he can't live without medicine. It's terrible that he must now get sent to a camp to work! They said Father would be released after interrogation. We had hopes of his release. I didn't go out into the street at all for fear they'd pick me up too; my brother and Anciel are the only ones to take them food. Anciel came in from the street, saying they'd picked up his brother-in-law as well. There was dreadful panic, everyone hid wherever he could. The relatives or wives of the arrested men wept terribly. How can you help weeping? The Bieliny police have also made raids. When it got a bit quieter, two lorries came up and one had a trailer. When I saw it I immediately thought they were taking Father away in it, and began weeping terribly. Father told my brother he should bring him food, some clothes and a little mug. And again I couldn't help crying when I saw him taking all those things. Mother was the whole time at the Jews' Council, making representations on Father's behalf, but all they'd say was that they'd be releasing him. My brother came to see about a warm cap, but it was already too late ... The lorry was already at the other market-place. I burst out crying, and as they came up I cried out: 'Papa!— Papa, where are you? If only I could see you once more' ... and then I saw him on the last lorry; his eyes were red with weeping. I kept on looking at him until he disappeared round the corner, then I had a sudden fit of crying, and I felt how much I love him and how much he loves me.

8 May

The rumour's going round that today there'll be another raid because they're still 120 men short.

Auntie came, saying they're also picking up people like me. At first I didn't know what to do, but then I suddenly realized I had to hide. I went to our Polish neighbour's wife and stayed there. The slightest rustling, and I was terrified it was them coming in! This neighbour said the police had gone into the woods, and the very moment she said this we heard several shots. Someone must have been shot dead, I thought. I wasn't there long before the lorries drove off; only two were full, the third was empty. I went straight home; now I could be quiet at home for not a soul came in. I didn't go out into the street again the whole day. In the evening I went to pray—after all it *is* Friday. We used to always go with Father; however things might be, whether happy or sad, we were still with Father, now ... When we returned from praying I was dreadfully sad. How could I help being sad?— supper was prepared somehow or other, the table laid; after all it is a feast-day. But when I see Father's place, and he's not sitting there, then grief and sorrow break my heart. ...

21 May

At half-past eight the lorry with the Jews arrived. When I saw the lorry my heart began to pound like mad—perhaps Father's with them. As it came nearer I looked for Father but didn't see him. I ran after it; the lorry stopped by the Jews' Council and all the men immediately jumped out, but Father wasn't with them. I started weeping to see so many men arrive, but no Father. Some were quite healthy and yet *they'd* come back—that gave me quite a shock. Father sent several cards by means of acquaintances, asking us to send him some potatoes, bread-dough and groats. We made up a parcel right away and gave it to the lorry-driver. We quite forgot that today is Whitsun and made no preparation—we were entirely taken up by the one concern. It's never happened before that Father hasn't been at home for a feast-day, and today he's not only not here but in a camp.

22 May

While praying I felt a deep yearning for Father. I saw other children standing with their fathers, and the parts of their prayers that they didn't know were told them by their fathers, and who is there to tell me? . . . only God alone. God give me good thoughts and lead me in the right way. Never before have I felt my prayers to be such a burden to me as today. How could they have been so before? If only God would allow Father to return soon safe and sound. We rang up Suchedniów, and the woman said the matter's not settled yet.

1 June

A happy day. We were expecting a letter from Father, but none came, only a postcard from my cousin with greetings from Father, nothing else. We made up a large parcel for Father, because the Council is going to Skarzysko tomorrow. We've packed a light jacket, linen, shoes, some potatoes, bread and other odds and ends. I waited impatiently for 3 o'clock to come—that's when the mail's delivered. Perhaps there'll be a letter from Father, perhaps there's a chance of him being released. Toward evening I went to our neighbour's to make slippers for my sister. While I was working I heard a lorry approach, and singing. I immediately thought it was the Jews coming from Skarzysko. I ran out, and right enough!—there they were, driving up. From far away you could see them waving their arms, their caps; I saw my father waving too. I threw everything down, ran to meet them and arrived at the same time as the lorry. I immediately took Father's bundle from him, and he got down from the lorry. Mother took the bundle off me and I went to the police to recover the parcel. I entered our flat and couldn't even greet Father, I was so glad. No one can imagine our joy, only someone who's been through the same experience will understand. It was all like in a film, we experienced so much almost in a second. The place was immediately full of people—they all came for the good news. Father had injured his arm—that's why they'd let him out ... At first I was very frightened, thinking he'd been very badly wounded. It's hard for me to describe everything Father related. I'll begin at the beginning. The first week was the worst, until he'd got used to things. The work wasn't so terrible, only the discipline; if a man doesn't march well or sing, he gets beaten. Reveille is at 4 a.m.; at 5 p.m. work ceases. For thirteen hours at a stretch the men aren't allowed to take a rest; anyone who sits down receives a terrible beating. There was no end to his account; we stayed up till 2 a.m.—it's impossible to describe how it was. Father didn't look too bad, he'd had as much to eat as he needed. I'm so glad, I've forgotten to write down the most important and most terrible news of all. This morning two Jewish women, a mother and a daughter, had gone out into the country. Unfortunately the Germans were driving from Rudki to Bodzentyn to fetch potatoes and ran across them. When the two women caught sight of the Germans they began to flee, but were overtaken and arrested. They intended shooting them on the spot in the village, but the mayor wouldn't allow it. They then went into the woods and shot them there. The Jewish police immediately went there to bury them in the cemetery. When the cart returned it was full of blood. Who ...   (End of diary)

Helga Kinsky-Pollack

AUSTRIA ∽ 13 YEARS OLD

*B*orn in Vienna in 1930, Helga Kinsky-Pollack was deported to the Terezín transport camp (in what is now the Czech Republic) when she was thirteen. She was separated from her parents and subjected to fierce discipline, disease, hunger, and overcrowding. From Terezín, Helga was sent to Auschwitz and then forced into slave labor in the Flossenbürg concentration camp. Finally, she was returned to Terezín just before liberation. Helga survived all this and was able to hold on to the diary she had written during her first imprisonment in Terezín. The following are a few of her entries from 1943, which were translated into English and published in the book Terezín in 1965.

Tuesday, March 16, 1943
... I went to see my uncle in the Sudeten barracks and there I saw them throw out potato peelings and ten people threw themselves on the little pile and fought for them ...

Friday, April 2, 1943

This day is filled with joy. The Germans themselves admit their losses at the front. This afternoon I moved to another bunk, in the bottom tier next to Ella Steiner. I'm happy. I had an unpleasant neighbour, Marta Kenderová, who always scolded me if I sat on her bunk . . .

Tuesday, April 6, 1943

Tomorrow SS-man Guenther is coming and no children can go out on the street tomorrow. Daddy doesn't know this and I'll die of hunger by evening . . .

Wednesday, April 7, 1943

I missed Daddy yesterday, but I didn't give in to my sadness, because the other children couldn't see their parents either and won't see them all day.

Saturday, April 10, 1943

We aren't allowed to go out of the barracks. We can't go into the street without a pass and children don't get a pass. They say this can last a week or even several months. I thought I wouldn't see Daddy for a long time, but he has been to see me twice. I seem like a bird in a cage. This is all because two prisoners escaped from the ghetto . . .

Thursday, May 6, 1943

It's terrible here in Terezín. A regular Tower of Babel. There are Germans, Austrians, Czech, Dutch, some French, I even know a Finnish girl, etc. There are Aryans, Jews and mixed. Next to my bunk there was a girl Antonie Michalová to whom fate was very cruel. She arrived three weeks ago

from Brno; her father is an Aryan and her mother Jewish.
She is completely alone, badly provided for, and does not
feel right in a Jewish environment. She cries almost all day
long. Her father was allowed to accompany her to Prague,
where there was a terrible leave-taking, according to the account of a girl who came with her.

Saturday, July 31, 1943

This is the second day I've been sleeping in the corridor
because of bedbugs. There are seven of us girls sleeping outside and we've all been bitten.

We have permission to sleep in the garden, because it's
impossible in the corridor. Spraying with Flit didn't help at
all. I caught six fleas and three bedbugs today. Isn't that a
fine hunt? I don't even need a gun and right away I have
supper. A rat slept in my shoe. Walter, our Hausältester,
killed it. Now I'm going to pitch a tent for the night with
Ella and Irča.

Thursday, August 26, 1943

It's terrible here now. There is a great deal of tension
among the older, sensible children. They are going to send
transports to a new ghetto—into the unknown.

And something else, 1,500 children will arrive tonight.
They are from Poland. We are making toys and little bags
and nets for them, etc.

I have diarrhea. Of 27 children, 19 have diarrhea and 16
are sick in bed. Two toilets for 100 children aren't enough,
when there is infectious diarrhea in every 'Heim'.

What those toilets look like!!!

Friday, August 27, 1943

The children came at three this morning. They are full of lice. They only have what they are wearing. We are collecting things for them.

Saturday, September 4, 1943

Tomorrow they load the transport. From our room only Zdeňka is going so far. They are sending them in several batches. Zdeňka is acting very bravely.

Sunday, September 5, 1943

This was a day, but it's all over now. They are already in the 'šlojska.' From our room Pavla, Helena, Zdeňka, Olila and Popinka are going.

Everyone gave Zdeňka something, she's such a poor thing. I gave a half loaf of bread, a can of meat paste, linden tea and sugar. Her father came to pack her things and Zdeňka gave him bread, sugar and a tomato. He didn't want to take it, but we made him and said that we would bring Zdeňka some more food. He wept and thanked the children and the assistants for the care they had given Zdeňka. We all cried. Her father, mother, and brother didn't even have a bit of bread. We fixed them up so that from having nothing they had in a little while a full little suitcase and a small bag full of food.

At six in the evening they reported for the transport. Each one somewhere else. The parting was hard. After eight in the evening I went to look for Zdeňka. She was sitting on her luggage and she cried and laughed at the same time, she was so happy to see someone before she left. I slept all night, but I had terrible dreams and had rings under my eyes in the morning.

Monday, September 6, 1943

I got up at six to see Zdeňka again. When I came up to the Hamburg barracks the last people were just going through the back gates and getting on the train. Everything was boarded up all around so no one could get to them and so they could not run away. I jumped over, ran up to the last people going through the gates. I saw the train pulling away and in one of the cars Zdeňka was riding away.

Eva Heyman

*E*va Heyman, a Jewish girl who lived with her family in Hungary, began her diary on her thirteenth birthday, in 1944, as she watched Hitler's troops take over her country. Judging by events in Budapest, which she fondly called "Pest," she could see that the air raids and intense persecution of the Jews were only days away from Nagyvárad, the city in which she lived and called by its diminutive, "Várad."

Especially because Eva's family was so politically active, they expected the worst. And that is what occurred. Along with her grandparents, Eva was murdered at Auschwitz in October of 1944.

Mariska, Eva's loving and faithful Christian maid, kept Eva's diary safe after she was deported to the death camp. She eventually gave it to Eva's mother, Ági Zsolt, who had been interned in Bergen-Belsen and then rescued and sent to Switzerland.

Three years after the war was over, Ági saw to it that

her daughter's diary was published. Then, overwhelmed by grief, Ági committed suicide. Her body was found lying next to a picture of Eva.

Eva had foretold her own death many times. Ever since the Nazis had shot and killed her best friend Márta, she had been convinced that, despite how desperately she wanted to live, the Nazis would kill her too. Her diary, which she called "my best friend," gave her the courage to go on living every day in the face of death.

Eva's diary was first published in Hungarian. The whereabouts of the original manuscript is unknown. It was published in Hebrew in 1964 by Yad Vashem in Israel, and then translated into English by Moshe M. Kohn and published by Yad Vashem in 1974. It remains in print in an American edition published by Shapolsky Publishers in 1974 and 1988.

March 18, 1944

There are constant air raid alarms in Pest. Dear diary, I'm so afraid that here, too, there will be air raids. I can hardly write, because I kept thinking about what will happen if they bomb Várad, after all. I want to live at all costs.

March 25, 1944

No changes yet. I've even been back to school, but they're stopping classes and I won't have to go anymore. I was on my way home when the German soldiers came marching in, with cannons and tanks, the kind I've seen in the newsreels. In Budapest there are constant air raid alarms, and all day the radio keeps issuing air raid warnings, always opening with the code words for places in danger of bombing: Warning to Bácska Baja. And then we turn off the radio, because I'm afraid. Anyway, if they were flying toward our town, the sirens would sound. Grandma says that the Aryans are greeting her coolly in the street, or turning the other way. There is a new government already, and Sztójay is Prime Minister. I don't know the rest of it, but Ági says that this is the end of everything; we won't see the end of the war.

Grandma gets drugs all the time, and then she doesn't talk to a soul, just keeps staring straight ahead, and she sits that way for hours in her easy chair. Dear diary, I'm so miserable. Why did those German cadavers have to come here!

The Englishmen and the Americans should have invaded a long time ago, and I don't understand how they're going to do it. No matter how hard I think about it, I can't imagine it! And Grandma always says that the invasion won't succeed anyway, because the Germans are still very strong. Still, I think that the Russians are much, much stronger, because they are already inside Rumania, and Rumania is much nearer than any beach on which it is possible to plant a flag.

March 26, 1944

The radio keeps issuing warnings about air bombings, or it curses the Jews, but much more furiously than before. I'm not even afraid of bombings anymore, because I would rather have bombings; then they would stop cursing the Jews. And on the radio they keep announcing all kinds of regulations about the Jews, all the things they are not allowed to do. Ági spoke to Budapest today, too. She says that all their friends have already been captured by the Germans, who kill all of them, including children. Dear diary, until now I didn't want to write about this in you because I tried to put it out of my mind, but ever since the Germans are here, all I think about is Márta. She was also just a girl, and still the Germans killed her. But I don't want them to kill me!

March 28, 1944

Aunt Friedländer was just here. Early this morning the German and Hungarian police took Uncle Sándor and everyone they knew who is a Socialist or Communist. They searched his whole apartment, and since then she doesn't know what has happened to Uncle Sándor. At our place the fire is going in three stoves today. Ági is burning all the books and the letters that Uncle Béla wrote to her before she married him. There is a terrible smell of burning paper in the house! We heard on the radio this evening that in Budapest all the books ever written by Uncle Béla were taken to some kind of a mill, because his books mustn't be read anymore, and they are harmful to people. But not only Uncle Béla's books are harmful, also those written by other people. For example, those of Ferenc Molnár, of which I've already read "The Pál Street Boys." I really don't know how that can be harmful to people. I cried so hard when little Nemecsek was killed in the book. I always cry when I read about someone dying. I don't want to die, because I've hardly lived!

March 30, 1944

Now the worst is only starting. This afternoon Grandpa came home with the news that the Germans are throwing the Jews out of the finest houses, and they are allowed to take along only the clothes they wear, and nobody asks them where they will sleep. The others take in the dispossessed people, but Grandpa says that it has already happened that an hour later the people who have taken others in are also thrown out, and then there are even more families out in the street without a place to live. That was all that poor Grandma Rácz needed. Until now, only Ági used to scream every time the doorbell rang and would hug Uncle Béla as though she was going to strangle him. Now Grandma also sobs and says: We are going to be wanderers without a roof over our heads! They're throwing everybody out in our neighbourhood, too. This afternoon I saw the Waldmanns from the window of our children's room. Carrying a little handbag and a basket, they went out through the gate, and outside three German officers were standing. One of them kicked Uncle Waldmann in the behind as he came out through the gateway of his house in order to hand that pretty little house over to the damned Germans. But I didn't speak about it to anyone, not even to Uncle Béla. Uncle Béla is the calmest person in the family; so is Grandpa. Grandpa said to Ági: "Daughter, nothing matters to me any more. I am sixty-one. I am so weary. I have worked so hard all my life, and I have had so little joy—you know this very well." That was all Ági needed to hear to make her cry even harder. She tried to comfort Grandpa, and even I burst out crying when she told him: "Papa, I want us to live, I want you to live to a ripe old age. You'll see, everything will be for the best, if only we get through this . . ." That's what Ági said to Grandpa, kissing him all over his head and hands.

Uncle Béla said that everybody should prepare a small bundle of the most essential items, because we can be thrown out into the street at any moment, the way the Waldmanns were.

I don't go out into the street at all since the Germans

came. My father comes to visit us. Though I would like so much to be with children, because then I might forget—at least for a while—that the Germans are here. My father is comparatively calm. Today he asked Ági if she didn't want me to become a Catholic, too, as he has been for some time. It doesn't matter to Ági. She is for anything that might help me, but unfortunately there is the Race Law, and it doesn't matter what a person's religion is. At first I didn't understand what this Race Law was, but afterwards I realized that Hitler probably invented it. It is called the Nuremburg Laws. I've heard and read a lot about them. The main thing is that a person must be an Aryan, and it doesn't matter whether he is Protestant or a Catholic. In short, dear diary, I'm not becoming a Christian, even though Uncle Béla has heard that many people want to. But the Christian priests in Várad still insist that a person can become a Christian only after studying for six months. Uncle Béla also said that the Church has failed shamefully! I always thought that priests are holy people and help anybody who is in trouble. But it seems that they help Aryans only. They don't help Jews. Who helps us?

March 31, 1944

Today an order was issued that from now on Jews have to wear a yellow star-shaped patch. The order tells exactly how big the star patch must be, and that it must be sewn on every outer garment, jacket or coat. When Grandma heard this, she started acting up again and we called the doctor. He gave her an injection. She is asleep now. Grandma doesn't know yet that the telephones have been cut off. Ági wanted to telephone to the doctor but couldn't. Then Grandpa told her that the telephones had been taken away from the Jews, and he said that he would go and get the doctor.

April 1, 1944

We are the only ones in the neighbourhood who haven't been thrown out of our home yet. Until the order about wearing the star goes into effect, I'm moving to Anikó's house. Grandma Rácz has her attacks very frequently now. When that happens I start to shake, and Ági doesn't want me to see these attacks.

Aunt Bora was here today and asked Ági if I could stay with Anikó, because Anni is so unhappy, practically in a state of depression. God, today is April Fool's Day; on whom should I play tricks? Who thinks about that at all now? Dear diary, soon I'll be going to Anikó's house, and I'm taking along the little suitcase which Mariska packed and my canary in the cage. I'm afraid that Mandi will die if I leave her at home, because everybody's mind is on other things now, and I'm worried about Mandi. She's such a darling bird. Whenever I come near her cage she notices me right away and starts singing. Mariska will bring me to the Anikós, because she is an Aryan and with her I'll be safer in the street.

Dear diary, I'm taking you along to Anikó's house. Don't worry, you won't be alone; you're my best friend.

April 7, 1944

Today they came for my bicycle. I almost caused a big drama. You know, dear diary, I was awfully afraid just by the fact that the policemen came into the house. I know that policemen bring only trouble with them, wherever they go. My bicycle had a proper license plate, and Grandpa had paid the tax for it. That's how the policemen found it, because it was registered at City Hall that I have a bicycle. Now that it's all over, I'm so ashamed about how I behaved in front of the policemen. So, dear diary, I threw myself on the ground, held on to the back wheel of my bicycle, and shouted all sorts of things at the policemen: "Shame on you for taking away a bicycle from a girl! That's robbery!" We had saved up for a year and a half to buy the bicycle. We had sold my old bicycle, my layette and Grandpa's old winter coat and added the money we had saved. My grandparents, Juszti, the Ágis, Grandma Lujza and Papa all had chipped in to buy my bicycle. We still didn't have the whole sum, but Hoff-mann didn't sell the bicycle to anyone else, and he even said that I could take the bicycle home. My father would pay, or Grandpa. But I didn't want to take the bicycle home until we had all the money. But in the meantime I hurried over to the store whenever I could and looked to see if that red bicycle was still there. How Ági laughed when I told her that when the whole sum was finally there. I went to the store and took the bicycle home, only I didn't ride it but led it along with my hands, the way you handle a big, beautiful dog. From the outside I admired the bicycle, and even gave it a name: Friday. I took the name from Robinson Crusoe, but it suits the bicycle. First of all, because I brought it home on a Friday, and also because Friday is the symbol of loyalty, because he was so loyal to Robinson. The "Bicycle Friday" would be loyal to "Éva Robinson," and I was right, because for three years it never gave me any trouble, that is, it never broke down, and there were no expenses for repair. Marica and Anni also gave their bicycles names. Marica's was called Horsie, and Anni's was called Berci just because that's such a funny name. One of the policemen was very annoyed and said: All we need is for a Jewgirl to put on such a comedy when her bicycle is being taken away. No Jewkid is entitled to keep a bicycle anymore. The Jews aren't entitled to bread, either; they shouldn't guzzle everything, but leave the food for the soldiers. You can imagine, dear diary, how I felt when they were saying this to my face. I had only heard that sort of thing on the radio, or read it in a German newspaper. Still, it's different when you read something and when it's thrown into your face. Especially if it's when they're taking my bicycle away. Actually, what does that nasty policeman think? That we stole the bicycle? We bought it from Hoffmann for cash, and Grandpa and all the others worked for this money. But you know, dear diary, I think the other policeman felt sorry for me. You should be ashamed of yourself, colleague, he said, is your heart made of stone? How can you speak that way to such a beautiful girl? Then he stroked my hair and promised to take good care of my bicycle. He gave me a receipt and told me not to cry, because when the war was over I would get my bicycle back. At worst it would need some repairs at Hoffmann's.

Ági said that we had been lucky this time, but that next time we should let them take whatever they wanted. In any case nothing could be done about it, and we shouldn't let those stinking scoundrels see how much we suffered. Still, I don't understand Ági. What do I care whether they know or don't know that we suffer. It isn't hard to see that if everything you own is being taken away from you, and soon you won't even have money to buy food, you suffer. But what does it matter?

April 9, 1944

Today they arrested my father. At night they came to him and put a seal on his door. For several days now I've known that a few hundred people are being held prisoner in the school in Körös Street, but until now they only took the very rich people.

I learned from Aunt Lili that my father has been taken away and locked up in the elementary school in Körös Street. Aunt Lili was terribly upset. Grandma Lujza sent her to us, because she has heard that it is possible to bring lunch to my father and they want me to bring the food, because if adults bring it the policemen don't allow them near the place, or they pretend that an accident happened and the food was spilled, while the prisoner goes hungry!

At twelve o'clock the meal was ready. I took potato soup, meatballs with pumpkin, and Linz pie. On the way many people stopped me to ask whether Grandpa was in prison and whether I was bringing him lunch. I said: No, I'm bringing it to my father. But I was very much afraid, because from their questions it occurred to me that Grandpa can also be put in prison, and then I really don't know what will become of us and what will I do with Grandma Rácz and Ági.

From the bridge I already saw a crowd standing and waiting in front of the elementary school building in Körös Street. When I got there, I saw that I knew nearly every single one of the people. And it seems that Grandma Lujza was right when she said that it is better for a boy or a girl to bring the meal. A crowd of boys and girls were standing and waiting in front of the school, holding food containers. While waiting to get in, I found out that my father was being held as a hostage.

While we waited, Aunt Ági explained to me that hostage
means security, that is, my father has now become a security;
only I don't understand how a human being can be a security. At last they let me go in to my father. Most of those
securities sat in the yard on the ground. The sick ones lay in
the classroom on the bare floor. Papa said that it wasn't so
terrible, but it was boring and uncomfortable because there
was no place to sit down alone, and he didn't feel like talking
to anyone, so he had no choice but to pace back and forth
in the yard of the elementary school. When I left him, it
occurred to me that when I was going to elementary school,
we children always used to be inside the gate and the parents
would wait outside the fence to take us home after school.
Now only adults, even old people, are inside the school
fence, and we children are outside. There is no getting away
from it: the world is topsy-turvy.

April 10, 1944

I have only just found out, dear diary, that Mariska has
been ordered to leave us by April 15. Jews can't have house-
hold help. I'm so sorry that Mariska is leaving us. She is
really very good to me, especially when Grandma has an
attack. Of course, now we will have a lot of work. The trouble is that even though Grandma works all the time, she
keeps doing the same things over and over again. For example: she washes the porch floor fifteen times, or cleans the
same window three times but doesn't remember to dust the
furniture in the parlour. Ági doesn't count, because she can
hardly stand on her feet, and even when she is healthy, she is
totally helpless. Ági really doesn't understand a thing about
running a house. Uncle Béla always says that she knows how

to save, and that is also a fine quality. Whereas I am very agile. This, dear diary, you know well. And I enjoy working very much. I would even do housework for ten years, if only we shouldn't have to leave the house and Grandma should get better and Uncle Béla and Grandpa shouldn't be taken away from us! It's bad enough for a girl of thirteen that her Papa and her bicycle have been taken away from her. I haven't yet written in you, dear diary, what else happened when they arrested Papa. He was taken away at five o'clock in the morning and they put a seal on his door, but they forgot Juno, Papa's puppy, inside. The poor dog kept yelping inside till the neighbours nearly went out of their minds, but nothing could be done, because the apartment was sealed, and only the police can open such a seal. Aunt Lili, my father's sister, approached the police about the dog, and today my father's apartment was finally opened for a minute; dear diary, miracle of miracles: Juno was alive. It seems he discovered the giblets that were kept in the pantry. But we don't really know, because only the policemen could go into the apartment, and they brought the dog out. Now Juno is living with Grandma Lujza, but he is so sad that he hardly eats anything at all. That dog is so loyal to Papa, more so than a lot of people, says Ági.

Dear diary, Papa is kept in prison all the time, without any change. I still bring him lunch, and every day there are more and more prisoners there. Sometimes I wait for hours for my turn to come to bring in the food, and even then I don't always get to talk to him. When I'm coming home late, Ági already sits in the gate arch to hear my footsteps come up the street, because she's afraid that one day I'll become a

security like my father. Life is really hard, dear diary;
Good night.

April 18, 1944

Just after sunset Ági's Christian cousin, Sányi Kaufmann,
came from Pest, where he works as a clerk in the Pannonia
Hotel. He brought Ági and Uncle Béla forged documents
which he stole from the hotel, and he wanted to smuggle
them to Budapest via Békéscsaba tonight. Today was an
awful day, dear diary, because when Grandma heard what
was going on, she threw herself on the floor and literally
screeched. She said that Ági is a murderer, because if Ági
and Uncle Béla run away they will kill her in their place.
She screamed other terrible things, until Ági gave her her
word of honour that nobody would run away, no matter
what! Sányi said there is a "reign of terror" in Budapest, but
still, Budapest is a big city, and it will be possible to find
some Aryan Socialist or Communist who will be willing to
hide Ági and her husband. Sányi told all kinds of horror
stories about what was being done to "politicals" and Jews
in Budapest, until finally Ági told me to leave the room, and
Jakobi was offended by Grandma's words, but Ági took her
to the children's room and there she told her that Grandma
was out of her mind, and may the good Lord always help
Mrs. Jakobi for wanting to help an unfortunate child like me.
Ági didn't even tell Ági Friedländer, who is her best friend
in Várad, what a terrible thing had happened to Grandma;
she only said that Grandma's nerves were very bad. It looks
like Ági is ashamed that Grandma is out of her mind, even
though nobody can be blamed for it except that damned
Hitler.

This Mrs. Jakobi really isn't an evil woman, as poor Grandma said. She is a very good woman, and I don't even understand what Grandma meant when she did say that Mrs. Jakobi would sell me to men. Nobody is buying Jewish girls these days, and Ági even said that Grandma only says such things because she is sick right now. You know, dear diary, even though it would be very bad not to see Ági and all the rest for such a long time, I would go with Aunt Jakobi, or with Sányi, to any place in the world where they don't know that I'm Jewish and wherefrom I couldn't be taken to Poland like Márta was.

April 20, 1944

Every day they keep issuing new laws against the Jews. Today, for example, they took all our appliances away from us: the sewing machine, the radio, the telephone, the vacuum cleaner, the electric fryer and my camera. I don't care about the camera any more, even though they didn't leave a receipt for it, like when they took the bicycle. They also took Uncle Béla's typewriter, but he didn't care either. When the war ends we'll get everything back. Ági said we should be happy they're taking things and not people. She's right about that, because after the war I may even have a Zeiss-Ikon camera I'll be able to work with until I'm old enough to be a news photographer, but a mother or a grandfather can never be replaced.

Grandpa is very sad ever since he hasn't been able to work in the pharmacy any more. He looks at Ági in such an odd, sad way, and he keeps caressing her all the time, as though he is saying goodbye to her. Ági even said to him: Don't cling to me as though we are saying goodbye, my sweet Papa, because my heart is breaking. Ági wants to go on having a father forever. I can understand that, because I also want all of us to stay alive. Márta didn't want to stay here without her Papa and she went with him to die in Poland. Of course, she couldn't know in advance that she was being taken to her death. Dear diary, ever since the Germans came here I've often wondered: had Márta known in Várad what a horrible death was in store for her when she went with her father, would she still have gone? Dear diary, I admit that I very much want to live, so much so that if I were given the same choice as Márta, I would stay even without Papa and without Ági and without anybody at all, because I want to stay alive!

May 1, 1944

In the morning Mariska burst into the house and said: Have you seen the notices? No, we hadn't, we are not allowed to go outside, except between nine and ten! Aha, that's why we're allowed outside only between nine and ten, because we're being taken to the Ghetto.

Dear diary, from now on I'm imagining everything as if it really is a dream. We started packing exactly those things and exactly in the quantity that Ági read in the notice. I know it isn't a dream, but I can't believe a thing. We're also allowed to take along bedding, and right now we don't know when they'll come to take us, so we can't pack the bedding. I'm busy all day making coffee for Uncle Béla, but Grandma drinks cognac. Nobody says a word. Dear diary, I've never been so afraid.

May 5, 1944

Dear diary, now you aren't at 3 Istvan Gyöngyösi Street—that is, at home—any more, not even at Anikó's, nor at Tusnád, nor at Lake Balaton, nor in Budapest, places you've been with me too before, but in the Ghetto. Three days we waited for them to come and get us. There we sat in the apartment and watched for the policemen. Ági and Grandpa went out into the street between nine and ten in the morning to hear the latest news. The city was divided into sections, and a German truck would wait in front of the houses and two policemen would go into the apartments and bring the people out. The notices tell what we can take with us. Dear diary, I'm still too little a girl to write down what I felt while we waited to be taken into the Ghetto. Between one order and the next, Ági would cry out that we deserve what we get because we are like animals, patiently waiting to be slaughtered in the slaughterhouse. But now and then, after Ági burst into such an outcry, Grandma Rácz would have an attack, and then Ági would calm down. And there was such silence, dear diary; even Mandi didn't sing. But it wasn't silent the way it usually is at night, but of a kind that I couldn't even imagine till now. From time to time, when the bell rang, I would be almost happy. I knew that we were being taken to the Ghetto, but felt that if this silence would go on much longer we would all go crazy. Then everything happened like in a film.

The two policemen who came to us weren't unfriendly; they just took Grandma's and Ági's wedding rings away from them. Ági was shaking all over and couldn't get the wedding ring off her finger. In the end, Grandma took the ring off her finger. Then they checked our luggage and they didn't allow us to take Grandpa's valise because it is genuine pigskin. They didn't allow anything made out of leather to be taken along. They said: There is a war going on and the soldiers need the leather. They also didn't allow me to take my red purse. We took washing kits and Grandma's thick cloth bag.

One of the policemen saw a little gold chain on my neck, the one I got for my birthday, the one holding your key, dear diary. Don't you know yet, the policeman said, that you aren't allowed to keep anything made of gold?! This isn't private Jewish property anymore but national property! Whenever something was being taken from us, Ági would always pretend not to notice at all, because she had an obsession about not letting the policemen think that it bothered us that our things were being taken, but this time she begged the policeman to let me keep the little gold chain. She started sobbing and saying: Mr. Inspector, please go and ask your colleagues, and they will tell you that I have never begged for anything, but please let the child keep just this little gold chain. You see, she keeps the key to her diary on it. Please, the policeman said, that is impossible; in the Ghetto you will be checked again. I, so help me God, don't need this chain or any other object that is being taken from you. I don't need any of it, but I don't want any difficulties. I am a married man. My wife is going to have a baby. I gave him the chain. In Grandma's night table I found a velvet ribbon. I asked the policeman: Mr. Inspector, may I take a velvet ribbon along to the Ghetto? He said I could. Now your key hangs on that velvet ribbon, dear diary.

It seems that Mariska sneaked out of the house somehow when the policemen came, and I didn't see her anywhere. Although it's true that in all the excitement I forgot all about

Mariska. Mariska already took Mandi away yesterday. I trust Mariska to take care of her. She also loves Mandi very much. We tied the bedding in bundles. Grandpa and Uncle Béla took the bundles on their backs and carried them out to the open truck that stood by the gate. The truck driver was a German soldier, an S.S., I think, because he wore a black uniform. Dear diary, the most terrible thing happened when we got to the gate. Then I saw Grandpa cry for the first time in my life. From the gate arch you can see the garden, and the garden never looked so beautiful, even though no one had taken care of it for some days now. I will never forget how Grandpa stood there looking at the garden, shaking from his crying. There were also tears in Uncle Béla's eyes. And only now I noticed how Grandma had turned into such an old woman, just like Grandma Lujza, and Grandma Rácz is only fifty-four. She walked out of the gate as though she was drunk or sleepwalking. She didn't even look back, and there wasn't a tear in her eyes. Ági put her hands under the bundle on Grandpa's back so it shouldn't be so heavy for him.

Interesting, but it occurred to me only when we got to Szacsvay Street that we weren't going to have an apartment, because the commission had said: Your place to sleep will be at 20 Szacsvay Street. It makes a tremendous difference, dear diary, because a normal person has an apartment, while people talk about "place to sleep" only in connection with animals. I swear that Ági is right; as far as the Aryans are concerned, we've become like animals.

In the Vajda house, the basement was packed to the ceiling with logs of wood, and Ági said we would at least be able to heat water so that the children could wash. It is impossible to count how many of us there are in the house, because even in the halls and stairwells people sit on mattresses. Because of them it is impossible to move about, and we always trip over someone's leg.

At first, Chief Rabbi Vajdas said that the women and children should be separated from the men. But then none of the women wanted to leave their husbands, and the women said that we could undress in the dark, and that every effort should be made for families to sleep together. We were put in a room that had been used as an office. The bookshelves were sunk into the walls so it was impossible to take them out to the yard. The shelves are packed full of books. Uncle Béla said: I hope we shall manage to read them all till the end of the war. In the evening we wanted to turn on the lights, but it turned out that City Hall had cut off the electricity, because Jews aren't entitled to electricity.

May 10, 1944

Dear diary, we're here five days, but, word of honour, it seems like five years. I don't even know where to begin writing, because so many awful things have happened since I last wrote in you. First, the fence was finished, and nobody can go out or come in. The Aryans who used to live in the area of the Ghetto all left during these few days to make place for the Jews. From today on, dear diary, we're not in a Ghetto but in a Ghetto-camp, and on every house they've pasted a notice which tells exactly what we're not allowed to do, signed by Gendarme Lieutenant-Colonel Péterffy, commander of the Ghetto-camp, himself. Actually, everything is forbidden, but the most awful thing of all is that the punishment for everything is death. There is no difference between things; no standing in the corner, no spankings, no taking away food, no writing down the declension of irregular verbs one hundred times the way it used to be in school. Not at all: the lightest and heaviest punishment—death. It doesn't actually say that this punishment also applies to children, but I think it does apply to us, too. The gendarmes came into the house and took all the food we brought along from the pantry. There was a tremendous amount of food; so much that there wasn't enough place in the pantry, and a lot of it had been put on the roof and in the basement. From now on the women aren't allowed to cook; once a day we will get food from the gendarmes. They also took the logs out of the basement, the cigarettes they found, and even the thirty pengös each that we had been allowed to take into the Ghetto.

On the gate outside they've written down how many people live in the house and who they are. At last now I know that there are forty-eight of us living in seven rooms, and the hall and the foyer are also full of mattresses. Dear diary, I won't be able to go to Papa anymore, though he lives opposite Grandma Lujza and Aunt Lili, or to Anikó, who also lives in the same place where Papa is. Until now Mariska used to sneak in to us through the fence, in a spot where it was still open, and bring fresh bread, butter, meat, fruit and milk. We ate almost exactly the way we did at home, and I don't know what will happen now. The gendarmes certainly won't give any food worthy of the name.

When they searched the house, they took away the tremendous supply of cigarettes that Uncle Béla had. Ági cried more than I did when my bicycle was confiscated. The gendarmes only smirked at her and made such a mess that nobody could find his own things any more. Anyway there isn't any room even for the few things we took with us. Ági just sat on the mattress crying over her cigarettes. The gendarmes pushed her from every side but she didn't move. Dear diary, Ági looked at that cross-eyed gendarme with such a dreamy look as if he were the Almighty God at the very least. But he only laughed and said to Ági: You could go wild over a cigarette butt, couldn't you, you whore! ("Whore" means "wicked woman," Pista Mártón said.) But I know that Ági is upset over the cigarettes on account of Uncle Béla. It's true that she also likes to take a puff, but Uncle Béla is a chain smoker, and Ági says that this is his only addiction, and it's more important to him than life itself. I never want to smoke, so that I won't have any addictions.

But poor Ági, sometimes she just stares with such a sad look that people just don't want to believe their eyes—when the gendarmes had already loaded everything on the truck that waited in front of the house, taking everything they wanted, anything they could lay their hands on, unfortunately also taking the fat and the flour and also the sugar— they were already out of the house when the cross-eyed fellow came back and dropped about a thousand cigarettes into Ági's lap and gave her a good pinch in the face. Here, don't sit there so sad, he said, and ran out. After a very long time I saw Ági laugh again. I see that Ági doesn't care if the gendarme calls her whore and curses her for being a Jew, and speaks to her in the second-person familiar as though she were a child, just so long as this brings cigarettes. I even asked Uncle Béla why Ági behaved like that, and Uncle Béla answered: Ági doesn't think of the gendarme as a human being, she doesn't care how he speaks to her or what he

thinks of her; she is just afraid of him, and in this Ági is
right. But it hurt me that that disgusting cross-eyed gendarme could talk that way to my Ági.

We go to bed at 9 p.m., dear diary, and from now on we
are supposed to get up at five o'clock in the morning. This
has also been ordered by the gendarmes who took everything
away from us. I have no idea how things are going to be
now. Every time I think: This is the end, things couldn't
possibly be worse, and then I find out that it's always possible for everything to get worse, and even much much worse.
Until now we had food, and now there won't be anything
to eat. At least we were able to walk around inside the
Ghetto, and now we won't be able to leave the house. Every
child could wash up in warm water in the bathtub, and now
they've taken the wood from the basement, and we won't be
able to heat water to wash in any more. Until now there was
enough warm water for the adults, too, and they took turns
in the bathroom. It's true that Ági's and Uncle Béla's turn
only came in the evening, but even that was better than what
is in store for us now that there won't be any warm water
at all. Until now Mariska was even able to come to us and
we always had food, and now I really don't know what we're
going to eat. Ági doesn't care about anything except staying
alive, so she keeps saying, If we stay alive, we will be able
to fix everything.

May 14, 1944

Every evening we go to bed early, and we make our beds
while it is still light, because there is no electricity, of course.
Grandpa said that the gendarmes wanted to cut off the water,
too, but then there would certainly be a typhus epidemic in

the Ghetto, and the epidemic might spread beyond the Ghetto walls, and the Aryans would also get sick. That is why we have water! I don't know why, but I'm thinking less about Márta, less than I used to. Of course, I'm not saying that I never think of her. But still, I think about her less often.

Another interesting thing is that since we live in the Ghetto, I all the time dream. At home I would fall asleep as soon as I put down my head.

But at home I never dreamt at all. What I'm saying, dear diary, is that even though I don't think much about Márta, I dream about her at night. For instance, yesterday I dreamt that I was Márta and I stood in a big field, bigger than any I had ever seen, and then I realized that that field was Poland. There wasn't a sign of a human being anywhere, or of a bird, or of any other creature, and it was still, like that time we were waiting to be taken to the Ghetto. In my dream I was very frightened by the silence and I started running. Suddenly, that cross-eyed gendarme, who returned the cigarettes to Ági, grabbed me from behind by the neck, and put his pistol against my nape. The pistol felt very cold. I wanted to scream, but not a sound came out of my throat. I woke up and woke up Marica and told her what an awful dream I had had. Suddenly it occurred to me that that is the way poor Márta must have felt at the moment the Germans shot her to death!

May 17, 1944

I did write in you some time ago, dear diary, didn't I, that every misfortune can be followed by something worse? You see how right I am? The interrogation has begun in the Dreher beer factory. You know, dear diary, the gendarmes don't believe that Jews don't have anything left of their valuables. They say that they probably hid them or buried them in the ground someplace, or deposited them for safekeeping with Aryans. For example, we deposited Grandma's jewelry with Juszti, that's true. Now they come to the Ghetto houses and pick up people, almost all of them rich ones, and take them to the Dreher beer factory. There they beat them until they tell where they hid their possessions. I know that they beat them terribly, because Ági said that you can hear the cries in the hospital. Now everybody in the house is afraid that they will be taken to be beaten at Dreher.

May 18, 1944

Last night, dear diary, the same thing happened to me that happened to Marica. I couldn't sleep, and I overheard what the adults said. At first I heard only Ági and Uncle Bándi Kecskeméti, who know everything from the hospital. They said that people aren't only beaten at Dreher, but also get electric shocks. Ági cried as she told this, and if she hadn't told it, I would have thought that it was all just some story out of an awful nightmare. Ági said that from Dreher, people are brought to the hospital bleeding at the mouth and ears, and some of them also with teeth missing and the soles of their feet swollen so that they can't stand. Dear diary, Ági also told other things, like what the gendarmes do to the women, because women are also taken there, things that it would be better if I didn't write them down in you. Things that I am incapable of putting into words, even though you know, dear diary, that I haven't kept any secrets from you till now. I even heard—but this time it was Grandpa who told it in the dark—that in the Ghetto here, there are many people who commit suicide. In the Ghetto pharmacy there is enough poison, and Grandpa also said that it would be better if he took cyanide and also gave some to Grandma. At this Ági began to wail. I heard her crawl over to Grandpa's mattress in the dark and say to him crying: Patience, my dear Papa, this can't go on much longer! Even Grandma said: I really don't want to die, because maybe I will yet live to see a better world, and all those people who are now so inhuman and wicked will be punished.

May 29, 1944

And so, dear diary, now the end of everything has really come. The Ghetto has been divided up into blocks and we're all going to be taken away from here.

May 30, 1944

The people of Block One were taken away yesterday. All of them had to be in their houses in the afternoon. We've been locked up in here a long time, but now even those with special passes aren't allowed to go out anymore. We even know already that we can take along one knapsack for every two persons. It is forbidden to put in it more than one change of underwear; no bedding. Rumor has it that food is allowed, but who has any food left? The gendarmes took everybody's food away when they took ours. It is so quiet you can hear a fly buzz. Nobody cries. We don't even care that only Grandpa and Uncle Béla are allowed to take a knapsack.

Dear diary, everybody says we're going to stay in Hungary; the Jews from all over the country are being brought to the Lake Balaton area and we are going to work there. But I don't believe it. That train-wagon is probably awful, and now nobody says that we're being taken away, but that they deport us. I've never heard this word before, and now Ági says to Uncle Béla: Béluska, don't you understand? We are being deported! There's a gendarme pacing back and forth in front of the house. Yesterday he was in Rédey Park, from where the Jews are being deported. Not from the real railroad station, because then it would all be seen by the city, Grandpa says. As though the city cares at all. If the Aryans had wanted to, they could have prevented our being put in the Ghetto. But they were even glad about it, and now they also don't care what happens to us! That gendarme in front of the house, whom Uncle Béla calls a friendly gendarme, because he never yells at us and doesn't even speak familiarly to the women, came into the garden and told us that he will have to leave the gendarmerie, because what he saw in Rédey Park isn't a fit sight for human beings. They stuffed eighty people into each wagon and all they gave them was one pail of water for that many people. But what is even more awful is that they bolt the wagons. In this terrible heat we will suffocate in there! The gendarme says that he doesn't understand these Jews: not even the children cried; all of them were like zombies; like robots. They walked into the wagon so mechanically, without making a sound. The friendly gendarme didn't sleep all night, even though—he said—he usually falls asleep as soon as his head touches the pillow. It was such an awful sight that even he couldn't fall asleep, he said. And after all, he's a gendarme! Ági and Uncle Béla are whispering something to each other about our staying here in some kind of typhoid hospital, because they plan to say that Uncle Béla has typhoid fever. It's possible, because he had it when he was in the Ukraine. All I know is that I don't believe anything anymore, all I think about is Márta, and I'm afraid that what happened to her is going to happen to us, too. It's no use that everybody says that we're not going to Poland but to Balaton. Even though, dear diary, I don't want to die; I want to live even if it means that I'll be the only person here allowed to stay. I would wait for the end of the war in some cellar, or on the roof, or in some secret cranny. I would even let the cross-eyed gendarme, the one who took our flour away from us, kiss me, just as long as they didn't kill me, only that they should let me live.

Now I see that friendly gendarme has let Mariska come in. I can't write anymore, dear diary, the tears run from my eyes, I'm hurrying over to Mariska . . .   (End of diary)

Tamarah Lazerson

LITHUANIA ∞ *13 YEARS OLD*

*I*n 1941, thirteen-year-old Tamarah was living with her
parents in Kovno, Lithuania, when the Nazis occupied their town.
Her father, a psychiatrist, persuaded her to begin keeping a diary of
the historic events she was witnessing.

In August of 1941, the Jews of Kovno were forced to move
into a ghetto. Two thousand intellectuals were murdered immediately
and four thousand people were forced into slave labor. Eventually the
entire ghetto of thirty thousand Jews was burned to the ground and
Tamarah was separated from her parents. She escaped the Nazis but
she was so devastated by the war and the loss of her parents that
often she did not want to go on living. She thought of herself as an
orphan, and, in fact, the death of both her parents was later confirmed.

On May 8, 1945, the Nazis surrendered and Tamarah
began to hope again and to restore her own will to live. She ended
her diary the following September with a promise "to pave a new
road for myself to the future."

Tamarah went on to finish her studies in chemistry and to marry a fellow student, Michael Ostrowsky. Her Terezín Diary *was published in Israel in 1966.*

September 14, 1942

By chance I was conscripted to join a Jewish labor battalion. To my amazement the conversations centered around smuggling "bundles" into the ghetto, despite the threat of severe punishments. Our people endanger their very lives to obtain food. They hide their purchases in their clothing and smuggle them in at the gate or above the ghetto fence. And even if they are searched, they somehow get through. We are a remarkable people, indestructible. No decrees or edicts will break us. I declare this people will never be destroyed, despite their unspeakable suffering; therefore it is an eternal people and ultimately it shall overcome its enemies.

September 21

My old wound has reopened. The school year has begun. I am deeply pained that another year will go to waste. But what can I do? . . .

November 24

A long time has passed since I have read a book. It's terribly hard to obtain them now. To add to our troubles, the electricity has been cut off. My room is dark and unheated. Nothing to do but to crawl into bed. At seven o'clock, and sometimes even earlier, I'm in bed. These are my worst hours. Memories overwhelm me and there's no way to shake them off. I remain sleepless and toss about half the night.

April 4, 1943

I am now working in a trade school and am very pleased. The lectures are interesting. We take notes diligently and then study them at home. I cannot recognize myself, for I am now preparing for life in Eretz Yisrael. Today I handed in quite a long essay for our wall newspaper. I ended it with the slogan: "Eretz Yisrael awaits us!" I am happy!

May 20

I am very pleased with myself. It seems to me that I had strayed and have been wandering about aimlessly. And now at long last I have found an aim in life. I am no longer forlorn—an individual without a homeland and a people. No! I have found an aim: to struggle, to study, to devote my strength to advance the well-being of my people and my homeland. I am proud of it. I am no longer blind—God and fate have opened my eyes. I now see that my goals in life were false, and I have atoned. My heart tells me that I am now on the right road. I trust that I shall not be blinded again. Hurrah! Long live the Homeland, our hope and our faith. . . .

August 10

Yesterday a group of Hitler Youth hikers visited our Jewish workshops. For them it was an entertaining excursion— a lark.

August 15

I am working in a tailor shop and am continuing my Hebrew studies. I am absorbed in the cultural life of the ghetto. A large number of our youth participate and are avid to learn. They deserve praise. I myself take part in three study circles and am pleased. As may be expected, there are two kinds of young people in the ghetto. Some are permeated with love and longing for Eretz Yisrael and all that the Zionist ideal implies. They are thirsty for knowledge and pursue idealistic, meaningful activities. The others are unbridled and completely given over to satisfying their lusts. This is utterly disgusting and painful for me to observe. They are degenerates.

September 8

I am busier than ever and have little time to write. I now belong to four study circles, two of which I lead. I am engaged in important work. Celia and I have become attached to the pitiful children of Zeznier. We help them; they are so dependent on us. We comfort them, teach them Jewish values, and inspire them with goals for living. I am alive and dynamic. I feel that I am needed and useful.

[During this period the ghetto was being emptied, and many of its inhabitants were deported.] I am deeply distressed about the future of our generation. I'd like to write a poem, "The Mother and the Child," but I haven't the time or the inspiration. I have no books and am very bored—especially on Sundays. No one visits me, and I am no longer occupied in cultural activity. The big tenement houses are becoming empty and dark. The weather is cold. It is raining; my feet are frozen; my spirits are very low.

November 14

SS commander Wilhelm Geke is "busy" in the ghetto. His aim is to convert it into a concentration camp. He has promised to build a new hospital. I am deeply suspicious of his promises.

All who can do so escape from the city. Mothers place their children with Lithuanian friends because concentration camp means death to all. . . .

December 5

I am struggling with myself. Again the wound in my heart opens. Three years lost. O God, I recall the past. I advanced from class to class, ever higher, and suddenly the ban—a fatal blow to my future.

Three years. It's hard to take. Be it as it may, if I'm alive I shall yet catch up. I know I can be a person of value to mankind. . . .

I am weighed down by my enslavement and have no time or strength to write, to think, or even to read. I am mired in a morass, into which I sink as I daily labor from early morning to night with the slave gang. Around me is darkness. I thirst for light. . . .

April 7, 1944

Five months have passed. The landscape has changed. The ghetto went up in flames and has left behind ruin and devastation that boggle the mind. Not a building in sight. Where once proud edifices stood erect, only blackened chimneys remain. The place is now a graveyard. The blackened skeletons stretch skyward, calling down revenge for the outrage committed against them and their former inhabitants.

We are now free. It is five months since I have thrown off the prison shackles. The rescuers came to save me, but woe is me! Only a handful escaped, smoldering embers from the great conflagration.

My life has now taken on a new direction. I am a lone orphan, a stray stone. My parents were uprooted during the golden summer days. They were put to death. Ah, my poor father, doomed mother. They could not escape. I am left with an agonizing pain and an aching heart. Only little Vitas, my beloved younger brother, is left alive! With him I do not feel quite so desolate. How fortunate am I that he succeeded in escaping! We are but two remaining limbs of a time-honored stock.

Before me pass scenes of our happy past. Why do I say a "happy past"? Even though my hands and legs were manacled, my heart was free. Now even my poor heart is chained. Alone in the thick forest, I seek the way to a sympathetic heart—my mother's. Physically I exist, but spiritually? . . . I learn; I live, I swallow bitter grub. I subsist.

"Daughter mine, what else do you need?"

"You, mother mine," I reply silently in a corner of my heart.

Today I saw a dead body. A human being, beautiful and blooming, suddenly cut off by death, lying in a casket. He was Dr. Stokes. His hands, white as snow, rested on his breast, and his bluish lips looked as if they were about to smile. He is smiling, but not at life. He has experienced death but he looks as if he were still alive. He *is* dead. Explain to me O World, can it be that a man is so helpless before his fated end? If so, why struggle and suffer? Man's destiny is to end in a coffin, legs stretched out, lifeless. Not a teardrop will accompany you on your last journey. But why tears? Is it easier to observe the unspeakable distress of a mother near the dead body of her offspring? No, a hundred times no!

The ground will welcome you, the tired, to her bosom. The heavens will let fall, at the very least, a tear—and thus your life will end. Why sink into despair? Why mourn? Why love and hate? No need! Manifestly we are but withered grass in the parched fields of life.

December 29

I note with a pained heart that I am beginning to forget Yiddish, which is dear to me. What's with you, Tamarah? Have you already forgotten the affliction that you have borne together with your people? Now that you live among gentiles, have you blotted out the oath you took on that black and sinister night? Remember! There is still time. Open your eyes and see the torment of your people. A voice calls out of the darkness: Right the wrong! I hear the voice, and my heart is torn. I awake. About me the night is thick with darkness. I see the horrible devastation of war and hear the weeping of children. O my people Israel! I can't forget you. An inner voice calls me to you. I am coming. I am ready to crawl on my knees and kiss your sacred soil. Only tell me that you hear my call. Say you will not spurn your daughter who yearns to return to you. I struggle with myself. I am all wrought up. I am consumed with fears. I await your answer.

January 14, 1945

Boredom and cold; it is bleak outside and in my heart. Vitas left for some place afar, and I do not know where. Uncle and aunt are somewhere in a desolate land, and I am here alone, a stranger. O God, what a burden it is to be solitary among aliens, fatherless and motherless. There is no one to whom you can run for solace, to embrace, to kiss. Around me are apathetic faces of people. How long can this continue? How can one stand up under it and endure? I want to die so that my sufferings will end. Not to live any longer, not to feel the oppression, the hate. What have I done to deserve all this? Why have I borne suffering all these years? When will it all end? When will the tears cease flowing? When will the sun rise? Never! Only when the soul rises heavenward will I find surcease. Why is life so cruel? Is there any happiness on this earth?

May 9

Yesterday Germany surrendered unconditionally. The war is over. Red flags fly triumphantly over Kovno. At long last the ugly Fascists have been decisively defeated. . . . Whatever may come, I am delighted that the dictator has been brought to his knees. The arrogant fiend who touted "Germany, Germany above all" now has to stoop to the barbarian of the East—the USSR.

You have lost; just as proud and mighty Rome did not rise out of its ashes, so Germany will not raise her head again above the nations of the world. She has fallen. Her strong might has been crushed forever. Long live peace! Honor to the heroes who raised the flag of victory over the contemptible towers of Berlin.

August 10

Yesterday I met Gershowitz. He was a battalion head in Camp Landsberg. There my poor father toiled until he breathed his last. How much he suffered! He was not built for back-breaking labor; he was not suited for slavery. He was aged and weak. This tragic news was confirmed later. The last small spark of hope in me has flickered and died. His book of life is closed. There is no return. I must fortify myself with strength and patience and pave a new road for myself to the future.

Yitskhok Rudashevski

LITHUANIA ∞ 14 YEARS OLD

Y itskhok Rudashevski, an only child born in 1927, lived with his parents in the town of Vilna on the Lithuanian/Russian border. His father worked as a typesetter for a Yiddish newspaper and his mother was a seamstress. His maternal grandmother lived with the small family and Yitskhok was very attached to her.

The German army took over Vilna when Yitskhok was fourteen years old. As he describes in his diary, he and all the Jews of Vilna were systematically humiliated, economically disempowered, and finally confined to a ghetto. Nevertheless, Yitskhok and his young friends strove to continue the cultural and educational activities that they had loved before Vilna was occupied by the Germans. In clubs, performance groups, and ad hoc schools, the children made every effort to continue learning and practicing their arts.

One of the ways Yitskhok tried to remain intellectually alive was to think about the historical events he was living through and to write about them in his diary. He faithfully recorded events *in the Vilna Ghetto from June 1941 to April 1943. When it became clear that Hitler planned the total "liquidation" of Vilna, Yitskhok and his family went into hiding much as Anne Frank and her family did. On the fifth or sixth of October of 1943, the Germans discovered their hideout and took them to the slaughterhouse at Ponar, where they were murdered.*

Yitskhok's cousin, a girl named Sore Voloshin, found an opportune moment and escaped the Germans on the trip to Ponar. She ran into the woods and joined a partisan unit engaged in fighting the Germans. After the war was over, she returned to the hiding place she had shared with Yitskhok and his family. There she found his diary, covered with dirt and mud, and she read it for the first time. She showed it to members of her partisan unit, who saw to it that it would be preserved.

Yitskhok's 204-page diary manuscript, written entirely in Yiddish, is preserved in the archives of the Yivo Institute for Jewish Research in New York. It was first published as a book in Hebrew in 1968 in Israel. The only English edition of the diary was published in Israel in 1973. Very few copies of the diary are still available.

It is Sunday the 21st of June [1941]

A beautiful summer day. Our "ten" is supposed to meet today. I am going to Gabik to have him announce it to some comrades. I met him in his garden busy with a garden bed. Our cheerful conversation was interrupted by the howling of a siren. The siren was so inappropriate to the peaceful joyous summer which spread out around us. The siren cruelly cut the blue air and announced something cruel. The evening of this beautiful summer day is marred. Bombs are bursting over the city. The street was full of smoke. It is war. People have been running around bewildered. Everything has suddenly changed so much. The blue, happy sky has become transformed into a mighty [volcano] which has showered the city with bombs. It has become clear to all: the Hitlerites have attacked our land. They have forced a war upon us. And so we shall retaliate, and strike until we shall smash the aggressor on his own soil. I keep looking at the calm Red Army soldier who is standing on guard in our yard. I feel that I can be sure of him, I see he will not perish. He will perhaps be killed, but the star attached to his hat will remain forever. We are in a cellar. The roar of the propeller-machines prevents us from thinking, and suddenly—a whistle and sharp report, a second, a third, a full hail of them. It becomes calm. I think about our future life. I think that we pioneers will not remain aloof in the struggle. I feel that we shall be useful. Soon, at 6 o'clock, a meeting of our "ten" was supposed to take place. I decide that we must attend it. I had a foreboding that hard tasks await us. The struggle is beginning, the Soviet Union will arise. With these thoughts I went to our meeting place in the little park on the railway street. I carry with me *The Hero in Chains*. We shall read together about Gavroche, the child of the Parisian proletariat who fell on the barricades beside the adult fighters. I approach the little park. No one is there. A little later Serke comes. We talk about the latest events. We were dispersed immediately by the first German bombs. Of all the comrades, two of us came, and that because we live near the railroad. Now as I write I think we have become quite different pioneers. I feel that if they will need us, we shall come, even if it will be our last pioneer meeting.

Serke and I sit for a while in the little park. The bombing stopped as if the sky had cleared. Suddenly we hear the siren again. We run home. Explosions shatter the air again. Outside there is a banging and howling. In the cellar I see before me frightened people with bundles. No one knows what is in store for us. The anxious evening arrives. People await the coming night with terror. I go out into the street. Autos keep moving. The black sky is aflame with red light. There must be a great fire somewhere.

Monday was also an uneasy day. Red Army soldiers crowded into autos are continually riding to Lipovke. The residents are also running away. People say with despair that the Red Army is abandoning us. The Germans are marching on Vilna. The evening of that desperate day approaches. The autos with the Red Army soldiers are fleeing. I understand that they are leaving us. I am certain, however, that resistance will come.

I look at the fleeing army and I am certain that it will return victoriously. The night was a restless one. Autos are roaring in the street. From time to time a burst of shooting begins. A neighbor notices a red star in my lapel. He tells me to take it off. I cannot make peace with the thought: is it really so? I am full of sorrow and pain that it is ending thus. I feel that he is right.

It is Tuesday, the 24th of June

I observe the empty, sad streets. A Lithuanian with a gun goes through the street. I begin to understand the base betrayal of the Lithuanians. They shot the Red Army soldiers in the back. They make common cause with the Hitlerite bandits. the Red Army will return and you will pay dearly, traitor. We shall live to see your end.

At dawn a motorcycle rides through the street. A gray square-rimmed helmet, spectacles, a greatcoat and a rifle. Unfortunately, the first soldier of the German usurping army that I have caught sight of. The helmet flashes coldly and evilly. A little later I go down to the street. Today at ten o'clock we were supposed to have a meeting of the "tens." Today the school library is open. I know that I will find no one there. However, I go to the school anyway. All this has happened too suddenly. It is hard to comprehend that everything has actually come to a dead stop. I approach the school. The school is sealed up. I meet a comrade. And we walk like strangers over wide streets. The German army is marching. We both stand with bowed heads. A black mirage of tanks, motorcycles, machines.

I recall how last year almost at the same time I met the Red Army in a small Lithuanian town where we ran several kilometers to meet the first Soviet tank which had stopped there. A year has passed and now German tanks are riding over the Vilna streets. And it seems to me that there is some grievous error which will soon be corrected. I imagine life under the Germans as a short provisional period. I look at the entry of the Germans and I am already thinking of their departure. I imagine them fleeing back, beaten up and without heads. The Red Army is here again. I went in to see my teacher Mire. She was sitting in a depressed mood. We understood each other.

I went to my friend Benkye Nayer. I met him heating the range with journals, books, notebooks. On coming home, I also heated the range ... The first day under the German conquerors passed. I lie at night and think. German autos keep riding day and night. I think how defenseless we are, isolated from each other, exposed entirely to the mercy of the Hitlerites.

Weeks drag on. I returned from the summer, from its surroundings, chained to the house, to the yard. We do not see our gang. There is absolutely no contact among our gang. Everyone is occupied with his day-to-day concerns. Jews are humiliated and exploited. One must stand in long lines to receive bread and other products. Jews are ousted from them. Germans go to the rows, throw out the Jews. Jews receive less food than the Aryans. Our life is a life of helpless terror. Our day has no future. We have one consolation. The Red Army shows a fighting spirit. It has become concentrated. It gives blow for blow, it is offering resistance. The Germans have realized that they will not accomplish this in short order. They are dealing with a courageous fighter who does not abandon our struggle.

Lithuanian "captors" walk around the houses to capture Jewish men, drive them to a station and send them to work. Many of them do not return. I sometimes go to the courtyard of the community at Strashun 6. I bring food there for father. Here many Jews are driven together. From here they are led to work. I enter the courtyard. The courtyard is full of a crowd of men, gray, gloomy, discouraged men, like a large, frightened, murmuring flock. From time to time a woman runs into the courtyard with a lamentation. Here each person comes with his misfortune to the small room where the first Vilna Jewish council is sitting. They think they will be helped here. Presently a German barges into the courtyard. The people rush towards him. They offer themselves to him, because they know that he is a good German.

The German selects a group of healthy men, selects them like horses, looking at the muscles of each, lines them up and orders them to go. The rest dash after him. The German drives them with his belt. . . .

It is dusk. "We have staved off another day," the women say to each other. The men of our courtyard arrive, perspiring and covered with dust. All day they have been dragging boxes into the storehouses for weapons.

Our hearts are crushed witnessing the shameful scene where women and older people are beaten and kicked in the middle of the street by small bandits. A performance. Germans stand and look at a throng of gentile women. I stand at the window and feel a sense of rage. Tears come to my eyes: all our helplessness, all our loneliness lies in the streets. There is no one to take our part. And we ourselves are so helpless! so helpless. Life becomes more and more difficult. People do not go anywhere. On scores of streets a Jew must not show himself. Only in the morning do frightened Jewish women slip out to do some shopping. The men go off to work. It rains incessantly. We are so sad, so lonely. We are exposed to mockery and humiliation. A new feeling of terror frequently overcomes the few neighbors of the yard. They are looking for weapons. The courtyard is full of Germans. There is a ring, the door is torn open and all hearts are pounding. Germans in helmets rush in, their weapons resound. Meekly the cupboards and drawers are opened to them. Cruelly they fling everything apart, fling, throw, go away and leave behind them a sad house with things scattered all over. We stand around with pale faces. We calm ourselves only when we learn that they have left. The mood becomes worse from day to day. People talk about the ghetto. In the rainy evenings we gather at a neighbor's house and talk about the news, the situation in the ghetto which has now become a reality.

The 8th of July

The decree was issued that the Vilna Jewish population must put on badges front and back—a yellow circle and inside it the letter J. It is daybreak. I am looking through the window and see before me the first Vilna Jews with badges. It was painful to see how people were staring at them. The large piece of yellow material on their shoulders seemed to be burning me and for a long time I could not put on the badge. I felt a hump, as though I had two frogs on me. I was ashamed to appear in them on the street not because it would be noticed that I am a Jew but because I was ashamed of what [they were] doing to us. I was ashamed of our helplessness. We will be hung from head to foot with badges and we cannot help each other in any way. It hurt me that I saw absolutely no way out. Now we pay no attention to the badges. The badge is attached to our coats but has not touched our consciousness. We now possess so much consciousness that we can say that we are not ashamed of our badges! Let those be ashamed who have hung them on us. Let them serve as a searing brand to every conscious German who attempts to think about the future of his people.

It is the end of the summer of 1941

We do not know what is in store for us. Never did I feel the coming of autumn as I did at that time. The days became more and more turbulent. The furniture of the Jews is being confiscated. People are talking about a ghetto. Suddenly the terrible news spread about the provocation on Daytshe, Shavler, Mikolayvske, Disner and other streets. At night the Jewish population of these streets was led out, we do not know where. Later it became known: to Ponar where they were shot to death. The situation has become more and more strained. The Jews in our courtyard are in despair. They are transferring things to their Christian neighbors. The sad days began of binding packages, of sleepless nights full of restless expectation about the coming day. It is the night between the fifth and the sixth of September, a beautiful, sleepless September night, a sleepless, desperate night, people like shadows. People sit in helpless, painful expectation with their bundles. Tomorrow we shall be led to the ghetto.

It is the 6th of September

A beautiful, sunny day has risen. The streets are closed off by Lithuanians. The streets are turbulent. Jewish workers are permitted to enter. A ghetto is being created for Vilna Jews.

People are packing in the house. The women go back and forth. They wring their hands when they see the house looking as if after a pogrom. I go around with bleary eyes among the bundles, see how we are being uprooted overnight from our home. Soon we have our first view of the move to the ghetto, a picture of the Middle Ages—a gray black mass of people goes harnessed to large bundles. We understand that soon our turn will come. I look at the house in disarray, at the bundles, at the perplexed, desperate people. I see things scattered which were dear to me, which I was accustomed to use. We carry the bundles to the courtyard. On our street a new mass of Jews streams continually to the ghetto. The small number of Jews of our courtyard begin to drag the bundles to the gate. Gentiles are standing and taking part in our sorrow. Some Jews hire gentile boys to help carry the bundles. A bundle was suddenly stolen from a neighbor. The woman stands in despair among her bundles and does not know how to cope with them, weeps and wrings her hands. Suddenly everything around me begins to weep. Everything weeps. The people weep looking at the bundles which they cannot manage. Here a woman's bundle burst apart. Eggs began to roll. The sun, as though it were ashamed at what people are doing, has clouded over. It began to rain. We too are carried along with the mass of Jews with their bundles. The street streamed with Jews carrying bundles. The first great tragedy. People are harnessed to bundles which they drag across the pavement. People fall, bundles scatter. Before me a woman bends under her bundle. From the bundle a thin string of rice keeps pouring over the street. I walk burdened and irritated. The Lithuanians drive us on, do not let us rest. I think of nothing: not what I am losing, not what I have just lost, not what is in store for me. I do not see the streets before me, the people passing by. I only feel that I am terribly weary, I feel that an insult, a hurt is burning inside me. Here is the ghetto gate. I feel that I have been robbed, my freedom is being robbed from me, my home, and the familiar Vilna streets I love so much. I have been cut off from all that is dear and precious to me. People crowd at the gate. Finally I am on the other side of the gate. The stream of people flings me into a gate blocked with bundles. I throw down the bundles which cut my shoulders. I find my parents and here we are in the ghetto house. It is dusk, rather dark and rainy. The little streets, Rudnitski, Shavler, Yatkever, Shpitalne, and Disner which constitute the ghetto look like anthills. It swarms with people. The newcomers begin to settle down, each in his tiny bit of space, on his bundles. Additional Jews keep streaming in constantly. We settle down in our place. Besides the four of us there are eleven persons in the room. The room is a dirty and stuffy one. It is crowded. The first ghetto night. We lie three together on two doors. I do not sleep. In my ears resounds the lamentation of this day. I hear the restless breathing of people with whom I have been suddenly thrown together, people who just like me have suddenly been uprooted from their homes.

The first ghetto day begins. I run right out into the street. The little streets are still full of a restless mass of people. It is hard to push your way through. I feel as if I were in a box. There is no air to breathe. Wherever you go you encounter a gate that hems you in. We drift to the gate which divides us from Strashun and I find relatives and acquaintances. Many of the people no longer have places to live in. They settle down on stairs, in stores. Suddenly the mass of people in the street starts to sway, people begin to run in fear. German officers are going to photograph them, the crooked little streets, the frightened people. They take pleasure in the Middle Ages which they have transported into the twentieth century!!!!

They leave soon. People calm down. I decide to hunt up my friends in the courtyard. I have an idea that all of us will be there. I soon find Benkye Nayer, Gabik, and several others. The first day is spent in settling down, hunting up one another. The second evening in the ghetto people feel a little more at home, calmer. My chums are figuring out how many weeks we shall be sitting here. At night things are turbulent again. German soldiers have slipped into the ghetto in order to plunder. There is a knocking at the gate. People begin to get dressed hurriedly in the crowded quarters and now three soldiers barge in. They search, crawl over the bedding with their feet. They look for rings on people's fingers, ransack, make a mess of the slumbering house and go away without taking anything. Women shout after them: "Thank you, dear sir, good night." I do not understand the reason for the thanks—because they have not been robbed?—considering that the robber is not interested in listening to anything anyway. I am disgusted with this. I am upset. The exasperated people wish one another a good, calm night and lie down again.

The first ghetto days speed by

Father goes to work again in the munitions storehouses. It is crowded and smoky in the house. Like many others I go hunting for firewood. We break doors, floors, and carry wood. One person tries to grab from the other, they quarrel over a piece of wood, the first effect of these conditions on the human being. People become petty, cruel to one another. Soon we notice the first Jewish policemen. They are supposed to keep order in the ghetto. In time, however, they become a caste which helps the oppressors in their work. With the help of the Jewish police, the Gestapo accomplished many things in the course of time. The Jewish police help to grasp their brothers by the throat, they help to trip up their brothers.

There is a great deal of restlessness also in our ghetto. The white certificates are being exchanged for yellow ones of which, however, very few are issued. Thus was born the yellow certificate, the blood-drenched delusion, this little piece of paper constituting such a tragedy for the Vilna Jews. The days are full of expectation. Days before a storm. The people, helpless creatures, stagger around in little streets: Like animals sensing the storm, everyone is looking for a place to hide, to save his life. They register as members of the family with the owners of the yellow certificates. Fate suddenly split the people of the ghetto into two parts. One part possesses the yellow certificate. They believe in the power of this little piece of paper. It bestows the right to life. The second part—lost, despairing people—people who sense their doom, and do not know where to go. We do not have a yellow certificate. Our parents are running around like hundreds of others, as though in a fever.

Something terrible is hovering in the air. Soon, soon something will explode. A troubled evening approaches. The streets are full of people. The owners of the yellow professional certificates are registering. Whoever can do so, hides. To hide, to bury oneself: in a basement, in an attic, to save one's life. Scores of people plead with those who are standing in line, the chosen ones, to be registered on their yellow certificate. People offer money and gold for the privilege of being registered.

The tenants of the house go into a hide-out. We go with them. Three floors of warehouses in the courtyard of Shavler 4. Stairs lead from one story to the other. The stairs from the first to the second story have been taken down and the opening has been closed up with boards. The hide-out consists of two small warehouses. You enter the hide-out through a hole in the wall of an apartment which borders on the uppermost story of the hide-out. The hole is blocked ingeniously by a kitchen cupboard. One wall of the cupboard serves at the same time as a little gate for the hole. The hole is barricaded by stones. The flat through which you enter the hide-out is located near our apartment. Little groups of people with bundles go in. Soon we also crawl through the hole of the hide-out. Many people have gathered in the two stories of the hide-out. They sneak along like shadows by candlelight around the cold, dank cellar walls. The whole hide-out is filled with a restless murmuring. An imprisoned mass of people. Everyone begins to settle down in the corners, on the stairs. Pillows and bundles are spread out on the hard bricks and boards and people fall asleep. The candle lights begin to die out. Everything is covered in darkness. You hear only the snoring of the sleepers, a groaning, a restless murmuring. It is stifling. An odor of a cellar and of people crowded together. From time to time someone lights a match. By the light I see people lying on the bricks like rags in the dirt. I think: into what kind of helpless, broken creature can man be transformed? I am at my wit's end. I begin to feel very nauseated. I barely lived to see the dawn. The people are crawling out. The dawn brings a new piece of news. Persons with yellow certificates must leave the ghetto with their families. They will leave and now the game will begin. I look at the mass of people with bundles that is streaming to the gate. They are headed for life. How I envy them! I too would like to leave the accursed ghetto which is becoming a terrible snare. I wish like them, the people with the yellow certificates, to go away, to leave the storm behind me, to save my life.

We are in the hide-out again. We expect something any moment. While lying thus on bundles I fell asleep. A noise, the sound of people crowding each other woke me. I understood that the Lithuanians were already in the ghetto. The hide-out is becoming fuller and fuller. We are finally so tightly crowded together that we cannot move. The hide-out is being hammered up. My parents are somewhere upstairs. I am downstairs with my uncle. The hide-out is full of a restless whispering. Candles are being lit. People reassure each other. Suddenly there is a sound of steps. People mass together. An old Jew has remained hanging in the narrow passage of the second story. His feet are dangling over the heads of the people below. He is taken down. People call: "Bring water!" But gradually everything becomes still. Everything becomes completely enveloped in a black, dreadful silence, a silence from which there shouts forth the great tragedy of our helplessness, the destructive storm which is now pervading the ghetto. You hear a faint sound, as though a tempest were being rent with shouts, with shots. My heart beats as though with hammers to the cadence of the storm outside. Soon I feel that the storm is approaching us. My head is dizzy, a cold perspiration oozes forth, my heart stops beating entirely.

We are like animals surrounded by the hunter. The hunter on all sides: beneath us, above us, from the sides. Broken locks snap, doors creak, axes, saws. I feel the enemy under the boards on which I am standing. The light of an electric bulb seeps through the cracks. They pound, tear, break. Soon the attack is heard from another side. Suddenly, somewhere upstairs, a child bursts into tears. A desperate groan breaks forth from everyone's lips. We are lost. A desperate attempt to shove sugar into the child's mouth is of no avail. They stop up the child's mouth with pillows. The mother of the child is weeping. People shout in wild terror that the child should be strangled. The child is shouting more loudly, the Lithuanians are pounding more strongly against the walls. However, slowly everything calmed down of itself. We understand that they have left. Later we heard a voice from the other side of the hide-out. You are liberated. My heart beat with such joy! I have remained alive!

To save one's own life at any price, even at the price of our brothers who are leaving us. To save one's own life and not attempt to defend it . . . the point of view of our dying passively like sheep, unconsciousness of our tragic fragmentation, our helplessness.

We creep out of the hide-out after a six-hour imprisonment. It is eight o'clock in the evening. Everything resembles the aftermath of a catastrophe. The tenants' belongings are scattered over the courtyard. Smashed locks lie around under our feet, everything is turned upside down, topsy turvy, broken. All doors are wide open. The house is unrecognizable. Everything is scattered far and wide, many things are broken. A bottle of spirits lies smashed in the middle of the room. The bundles are ripped with knives. I go out into the street. It is dark. The street is full of the tragedy which has just happened here. On the pavement lie bundles, a bloody reminder of the people who have just been dragged away to their deaths. I enter the courtyard where my cousins live. I notice two large bright windows. I look inside. A house in the wake of a pogrom. Electricity is burning and no person is to be seen. I step on things. It is quiet. A clock strikes forlornly. No one is here.

We live in the ghetto as owners of white certificates. The mood of slaughter has not yet disappeared. What has been will soon be repeated. Meanwhile life is so hard. The owners of the white certificates do not go out to work. In the ghetto everything costs a lot. Toward evening I walk around through the ghetto. From the gate the owners of the yellow certificates arrive with bundles. I look at them with envy. Suddenly there is a noise. You hear people shout: "We wish, we also wish to eat!" The people who are walking, who are shouting, tear the bundles from the new arrivals. I see a person with hungry eyes cutting open a bag of potatoes on his shoulder. Potatoes scatter over the street! . . . We also wish to eat. There is a noise. Police are beating, chasing people. Things calm down. At night people sleep mostly in the hide-out. We are so anxious to get undressed, to lie down in bed. It is cold in the hide-out, it is hard to lie there. Mice squeal all around. There are "aristocrats" in the hide-out, who managed to make soft berths for themselves here. Mother went away to a work-unit. Perhaps it will be possible to obtain a yellow certificate there. Meanwhile a command was issued in the evening that all owners of white certificates must go over immediately into the second ghetto which is assigned to them. Now our street, Shavler, must move. We feel that one ought not to go to the second ghetto. Meanwhile we are again packing bundles, which keep diminishing during the disturbances. Our courtyard is full of people with bundles. The policemen are urging us on to go more quickly. The frightened people feel that they ought not to go. I sensed the craftiness of the exterminators.

I meet mother. She brought a yellow certificate which grants the right to life. And I passed over to the group of more or less calm people, to the yellow certificates.

We take little bundles and join the stream of lucky ones who are leaving the ghetto. We are accompanied by our cousins who are registered with us. It is a cloudy, muddy day. A wet snow is falling. It should take a long time until we shall reach the gate because there is strict inspection there. Around us people are crying. They are taking leave of their relatives who remain here in the ghetto in hide-outs. We learn that old people who are registered as parents are not admitted through the gate. Grandmother cannot go with us. We are in despair. People are no longer admitted into the hide-out which is in the courtyard. They have locked themselves tightly inside. What is one to do? Meanwhile the stream of people began to sway. Our unit goes through the gate. The stream of people has swept us along. We quickly say good-bye to grandmother:—forever. We leave her alone in the middle of the street and we run to save ourselves. I shall never forget the two imploring hands and eyes which begged: "Take me along!" We left the ghetto. We emptied it to enable the wild Lithuanians to break into the defenseless little streets. We go to the gate, a crowded mass of specially selected people who are running away from their closest relatives, and are leaving them to God's mercy. German officers stand on both sides of the highway. They chase and drive us. At the barrier is the checkpoint. Several elderly persons are thrown into the neighboring guarded gate. We rush our way through. Our certificates are being checked. The Lithuanian officers hurry us on to the gate. They raise their rubber clubs. They are driving the selected people to life. . . .

We are already on the street. We see the executioners. Our hearts pound. Detachments of Lithuanians encircle the ghetto. Very soon they will slip inside. They let us go wherever we wish: either into the units or to the second ghetto. The streets become full of little groups of Jews like flocks that have gone astray. We walk in the middle of the street. Autos fly past and spatter us with mud. Mother and I go to the unit "tailor shop." We sat there all day. I sit, look at the satiated, contented Germans who keep moving back and forth. I look at the harassed Jewish workers who are waiting for the relatives they have left in the ghetto. Money is offered the German gendarmes to rescue the brothers, sisters and parents of the workers who have remained there. In the evening we go to the second ghetto. We meet up with uncle. For more than a week he stayed in the second ghetto in a hide-out in a little room, blocked by a cupboard. We lie on the chairs in the house where uncle lives. We are frozen and weary. Mother is crying. We cannot forget that we have abandoned grandmother. With heavy hearts we lie down to sleep in the new place.

I walk around over the little streets of the second ghetto, the little streets of the old Vilna ghetto. Never was there vented on them so much devastation, desolation as now. The old synagogue courtyard is pogromized. Phylacteries, religious books, rags are scattered under one's feet. Everything in the second ghetto is demolished, broken and abandoned. Everything is pervaded by the despair of those who have been wrenched away from here. The word Ponar hovers among the old ghetto streets. After staying three days in the second ghetto we return to the gate of the first. We are not checked. In the ghetto there is devastation. Overturned doors, torn up floors. We come home. Everything is gone to rack and ruin. From the hide-outs people emerge like corpses, pale, dirty, with black rings under their eyes. For three days people lay choked up in holes and cellars. Grandmother is not here. The house fills with weeping and shouting. I run away from the house. I walk over the little streets. A feeling of pain, of resentment burns in me. I feel we are like sheep. We are being slaughtered in the thousands and we are helpless. The enemy is strong, crafty, he is exterminating us according to a plan and we are discouraged.

The Jews must live in blocks according to the units where they are working. We too must move to the block. Life has gradually begun to "return to normal." The handful of surviving Jews has begun to become accustomed to the new conditions. My parents work and I have become the "mistress" in the house. I have learned to cook, to wash floors, and on this I spend my days. In the evening I go to meet my parents. Jewish groups of workers return embittered from the city. Gray masses continue to stream through the gate, free labor for the exploiters.

It is forbidden to transport food from the city through the gate. The Jewish workers find a way out and smuggle the necessities concealed under their things. They are searched at the gate and [whatever is found] is taken away. This respectable work actually is being carried out by Jewish police. Winter is approaching with its new daily cares: warm clothes, wood. Along with the winter there appeared a new certificate. The pink family certificate which was received only by family members of the owners of yellow certificates. Things became troubled again. And at the end of December a new raid was launched which wrenched away another few hundred people.

A frosty day. We are not permitted to walk in the streets. Lithuanians walk through the houses and take away those who do not possess pink certificates. We sit in the house and see through the windows how people are being led to death.

The only consolation has now become the latest news at the front. We suffer here, but there, far in the East, the Red Army has started an offensive. The Soviets have occupied Rostov, have dealt a blow from Moscow and are marching forward. And it always seems that any moment freedom will follow it.

The 23rd of March [1942]

Suddenly an explosion of bombs which lasts several hours. I stand in the cellar and hear the explosions and think that those are our Soviet aviators. For several hours they hurled bombs upon the city and left. In the city they created havoc among the Lithuanian barracks. In this way they announced that they are strong and will [return].

How terrible the ghetto streets look under the cloudy sky which flares up every once in a while with a dazzling redness.

Saturday the 12th [of September]

Today is a holiday. The Jewish New Year, Rosh Hashanah. It is a cool day, like all the other days recently. The sky is clear. In the morning I go down to the street. A holiday spirit which is anything but cheerful is diffused over the few little

ghetto streets. Something somehow is missing. I am reminded of the past. From somewhere a sound of loud, quick
praying is heard. Here and there Jewish women walk past
with festive kerchiefs on their heads, with prayer books
under their arms. I recalled my grandmother, how she too
used to go to synagogue this way once a year. On the detest-
able ghetto gate near the sentry a large poster hangs: A New
Year's greeting. The gate guard wishes us a Happy New
Year. This New Year's greeting on the gate ringed with
barbed wire, bearing the signature of the ghetto guard, made
a strange impression upon me. They wish us a Good Year
on the banner of the ghetto gate which symbolizes the dark
and languishing life of the ghetto. And who wishes us this?
In fact those, who, although not of their own will, were nevertheless the very people created to guard us and keep us
far from freedom. However, let us assume that through this
gate we shall return to freedom.

It is twilight. I go out into the street. The streets are lively.
People are walking around dressed up. Today is a holiday.
This is evident in every house you enter, the poverty has
been scrubbed away. Formerly this would not have made an
impression on me. However, now I felt strangely good because the everyday gray day is so much in need of a little
holiday spirit which should drive away for a while the gray
commonplaceness of life. People walked around until late on
the little Vilna ghetto streets. A strangely sad holiday mood.
And now the crowds thin out more and more. A cold starry
sky overhead. From time to time a star flies past across the
sky on its silvery way and suddenly falls down.

In the house we had a little fun. The workers in our house
belong to the famous "Schneiderstube." Mother works there

too. The workers tell about the events of the whole week. If they meet some fool of a German who wants a cap, the fellows make fun of him, they bring out a Jew and introduce him as the best "capmaker of Poland." The German believes it. Then they tell him that this diligent Jew can make beautiful caps only when he receives a little food. He is persuaded. He takes out material which can suffice for three hats and gives it to them. And they tell him that this is nothing. When the time comes for delivery, he is simply told: "Listen, do you have cigarettes? Give us cigarettes and you will have 'a delightful cap.'" Finally they make him a hat which looks like a blintz on him and he exclaims into the bargain, "Jews are a capable people!"

Thursday the 17th of September

It is getting colder and colder. How dismal and dejected the ghetto looks! A cold rain whips through the small narrow streets. You become sad and bored during the long hours that you hang around in one place. We do not go to school on account of an epidemic. It is a terrible time when you cannot settle down to some kind of work and you waste days on nothing. Toward evening when people return from work they sit down in their confined quarters and tell one another news—political and ghetto news. They tell that here and there people have secretly heard the radio and other such matters.

The Germans are now carrying out a mighty attack against Stalingrad (Tsaritsyn). Stalingrad has tremendous significance for both sides. By occupying Stalingrad, the Germans cut off the center of the Caucasus. By conquering Stalingrad, the Germans reach the Volga and occupy its largest, most important port. At the time when the Soviets have the full initiative in the middle and northern front—at Voronezh, at Rzhev, to the south of Ladoga, and across the Neva, near Stalingrad, a tremendous assault is in progress—the Soviets must be on the defensive at Stalingrad. At Stalingrad battles are proceeding on a tremendous scale. Both opponents have concentrated their strongest forces. In addition to its important strategic significance, Stalingrad has become a matter of prestige for both sides. The Germans wish to complete their summer campaign with the occupation of Stalingrad which would add glory to the German victories. The Red Army is fighting in the suburbs of Stalingrad with tremendous obstinacy and heroism. Tens of thousands are perishing in the gigantic battles at Stalingrad. The Soviet people are defending Stalin's city with body and soul. We who live in the ghetto read the reports daily, are eager for good news. Everyone's attention is now directed toward Stalingrad. Everyone is waiting for something tangible, for the final defeat of Germany. Everyone is waiting for the yearned-for peace when the weary world will straighten its back.

Saturday the 19th of September

It is cold and sad. When in the world will we get back to our studies? When I used to go to my lessons, I knew how to divide the days, and the days would fly, and now they drag by for me grayly and sadly. Oh, how dreary and sad it is to sit locked up in a ghetto. . . .

Sunday the 20th

It is Yom Kippur Eve. A sad mood suffuses the ghetto. People have such a sad High Holy Day feeling. I am as far from religion now as before the ghetto. Nevertheless, this holiday drenched in blood and sorrow which is solemnized in the ghetto, now penetrates my heart. In the evening I felt so sad at heart. People sit at home and weep. They remind themselves of the past.... Drenching each other with their tears as they embrace, they wish each other a Happy New Year.... I run out into the street and there it is also the same: sorrow flows over the little streets, the ghetto is drenched in tears. The hearts which have turned to stone in the grip of ghetto woes and did not have time to weep their fill have now in this evening of lamentation poured out all their bitterness.... The evening was dreary and darkly sad for me....

Monday the 5th [October]

Finally I have lived to see the day. Today we go to school. The day passed quite differently. Lessons, subjects. Both VIth classes were combined. There is a happy spirit in school. Finally the club too was opened. My own life is shaping up in quite a different way! We waste less time, the day is divided and flies by very quickly.... Yes, that is how it should be in the ghetto, the day should fly by and we should not waste time.

Wednesday the 7th

Life has become a little more interesting. The club work has begun. We have groups for literature, natural science. After leaving class at 7:30 I go immediately to the club. It is gay there, we have a good time and return home evenings in a large crowd. The days are short, it is dark in the street, and our bunch leaves the club. There is a racket, a commotion. Policemen shout at us but we do not listen to them.

Sunday the 18th

Jewish policemen donned official hats. I walk across the street and here go some of them wearing leather jackets, boots and green round hats with glossy peaks and Stars of David. Here goes Smilgovski (an "officer") in a dark blue hat and a golden Star of David. They march smartly by in unison. (Jackets are being "loaned" by force in the streets.) They impress you as Lithuanians, as kidnapers. An unpleasant feeling comes over me. I hate them from the bottom of my heart, ghetto Jews in uniforms, and how arrogantly they stride in the boots they have plundered! The entire ghetto is stunned. Everyone feels the same way about them and they have somehow become such strangers to the ghetto. In me they arouse a feeling compounded of ridicule, disgust and fear. In the ghetto it is said that the reason for the uniforms is that thirty Vilna policemen are riding to the neighboring towns to set up a ghetto in Oshmene. This is not known for certain.

Monday the 19th

The news in the ghetto spreads like a wind: today thirty Jewish policemen are leaving for the small towns for a certain kind of work by order of the Gestapo. A sorrowful mood prevails in the ghetto. Insult and misfortune have reached their climax. Jews will dip their hands in the dirtiest and bloodiest work. They wish simply to replace the Lithuanians. Our Jewish policemen are now leaving for Oshmene. They take along certificates. The Jews from the neighboring towns will be transported to Oshmene and there raids will probably occur, the same, sad, bloody story as in Vilna, and our police will be the most active participants in all of this. I stand at the gate. They are driving people away, but I see everything: thirty policemen as one man in leather coats and new caps, lined up in two rows, and a certain Weiss, The Gestapo-dog, is drilling them. And now they all pour into a closed auto. . . . They will come all dressed up to the unfortunate ones. The Gestapo people will thus kill two birds with one stone: first, they will carry out another bloody piece of work, certificates, ghettos, packing one's things. We who have suffered understand what that means. Second, they will demonstrate that Jews in uniform drive their own brothers to the ghetto, distribute certificates, and keep order with the knout. People say that they have already left with thousands. Vilna residents who have relatives in those towns have already paid large sums for their relatives to receive certificates there. For we, residents of Vilna, are aware that a certificate is a life-insuring note. The entire ghetto is in an uproar about this departure. How great is our misfortune, how great is our shame, our humiliation! Jews help the Germans in their organized, terrible work of extermination!

Wednesday the 21st

Today at the club we had a final rehearsal of the club's artistic efforts: recitations and dances that can be presented at any time. The club is preparing a performance for the workers in the unit "Beutelager." All the numbers have been examined by a jury committee. We sat until 11 o'clock and listened to tryouts. Splendid songs, bright, young voices. The poem by Gorki, "The Stormy Petrel," was beautiful. The poem "Hands" was also recited beautifully and the poem "Vilna". The poems, all such warmly felt, and intimate and strong ones, touched the heart.

Thursday the 22nd

The days pass quickly. Having finished my few lessons, I began to do a little housework. I read a book, wrote the diary, and off to class. The few lessons run by quickly: Latin, mathematics, history, Yiddish, and back home again. After eating I go to the club. Here we enjoy ourselves a little. Today there was a final rehearsal under the direction of Yashunski (the director of the educational division). They also presented the (puppet) theater of the club Miadim arranged by two boys. It is quite nice, although very primitive. The literary part is very weak, but it does not matter as long as one sees creativity. Our youth works and does not perish. Our history group works. We listen to lectures about the great French Revolution, about its periods. The second section of the history group, ghetto history, is also busy. We are investigating the history of Courtyard Shavler 4. For this purpose questionnaires have been distributed among the members, with questions that have to be asked of the courtyard residents. We have already begun the work. I go with a friend. The questions are divided into four parts: questions relating to the period of Polish, Soviet and German rule (up until the ghetto), and in the ghetto. The residents answer in different ways. Everywhere, however, the same sad ghetto song: property, certificates, hide-outs, the abandonment of things, the abandonment of relatives. I got a taste of a historian's task. I sit at the table and ask questions and record the greatest sufferings with cold objectivity. I write, I probe into details, and I do not realize at all that I am probing into wounds, and the one who answers me—indifferent to it: two sons and a husband taken away—the sons Monday, the husband Thursday.... And this horror, this tragedy is formulated by me in three words, coldly and dryly. I become absorbed in thought, and the words stare out of the paper crimson with blood. . . .

After school we went to the meeting of "Beutelager." It is an exemplary unit. Its brigadier, Kaplan-Kaplanski, arranges a gathering of the workers every Sunday. The gathering is cultural in nature. At today's gathering, Yashunski, the director of the educational department in the ghetto, delivered a report about the work. In the ghetto there are functioning right now three elementary schools with two kindergartens, a technical school, a music school, a *Mitlshul*, a nursery, and a dormitory for abandoned children. Each of these institutions has a rich history of martyrdom. Yashunski also spoke about the theater and sports in the ghetto.

In the second half, members of the club presented the best numbers of the final rehearsal. The gatherings of the "Beutelager" make a very good impression. How pleasant it is to spend a few hours in cultural surroundings.

Saturday the 31st

Toward evening our neighbor who works with my parents brought a Soviet leaflet. A holiday spirit broke out in the room. One person sits at the table and reads. All those around him open-mouthed and with bated breath. Such a little treasure which originates from far, far away, across battlefields, cities, and finally across ghetto gates entwined with barbed wire. "News about the Soviet Fatherland, death to the German aggressors." Everyone looks into the sheet of paper. It is such a rarity for everyone, such a holiday. In the leaflet it says we should not believe the German communiqués. The leaflet encourages the brothers and sisters of the temporarily occupied regions. The leaflet is from the 11th of August. There is nothing especially important in the communiqué from the front. The Kuban Cossack division under the command of Tutorinov distinguished itself at the Caucasus. Also the Soviet tank columns defeated the enemy at Bryansk. The leaflet tells about life in the Soviet Union. It is so pleasant for me to hear that life is still beating somewhere. The Russian people breathes, lives and fights. In the Soviet Union a great socialistic contest is proceeding on a gigantic scale in all regions. The factories and brigades which excel in the production of tanks and airplanes and in the extraction of oil are listed. People are writing about culture at the present moment. The education of children is still on the same high level. Tens of thousands of children of front soldiers are being maintained in nurseries. Recently two new films were produced which describe the great struggle: "The Commissar of Raykom" and "Partisans." The leaflet tells about the preparations in England for the second front. The workers of England and America demand from their governments that they undertake the decisive struggle against Hitlerism. The leaflet tells about the glorious work of the Russian partisans. The leaflet concludes with an appeal to the male and female partisans to carry on sabotage, to derail German trains! Our neighbor handed me the proclamation. I look closely at the modest piece of paper: it seems to me that embodied in it is all the exertion and self-sacrifice of the Russian people. I run with the leaflet to the club to show my friends. I keep it in my bosom. It seems to me that the writing warms me. The words are so close to me, so friendly. We stand in the corners of the club and read. Everyone felt for a while so joyous and cheerful—we received regards from our liberators.

Sunday the 1st of November

This is a beautiful day. Every day it has been cloudy and rainy. Today, as though suddenly, a spring day broke through between the autumn days. The sky is blue, the sun warms affectionately. And so indeed the ghetto people burst forth over the little streets to catch what are probably the very last sunbeams. Our police dressed up in their new hats. Here one of them is passing—my blood boils—in a leather overcoat, with an insolent air, his officer's hat askew. Its peak shines in the sun. The cord of his hat dropped over his chin, he clicks his shiny little boots. Satiated, gorged with food, he struts proudly like an officer, delights—the snake—in such a life, and plays his comedy. This is the source of all my anger against them, that they are playing a comedy with their own tragedy.

Monday the 2nd of November

Today we had a very interesting group meeting with the poet A. Sutskever. He talked to us about poetry, about art in general and about subdivisions in poetry. In our group two important and interesting things were decided. We create the following sections in our literary group: Yiddish poetry, and what is most important, a section that is to engage in collecting ghetto folklore. This section interested and attracted me very much. We have already discussed certain details. In the ghetto dozens of sayings, ghetto curses and ghetto blessings are created before our eyes; terms like *"va-shenen,"* "smuggling into the ghetto," even songs, jokes, and stories which already sound like legends. I feel that I shall participate zealously in this little circle, because the ghetto folklore which is amazingly cultivated in blood, and which is scattered over the little streets, must be collected and cherished as a treasure for the future.

Tuesday the 3rd of November

When I returned from school mother told me a few things she had experienced and heard. Mother is sewing for a German woman. The German woman is such a good, such a noble person, the Jewish workingwomen like her very much. She gave mother soap, flour, pieces of candy and bread. She is interested in the life of the ghetto. With all her heart she sympathizes with the Jews in the ghetto. "The war will end, the Führer is to blame for everything. You will be liberated, they need you, you are useful, industrious people. We Germans and you Jews will not suffer long!" A second story, in the Verzhbolov labor camp a German beat a Jew with a stick. Germans who were riding by jumped down from the auto, tore the stick from the hooligan's hands, and asked him with bitterness: "Why do you beat him? You dog, you have probably not been at the front, so you beat him. Had you seen how blood flows like water, you would not have beaten him. . . ." The stories sound half like legends. Every ghetto Jew enjoys expanding, enriching such a story; people revel in them. Thus, for instance, they tell that a German tore the badges off a Jew's clothes, saying that badges will soon no longer be needed! All these stories circulate among the people, or they change them, strengthen the impression, embellish them. But the spark of truth exists. We are touched by the thought that among the Germans there are great numbers who sympathize with us, and feel their shame in our anguish.

What a sense of gloom descends on the ghetto with the

arrival of winter! People run trembling and sighing across the streets. Everyone has his worries. Toward evening, however, things brightened up. The workers returned with happy, good, reliable news.

An American incursion has landed in West Africa, in Tunis, Algiers and Morocco. Spain and Portugal have received ultimatums not to obstruct the campaign. The English-American forces have opened a great campaign against the German and the Italian army in Africa. They are proceeding against the Germans from two sides. On the East the English attack from Egypt, and on the West the Americans from Tunis in the direction of Tripolitania. The Germans are suffering dreadful blows. The German-Italian army is in danger of falling into the sea. The Americans are operating with a strong aerial and naval fleet. After tremendous battles, the Americans and the English captured Tobruk and Salûm and a number of other positions. The Vichy government [issued] a command to the French naval fleet and land army to offer resistance against the English and the Americans. The French offered no resistance. The English-American fleet operates freely in the Mediterranean Sea. An incursion also penetrated into Corsica. The Germans fear an invasion of France and have taken control of unoccupied France. Raids into Italy are expected.

What happens in Africa is indeed very far from us. People say however that the campaign to liquidate the Germans in Africa conforms to the demand of the Soviet Union. For when the English finish in Africa, it is expected that a second front will be opened in Europe and then . . . we can still manage to leave the ghetto. We become encouraged hearing that the battle is proceeding, that our spark of hope still flickers.

Tuesday the 24th

The ghetto is in a cheerful mood and so are the children. The ghetto resounds with good news, the ghetto radiates with hope: we almost begin to imagine that presently . . . we shall leave our jail. . . . The Americans are marching on Tunis. The French fleet in Dakar has surrendered. The South African army attacks the Germans from the south. Rome is under continual bombardment. The most important thing: the German army suffered a defeat at Stalingrad. Two Soviet armies met encircling the enemy in the Stalingrad-Rostov region. Thousands of fallen and captured Germans. The Soviets are strongly attacking the central front: the ghetto feels with all its senses that the end is approaching or, rather, that our beginning is near.

In the evening I took a walk along the little ghetto streets. The evening is a marvelous one. There is a light frost. It is bright. The snow sparkles wherever it is not trampled upon. The evening is refreshing. I feel so lighthearted. The evening has bewitched me, as it were. The ruins on Yatkever Street glisten in the frost as though studded with diamonds. It is quiet and deserted. The snow-covered ruins stand under a frosty, blue sky where a great round moon hovers and appears intermittently through a different crevice in the wall of the ruin. On such evenings I used to like so much to walk with a companion somewhere in a quiet place beyond the city. It is so pleasant when your cheeks burn. You inhale frosty evening freshness with every breath. I feel the same today, even though I come across a ruin on the way, but my heart feels strangely good, because on such a night I can conceive of something new happening very soon. . . . I feel it is close at hand. I grope for it in the frost with my hand.

Monday the 30th

The ghetto resounds with good news. The Soviets have broken through the front at Latvia near Vyelikii Luki. They are coming, they are coming closer and closer.

Sunday the 7th [December]

In our circles on ghetto research we decided once and for all to complete the spadework, that is to say visiting homes with the questionnaires. We want to get started on processing the answers, to make history on the basis of the data.

Today my friend and I visited a new apartment. We received very good answers. Making the rounds among ghetto people and talking to them about their lives, we discern the ghetto person with his manner of thinking and speaking. Usually in our questions we are not concerned with the family. There are, however, people who wish to have a record made of their families, they wish to be part of history. Others, on the other hand, are terribly cautious and exceptionally diplomatic. In their answer there is no extraneous word: everything is weighed and measured. If we ask them where they lived before the ghetto, they do not answer. If you ask them in which unit they work, they do not answer. They regard us as people whose job it is to levy taxes. The ghetto person is full of distrust.

On the other hand, for instance, simple Jews today answered in such a friendly and pleasant manner. They were interested in answering us. [Perhaps they may not have understood what this meant.] However, they felt with all their hearts that they ought to answer us. They poured their hearts out to us, explained in full detail all their misfortunes, the complicated tragedies of including additional names to their own. "What do you say, children, this is what [the] Führer made of us. May the same thing happen to him. This will be a history of us. Write, write, children. It is good this way." We finish questioning a family and thank them. "Oh, do not thank us. Promise us that we shall leave the ghetto, and I shall tell you three times as much, wretched folk that we are." We assured the woman ten times that we shall leave the ghetto.

Wednesday the 10th of December

It dawned on me that today is my birthday. Today I became 15 years old. You hardly realize how time flies. It, the time, runs ahead unnoticed and presently we realize, as I did today, for example, and discover that days and months go by, that the ghetto is not a painful, squirming moment of a dream which constantly disappears, but is a large swamp in which we lose our days and weeks. Today I became deeply absorbed in the thought. I decided not to trifle my time away in the ghetto on nothing and I feel somehow happy that I can study, read, develop myself, and see that time does not stand still as long as I progress normally with it. In my daily ghetto life it seems to me that I live normally but often I have deep qualms. Surely I could have lived better. Must I day in day out see the walled-up ghetto gate, must I in my best years see only the one little street, the few stuffy court-yards?

Still other thoughts buzzed around in my head but I felt two things most strongly: a regret, a sort of gnawing. I wish to shout to time to linger, not to run. I wish to recapture my past year and keep it for later, for the new life. My second feeling today is that of strength and hope. I do not feel the slightest despair. Today I became 15 years of age and I live confident in the future. I am not conflicted about it, and see before me sun and sun and sun. . . .

Thursday the 11th of December

Today we had a club holiday in the kitchen of Rudnitski 6. We felt like having a little fun. So we wangled 100 kg. of potatoes out of the administration and we have a baked pudding. This was the happiest evening I have spent in the ghetto.

At nine o'clock we met in the kitchen.

People are already sitting at the tables. Many, many guests came. And here we sit crowded together. I look around at the crowd, all of our kind teachers, friends, intimates. It is so cozy, so warm, so pleasant. This evening we demonstrated what we are and what we can accomplish. Club members came with songs, recitations. Until late into the night we sang with the adults songs which tell about youthfulness and hope. Very beautiful was the living newspaper in which the club with its chairman and speakers was humorously criticized. We sat the meager tables and ate baked pudding and coffee and we were so happy, so happy. Song after song resounded. It is already 12 o'clock. We are, as it were, intoxicated with the joy of youth. We do not want to go home. Songs keep bursting forth, they simply will not stop. We disperse late at night. We have demonstrated that we are young, "within walls yet young, forever young." Our slogan with which "we go to meet the sun." Today we have demonstrated that even within the three small streets we can maintain our youthful zeal. We have proved that from the ghetto there will not emerge a youth broken in spirit; from the ghetto there will emerge a strong youth which is hardy and cheerful.

Today the ghetto celebrated the circulation of the one hundred thousandth book in the ghetto library. The festival was held in the auditorium of the theater. We came from our lessons. Various speeches were made and there was also an artistic program. The speakers analyzed the ghetto reader. Hundreds of people read in the ghetto. The reading of books in the ghetto is the greatest pleasure for me. The book unites us with the future, the book unites us with the world. The circulation of the hundred thousandth book is a great achievement for the ghetto and the ghetto has the right to be proud of it.

Sunday the 3rd of January 1943
At school today they are giving us oral marks for the first third of the school year. I have A's in Yiddish, Jew. history, history and biology. I have B's in mathematics, Hebrew, drawing, and physics; in Latin, German, C's.

My grades could perhaps have been better but even those mentioned above are proof that my time is not being frittered away.

Thursday the 7th
Today they give five deca of pork on the ration cards. I waited in line a short time and at last found myself inside the store. There is so much injustice evident among us Jews in the ghetto, so much that is not right, so much that is disgusting. For instance, in the distribution of meat on the ration cards. People freeze and stand in line. Policemen, privileged persons, walk in freely. During the distribution the

butcher throws the piece of meat to the person in line as if he were doing him a favor, exploiting a child, a person who is less vituperative, by giving him the worst. On the other hand, those who have "pull" with the butcher (for "pull" the ghetto person lowers himself into the merest nonentity, because in the ghetto the vitamin P, as it is called, is victorious; "pull" or "pleytses," in other words, *strong* shoulders), get a somewhat fatter piece. In the store they allot the few deca of pork. Every so often a policeman struts in, some "well-known" man, a genteel lady, a matron, people with briefcases, they turn to the supervisor of the store or directly to the butcher to "take care of them." The butcher extends his sweet, wheedling face to them in such a disgusting manner, cuts out a piece of thick, white fat for them (I think that they have enough even without that at home). The crowd of frozen women stands in "line," hushed, wrathful, devouring the meat.

Friday the 8th

New students are being accepted in the technical school in the ghetto. I am now going through a big struggle, whether to learn a trade or to continue to study in the high school as I have done until now. I cannot make up my mind. On the one hand, there is war; it is easier at the moment for the person who has some kind of trade or other. I am growing up and sooner or later I shall have to go to work. On the other hand, I imagine that attendance at the technical school means an interruption of one's studies. For after the four-month vocational course the goal is to go to work, and once I start working I shall never return to school again. After long hesitation and long reflection I decided to make use of every moment. I need to study; I still have suitable conditions, so I must not interrupt my studies. My determination to study has developed into something like defiance of the present which hates to study, loves to work, to drudge. No, I decided. I shall live with tomorrow, not with today. And if for every 100 ghetto children of my age 10 can study, I must be among the fortunate ones, I must take advantage of this. Studying has become even more precious to me than before.

Today is the first public appearance of the club. They are staging the splendidly prepared numbers: "The Enchanted Tailor," "Guards," by Peretz, "Dolls," produced in the children's club and "Mered," a Hebrew recitation. Our dramatic circle deserves high commendation! Under the most difficult club conditions, they have produced some rather good, beautiful numbers, all on the level of a good performance in peacetime with make-up, decorations, light effects.

Saturday the 9th

This evening the great club festival takes place. Our fresh clubrooms are full of members and guests. Our auditorium prides itself on having a stage of its own, with transparent curtain and reflectors. There are some beautiful pictures on the wall. It is warm and pleasant in the auditorium. A cultural and warm atmosphere hovers within the freshly painted walls. "Within the walls yet young" is the headline of our wall newspaper which shines down from the wall. A splendid newspaper. The articles are in the form of walls and a street leading to the ghetto gate. The whole appearance of the paper symbolizes the headline and the content of the articles and poems also prove the correctness of the newspaper headline. A beautiful bulletin gives an account of the work that has been done.

Finally people take their seats. Up on our own stage, our own people on the dais, our young club manager, Leo Bernshteyn, through whose efforts the club has become a reality, our heroic chairman Avreml, Reyze, our secretary, and a whole group of lecturers. The mood is an exalted one. Greetings and speeches. A present is given to Leo Bernshteyn and Reyze. The teacher Rokhl Broydo correctly asserted that "When a people has a young generation it is a sign of its progress. We have a youth, its flag is drenched in blood, it is red, but we hold it firmly; the youth in the ghetto, that is the firm bridge to the future!"

We applauded long and heartily.

Until 12 at night our dramatic circle showed what it could do. It is a pleasure to see how well our members are performing. We have every right to be proud of them. Such beautiful numbers, decorations, costumes, and everything accomplished so well, so consistently.

A present is also given to Pilnik, the favorite of the club, the chimney sweep director, who set up the performance. We remained in the club until half past two, intoxicated with youthful joy. After the program some entertainment, a living newspaper, songs, recitations. Pilnik presents one song after another. We are young, the young hall is saturated with youthful joy and work. Our spirit, which we bear proudly within the ghetto walls, will be the most beautiful gift to the newly rising future. Long live youth!—the progress of our people.

Wednesday the 27th

Today our class visited the ghetto workshops on Rudnitski 6. Here on Rudnitski 6 the ghetto industry is concentrated. Here our professionals work. This is the foundation of our existence. The ghetto has exerted its entire effort to create what we have seen here today. We go from department to department, workshops for locksmiths, mechanics, tinsmiths. The work sings to the accompaniment of the tools. There is knocking and clanging. Everything bears the stamp of serious work. Here they are repairing parts of machines. And here they are producing iron badges with numbers which every Jew like a cow will put on around his neck. Here is a forge with two fires. The air here is warm, saturated with iron and lime. And the fire blazes in the dark ovens and the Jews stand silently and strike monotonously with their hammers. The Jewish smith stands and makes horseshoes for the German army. A large forge with six fires is being built in the yard. We go to other departments. One of the engineers is showing us around. He is angry, strict, shouts at the workers like a boss. Murer's command here extends over everything.... The only workers who do not take the engineer seriously are the specialists because they know that they are needed. Murer knows them and will not exchange them for anyone else. For example, a worker severely reproached the engineer, who acted as our guide, for turning the machine without his permission.... Here is the department for wood turning, for the clog industry. How beautiful, how enticing is the work, the carving, how things are being created before my very eyes! But for whom....

Now a new department is being built where the only specialist, a Vilna Jew, will make artificial hands and feet. "Let's hope that the department will have large orders," people joke.

As I left the workshops I carried away the impression of the power of the will to live which emanates from everything here. It seems that everything I have seen here was created solely by will. I think about the fate of our work. Wolves and dogs benefit from the products of our work. But our will to live that I have discerned today proclaims distinctly that the dark game will cease, that finally a specter such as the one named Murer will disappear. . . . "You should be workers and not oppressors," a smith said to us today. Yes, we too shall be workers, but we shall work in different times.

Thursday the 28th

The hope that lives forever in the ghetto person flared up strongly these days. The proud German military reports have, alas, turned into women's prayers. The German military report concedes the mighty Soviet offensive on the fronts. The Soviets have begun a great offensive on the sector between the Caucasus and the Don. The German victorious army which had threatened and entered the suburbs of Stalingrad is now hurled into a mighty ring of the Soviet armies.

The Soviet armored divisions are driving the Germans from the Caucasus. A crushing defeat threatens the Germans at the front where the German army fought so hard and succeeded only in winning the grave for itself. The German attack on Stalingrad has become transformed into a desperate resistance of surrounded men.

"The German soldier presents an iron heart to the flood of iron,"—that is what today's report reads. Yes, they admit that a flood of Soviet arms proceeds against them, that the

Soviets are stronger. They console themselves with the heroism and discipline of the German soldier. However, we know
better which soldier is more heroic.

This news warms our hearts. The Soviet offensive speeds
across the front. Now it is on its way, any moment now will
come the flaming freedom that it bears.

Sunday the 7th of February

We have good news. The people in the ghetto are celebrat-
ing. The Germans concede that Stalingrad has fallen.

I walk across the street. . . . People wink at each other with
happy eyes. At last the Germans have suffered a gigantic
defeat. The entire 9th German army is crushed! Over three
hundred thousand Germans killed. The staff taken prisoner.
Stalin's city is the enemy's grave. The winter offensive of the
Soviets produces splendid results.

I walk in the street. . . . Winter is beginning to take leave
of the little ghetto streets. The air is warm and sunny. The
ice on the streets melts and oozes and our hearts are filled
with spring. The snow within us melts too, and such a sunny
feeling envelops us. Liberation is near. I feel its proximity
with all my blood.

Sunday the 14th

All is well. All is gay. The Soviet offensive is proceeding
admirably. Kharkov and Rostov have been occupied. Goeb-
bels, the German minister of propaganda, delivered a speech
full of pessimism. We were delighted at his calls for help: he
appeals to all cultural nations to help Germany against the
Soviets because things are in a critical state. This time Goeb-
bels said a great truth, that if the German front collapses,

Bolshevism will flood the world. And he is not even ashamed to say that the German front is on the point of falling, that one must exert all one's strength before it is too late.

Thursday the 18th

I am busy for hours at a time. It is so hard to accomplish something at school and in the club, and at the same time to be involved with cooking and cleaning. First of all reports sneaked up on us. At school we are now covering the theme Vilna in geography. I am preparing a report "On Jew[ish] Printing in Vilna." For several months now there is no light in the evenings. In the evenings we lie around in the work-room, the reading room. I often reflect, this is supposedly the ghetto yet I have such a rich life of intellectual work: I study, I read, I visit club circles. Time runs by so quickly and there is so much work to be done, lectures, social gatherings. I often forget that I am in the ghetto.

Thursday the 25th of March

A command was issued by the German regime about liquidating five small ghettos in the Vilna province. The Jews are being transported to the Vilna and the Kovno ghetto. Today the Jews from the neighboring little towns have begun to arrive. It is rainy and gray outside. Sadly the peasant carts ride into the ghetto like gypsy covered wagons. On the carts Jews with children, their bag and baggage. The newly arrived Jews have to be provided with dwellings. The school on Shavler 1 has been pre-empted for the newly arrived Jews. The school on Shavler 1 was moved into the building of our school. They are teaching in two shifts. Today we went to class in the evening. Our studies somehow no longer have any form. We are all depressed. We are in a bad mood.

Sunday the 28th

The mood in the ghetto is a very gloomy one. The crowding together in one place of so many Jews is a signal for something. The transportation of food through the gate has become very difficult. Several people have already been arrested on Lukishki. People walk around gray and worried. Danger is hovering in the air. No! This time we shall not permit ourselves to be led like dogs to the slaughter! We have been discussing this lately at our [. . .] and are prepared at any moment. We have to improve ourselves. This thought strengthens our nerves, gives us courage and endurance.

Monday the 5th [April]

Sunday at 3 o'clock the streets in the ghetto were closed off. A group of 300 of the Jews from Sol and Smorgon have left for Kovno with a large transport of provincial Jews that arrived at the railway station. As I stood at the gate I saw how they were packing their things. Gaily and in high spirits they went to the train. Today the terrible news reached us: 85 railroad cars of Jews, around 5000 persons, were not taken to Kovno as promised but transported by train to Ponar where they were shot to death. 5000 new bloody victims. The ghetto was deeply shaken, as though struck by thunder. The atmosphere of slaughter has gripped the people. It has begun again. Once more the sparrow hawk spurs are in evidence. People sit caged in as in a box. On the other side lurks the enemy which is preparing to destroy us in a sophisticated manner according to a plan, as today's slaughter has proved.

The ghetto is depressed and mournful. We are unprotected and exposed to death. Again there hovers over the little Vilna ghetto streets the nightmare of Ponar. It is terrible, terrible. People walk around like ghosts. They wring their hands. Toward evening an urgent gathering. The situation has been confirmed. We have no one to depend on. The danger is very great. We believe in our own strength. We are ready at any moment.

Tuesday the 6th

The situation is an oppressive one. We now know all the horrible details. Instead of Kovno, 5000 Jews were taken to Ponar where they were shot to death. Like wild animals before dying, the people began in mortal despair to break the railroad cars, they broke the little windows reinforced by strong wire. Hundreds were shot to death while running away. The railroad line over a great distance is covered with corpses. We did not study in school today. The children run away from their homes where it is terrible to stay on account of the mood, on account of the women. The teachers are also despondent. So we sit in a circle. We rally our spirits. We sing a song.

In the evening I went out into the street. It is 5 o'clock in the afternoon. The ghetto looks terrible: heavy leaden clouds hang and lower over the ghetto.

Macha Rolnikas

LITHUANIA   ∞   14 YEARS OLD

A *Jewish girl who grew up in Vilnius (Vilna), Lith-uania, Macha Rolnikas was fourteen years old in June of 1941, when the Nazis occupied her town and she began keeping a diary.*

As she writes, she and her family were doubly targeted by the Nazis because they were Jewish and because her father was a liberal lawyer who often defended Communists. As soon as the Nazis occupied Vilnius, he left to join the partisan underground.

Macha describes some of the same features of the Vilnius Ghetto that Yitskhok Rudashevski does in his diary. But, so far as we can tell from their writing, they did not know one another. And, unlike Yitskhok, Macha was not deported to the death camp at Panerai (Ponar), where all faced certain execution.

Macha's book-length diary has, of necessity, been greatly abbreviated. Although she was taken to a work camp directly after she was separated from her family, this excerpt includes only those entries written while she was still in the ghetto and those that she wrote in Stutthof concentration camp. It concludes with her account of the long forced march of prisoners when the Nazis evacuated Stutthof because the Russians were closing in on the camp. Even at the expense of their own lives, the Nazis refused to let the prisoners go when Allied victory was already a certainty.

Of all the children's diaries in this book, Macha's is, perhaps, the most horrifying account of Nazi brutality. She was badly beaten, starved for days at a time, and forced to be an "undertaker" for her friends' dead bodies.

Even though her life hung by a thread, Macha survived. And she managed to insure the survival of her diary as well. After the war, Macha returned to Vilnius, where she was reunited with her older sister and her father. Her little brother and sister and her mother were not so fortunate. In Vilnius, she found the early parts of her diary where she had hidden them, and was able to put them together with what she had written since deportation. All of the entries were undated.

Macha graduated from the Gorky Literary Institute in Moscow by correspondence, then married and moved to Leningrad. Her diary, which was written in Yiddish, was first published in Hebrew and then in Lithuanian, in 1964. It is entitled I Must Tell *and is dedicated to the memory of Macha's murdered family members.*

Macha herself translated her diary from Yiddish into French, and it was published as Je Devais Le Raconter *in 1966 in Paris. This excerpt was translated from the French, especially for this book, by Christine Lienhart Nelson.*

[June 1941]

The Nazis have occupied the town. People are crying and talking about the Nazis' hatred of Jews and Communists.

And we, we are both. And on top of it all, Papa has been working very actively for the Soviets.

The invaders have posted a decree saying that all Communists have to register. Those who know any Communists or members of any leftist organizations have to inform, to let the Gestapo or the S.S. know at once. Mama is uneasy. She asked us to go through all of Papa's things. There are files about his defense of Communists. If they are found, we will be shot.

New decrees have been posted in the town: all the Jews—adults and children—must wear insignias, a white piece of cloth, ten square centimeters, and in the middle the yellow letter "J." Is it possible that the invaders no longer regard us as human beings and brand us just like cattle? One can not accept such meanness. But who dares to oppose them?

Everybody is hiding their belongings with non-Jewish friends. Mama moved almost all of Papa's books, his overcoat, suits, shoes and new silk shirts to my teacher Jonaitis's house. I slipped the first notebook of my journal in among Papa's books.

[Macha witnessed the following horrifying scene but was unable to help because she was behind the locked gates of the ghetto.]

A woman is crawling on all fours. Her hair is all tangled, her clothes dirty because of dragging herself along the ground, her eyes wide open, her face grimacing. Her bulging belly is resting on the ground. Covered with sweat, she stops every few minutes and, like an animal, pricks up her ears: is danger awaiting her somewhere? She is losing her strength. With each passing moment she feels a bit weaker. A great pain seizes her, shooting pains into her breast. She knows that her last moments are approaching, she is going to give birth.

All night long, rolled up like a ball, exhausted, full of pain, she felt the approaching delivery. She continues to advance on all fours. She flops down in the middle of the street very close to the entrance, crawls to the sidewalk so as not to get run over. She won't ever get up again. She turns over and over in pain, in a kind of convulsion, writhing like a snake. She startles and death comes and interrupts her anguish at the same moment as her little girl comes to this world of pain and shadows. She is found next to her and is taken into the ghetto and named Ghettala. Poor little girl.

We were told that all those with yellow certificates had to go and register with the Jewish Council. The people are tense; everybody hurried to register.

The huge staircase of the former high school is overrun by people. Tumult—the tower of Babel. Only six months ago, these same steps were filled with pupils. In the former class-rooms where the people are now fighting against death, an upright skeleton seems to be watching us. In a corner some parts of a stage set are lying around . . . little ballet costumes. But nobody notices them. I, too, have already forgotten that such things still exist.

I heard some extraordinary news: in the ghetto there is an organization that is secretly working with the Communists and preparing to fight against the invaders. It is the O.U.P.—

the Organization of the United Partisans. The members of this organization have already constructed a mine which they put under the railroad tracks near Vilaike!! Hooray!! Of course, it is forbidden to talk about this. Mama even forbid me to put it down in my journal. But how can one not mention such a piece of news!!!

They have started searching the apartments. I hid my manuscripts. It would be a disaster if they were found. We would all be deported. Mama told me not to write down everything—only the essentials—and to memorize the rest, because it is very likely that we will have to destroy everything in writing.

The Nazis have ordered mourning. For three days the theaters, the movies, the restaurants and other amusement places in Vilnius will be closed down.

Our hearts are beating with joy. The Fascists are in mourning for their destroyed divisions on the Volga. If we could have, we would have organized a dance. It has been a long time since I have felt such a desire to dance. With our hearts rejoicing, we celebrated the mourning of the Nazis.

Now we have been totally turned into dogs: they have hung metal tags around our necks.

I went to a wonderful dance performance. The dance that impressed me the most was called "The Yellow Star." A little girl comes running out onto the stage. She dances joyfully, carefree like a beautiful butterfly. Suddenly everything turns somber. Far above, a huge yellow star is gliding by. The music is terribly mournful. The little girl is afraid. On the black curtain behind her the star has a terrifying effect. It's like a huge spider in hiding. The little girl wants to get away. She struggles and begs, but all in vain. She falls as if struck by lightning. . . .

If one is to believe certain rumors, the ghettos of all the small towns in Lithuania are to be completely liquidated starting the first of April. As the forests are crawling with partisans, the Nazis fear that the Jews who live close by could join the resistance. So they will all be transferred to the ghettos of Vilnius and Kaunas. Yesterday a few groups of policemen came to start moving the people. Those that were told by the Nazis that they would be transferred to Kaunas were deceived. Only a few managed to escape the trap and survive.

Toward evening, the clothes of the executed were brought back to the ghetto on carts.

The cart comes up the narrow pavement. The clothes move like human beings. A sleeve is dangling down. Yesterday morning, a man slipped his arm into it while dressing. Now this arm is already frozen. A small coat—how old was the child who wore it? A cap. It seems to be covering a cutoff head. The cap slips . . . beneath it a shoe appears. One feels like crying, screaming, biting, shouting: "It's yesterday, only yesterday, that under these clothes hearts were beating, warm bodies were breathing. Yesterday they still were human beings! Today they are no longer!! They were killed!!! Do you hear me: killed." The ghetto is plunged into a state of mourning.

* * *

I am writing after a sleepless night. We don't know what the morning will bring. Maybe this is the last time that I can write. They have threatened to liquidate the entire ghetto.

Kittel [the commandant of the ghetto] came with some members of the Gestapo. He ordered the police to assemble all the inhabitants of the ghetto for an important announcement. The Jews of the Ghetto Vilnius, who had come here two years ago, would be evacuated to two labor camps, one in Estonia, the other in Lithuania. We had to be ready in four hours. I brought this sad news to Mama. My little sister Raia looked at us, alarmed. "And if this is a lie and they take us to Panerai?" she asked. How to answer her? That I have the same thought?

Mama told the children to empty their school satchels and she would give them each some clothes. "And my books, aren't we going to take them?" my little brother asked fearfully.

"You will read, my little one, when we are free," Mama comforted him.

Mama gets our things ready. The children follow her with their eyes. Seeing that she is crying, their large eyes, too, fill with tears. I try to convince them that there is nothing to cry about, that maybe they will take us to a camp. But I, myself, don't believe in this camp and my words do not calm them.

I stay near the window. In summer it will be beautiful here. Here and everywhere. The apple tree will be white with blooms. The petals will stir, shaken by the wind, as if they were alive. They will give off their perfume. The sky will be blue, blue. Infinitely large. How wonderful it would have been to gaze at it! Or to pin a flower in my hair. Now, if I live, I will know how to be happy.

Mama says it is time to leave. There are soldiers everywhere on the sidewalks. Many of them have dogs. Impossible to escape.

A lot of jostling. Those ahead of us are hardly moving and those behind are pushing. The men are left in the street and the women and children are led into a courtyard. The courtyard is big and filled with soldiers. Mama is crying. I beg her to calm herself at least for the children. But she can't. She looks at us and cries harder.

Night falls. As long as I can see, I look at the trees, the birds' nests, the branches, the houses in the distance and each window. Because soon I will see nothing at all anymore. Everything is alive—each leaf and each drop of water, even the tiniest fly. It will go on living tomorrow and we, we will no longer be here. No, no!!! I do not want to die! But the others, those who have already been executed, they didn't want to die either.

Little Rouben has fallen asleep, his head buried in my shoulder. His hot breath tickles my neck. The last sleep. And there is nothing I can do that this little warm, breathing body won't be lying in a narrow ditch tomorrow, slippery with blood. Other bodies will cover it—maybe mine, too.

Raia, she isn't sleeping. She is exhausting Mama with her questions: Will they take us to Panerai? How? On foot or in cars? Maybe they will take us to a camp?

Mama sobs, "To send three children to their death, my own children!"

Near us, on a branch, a sparrow has perched. It shakes its

head, turns around and flies away. It has flown to the other side, behind our guards. It, it has the right to do so.

The guards order us to get up and to go into the courtyard. The closer you get to the gates, the greater the throng. Mama is afraid that we will lose each other and asks me to go through the gate first. After me, my little brother will follow, then my sister, and Mama last. This way she will see us all.

I pass through. A soldier grabs me by my coat and pushes me through. There is no car to be seen. I turn around to tell Mama, but she is no longer there. I run to the soldier and beg him to let me back through the gate to where Mama is. I explain to him that a mistake has occurred, that I have been separated from my mother. There she is, over there. My family is over there and I have to be with them. I talk, I beg, but the soldier doesn't pay any attention.

Suddenly I hear Mama's voice. She tells me not to come to her! She asks the soldier not to let me come back because I am still young and I can work.

"Mama!" I shout as loud as I can.

But she shakes her head and in a hoarse voice cries: "Live, my child, you at least, live! Avenge the small ones!"

They are pushed back. I can no longer see them. I climb on a rock near the wall and look for them. But I don't see Mama. Where is she? Black spots spin around in front of my eyes. My ears ring, buzz. . . . Where is the river in the middle of the street coming from? But it isn't water, it is blood. There is a lot of it. It is frothing. And Rouben and Raia are waving their little hands, begging me to save them. But it is impossible for me to reach them. I seem to be swaying. The small ones are definitely drowning. I am drowning.

Why am I lying down? Where has the river gone? I am lying on the sidewalk. Women are bending over me. One is holding my head, the other is checking my pulse.

Where is Mama? I want to see Mama!!! But the women don't allow me to get up yet. I fainted. I have never fainted before.

We are led into a large courtyard, not far from the train station, no doubt, because there are railroad tracks and freight cars. We are ordered to climb in. And the soldiers push, hit, demand that we climb in faster. Where is Mama? What will happen to them all? I weep. What have I done? What have Mama and the others done? Where does this barbarous hatred come from, the rage to exterminate us because we are Jews?

The train is moving. We are rolling . . . and Mama? Where is she? Why did they separate us? Even dying, I would be less afraid if we were together.

[Stutthof]

As we pass the barracks, the prisoners speak to us and ask where we are from. They speak in Russian, Polish, even in Gypsy dialect, but above all in Yiddish. Near one barrack there are some extremely thin women—almost skeletons. They don't ask any questions. They only advise us to watch out for a certain man named Max. The chief of these blocks, Max is the devil in the disguise of a human being. He has already beaten some to death. He, himself, is a prisoner, locked up for eleven years for having killed his wife and children. The S.S. love him for his unequalled cruelty.

We have been here for nine days already. Max beats us

brutally. We are covered with bruises. You don't see any "unmarked" faces. I call these bruises "Max's autographs."

In three roundups the S.S. have selected victims in our block for the crematory furnace. We are lined up, they measure us and take away the thinnest. The first two times they led away thirty persons, and a couple of days ago, sixty. Escape!! We absolutely must escape from here!

I have been ill. The women were saying that in my fevers I was singing little songs and called the Nazis terrible names. They had never suspected that I knew so many swear words. Luckily my voice was weak and the Nazis don't come in here anymore. That kind of talk gets you shot on the spot. It seems that I have come out of it. I have overcome the illness.

Horrible! I slept covered by a corpse. During the night, of course, I didn't realize it. It was very cold and I curled up against my neighbor's back. I slipped my hands under her armpits. It seems to me that she even moved to squeeze her arms. And in the morning, I discovered that she was dead.

The supervisor came. She ordered all of us who had overcome the illness to line up. There are very few of us. The supervisor chose eight (including myself) and declared that we were the team of "undertakers." Up to now there has been so much chaos that the dead have remained in the barracks for several days. Now we were obliged to undress them at once, pull out their gold teeth and put them in front of the barracks door. I don't know how I can carry others when I can hardly stay on my feet myself.

We approach one of our companions who died today. I take her frozen foot, but I can't lift it. The supervisor slaps me and puts a pair of scissors and pliers in my hands. I must undress the dead woman and take out her gold teeth.

The dead woman is lying at my feet. I look and she is alive!! The open eyes are moving. But the supervisor hurries me to undress the woman. Timidly I touch her and she is cold. So why these eyes? Finally I realize that it is the little lamp on the ceiling swinging in the wind which reflects in her eyes. With a shaking hand I cut the dress. I lift the body to undress it, but it won't stand up and falls backwards. The head knocks against the floorboards with a hollow sound. I hold her close to me. In her mouth gold teeth are shining. I cannot make myself pull them out. Having reassured myself that the supervisor isn't watching, I quickly close the mouth again with the pliers. Perhaps they won't open it to look for teeth.

"You silly fool, what are you doing?" the supervisor yells and then she hits me. I fall on the body. She was just waiting for me to do that and starts hitting me with a club. She always aims for my head. It seems as if my skull is splitting in two. And she doesn't stop. There is blood all over the floor. She beat me until she herself was out of breath.

In our barrack forty to sixty women die every day. Near the door, stiff and blue bodies are piling up. A cart to which some prisoners are harnessed arrives. Two of them take the dried up and frozen bodies by the arms and feet, swing them and throw them on the heap of naked bodies. The crematory is working day and night. Next to it heaps of bodies are piling up. Every day nearly a thousand people die in the camp.

* * *

Early this morning the supervisor came and told us that those who were capable of walking must get ready to leave. So this is the end. Now that freedom is quite near, I am at the end of my tether. If only I had some strength! At least some small hope of being able to drag myself along.

Our hope of staying on the road for three days only was in vain. The days go by and we can't see the end of the road. We walk and walk. I need to be supported. I can no longer walk alone. We are given nothing to eat.

I have begun to swell up. The side I sleep on during the night is completely swollen. One eye is puffed up and I can no longer open it during the day. And my feet are awful to look at. They are so swollen that I can hardly get into the men's clogs I used to stuff with paper.

In order to feel my powerlessness a bit less and not to think of the torture that is caused by each step, I go on mentally writing my journal.

In the night we hear muffled explosions in the distance. It must be the front!!

We have been ordered to walk in silence. Even the guards have been forbidden to talk and smoke. My legs no longer obey me, they zigzag. I have already fallen several times, but the women pick me up and drag me along. They beg me to hold on, not to slip out of their hands, but I fall. I can't help it. This is the end . . .

The women are obliged to leave me . . . they are pushed ahead. They sigh and leave. I close my eyes so as not to see when I get shot.

What is this voice? Am I dreaming? A woman's voice. She

is asking me if I am alive. I open an eye. A woman has stopped. She asks me to stand up. I mustn't remain lying down or I will freeze. I must move. She has brought me a walking stick. She tells me not to be foolish now that freedom is so close. One must force oneself to hold on, no matter what. She tells me to hold on to her arm and to at least move a bit so as not to freeze.

We see a guard from camp arriving in a cart. He hits us and tells us to get in. The guards drive the carts toward a barn. Will they set it on fire? We will be burned alive!!!

They make us go into the barn. We find many women there, not all of them from our camp.

Someone taps me on the shoulder. Who? Again the Hungarian woman who saved me. She asks me if I understand Polish. She says that somebody is knocking on the wall and speaking Polish. Is he saying that the Red Army is in this village and the Nazis have all fled?

A siren. Something is coming closer. Why this uproar? Why is everyone crying? Where are they running? They are going to trample me. Help me get up. Don't leave me alone! Nobody pays any attention to me. They stumble over the dead, fall down, but get up again at once and rush outside the barn.

And I can't get up. Behind the barn I can hear men's voices. Soldiers of the Red Army? Is it them? I want to go out there! Toward them! How can I get up?

The Red Army soldiers rush into the barn. They come toward us, looking for the living ones, helping them to get up. They take off their caps to the ones who no longer need their help.

"Do you need any help, little sister?" I am lifted up, put

on my feet, but I can no longer move forward my legs are shaking so. Two soldiers cross their arms and make a chair and carry me.

Ambulances arrive in the village. The soldiers run. One offers to carry me, the other gives me some bread, the third one gives me his gloves. And their kindness makes me feel so good that I feel like crying. The soldiers comfort me, calm me down. One of them takes out a dirty handkerchief and, like with a little girl, he wipes away my tears. "Don't cry, little sister, we won't allow anyone to harm you again." And on his cap shines the red star. It's been such a long time since I have seen it!

Charlotte Veresova

CZECHOSLOVAKIA   ∽   14 YEARS OLD

Charlotte was born in a small town in Czechoslovakia in 1928. When she was fourteen, she was separated from her family and deported from Prague to Terezín, where she lived in a youth barracks and began her diary. She survived Terezín, and after the war she became a librarian. This excerpt from her undated diary was published in the book Terezín *in 1965, with no mention of the whereabouts of the original diary.*

It is three weeks now since I came to this extraordinary place, actually a ghetto. I read once about the former ghettos and it never entered my head that I would experience such a thing one day. It seems to me as if we had gone back a few hundred years.

Everything here is so strange—different from anywhere

else in the world. For instance, people walk in the street, not just on the pavement, but there are so many of us here that we would probably not fit on the sidewalk. Cars do not drive here, though, so nothing can run over us. We sleep in bunks and everywhere lots of people are packed in. Husbands and wives do not live together and their children live separate from them in homes, or whatever you call it. When you hear the word "home" you imagine something quite nice. Well, it's all quite different, because that is how it must be. Nevertheless I envy the others a little, because they can at least visit their parents. I am here completely alone. Without Mommy and Dad and without my big brother whom I miss so much.

I was fourteen years old not long ago and I had never been away from home before, not even over the holidays, because I have no grandmother or aunt whom I could have gone to visit. So this is my first trip away from my parents and it's so strange. I should be glad that my folks are not here, and actually it's better that way. They will send me parcels and that's fine and dandy, and soon the war will be over and I'll go home. Everyone said that I'm going for only a couple of months and perhaps I can hold out that long.

My father is Jewish and my mommy is Aryan, so my brother and I are mixed and children of mixed marriages must, according to some German laws, go to Terezín. Why, I don't know, nor why it has to be us and not Dad, it's all a big mix-up. They say Mom saves Dad from being sent in a transport, but not us. It isn't clear to me, but nothing can be done about it, it's the stupid regulations.

So I sit here in my bunk and write and am unhappy.

I still have no appetite. Most of the time I eat from my

EVA HEYMAN–AGE THIRTEEN
Eva called her diary "my best friend." She gave it to her Christian maid
for safekeeping when she and her family were deported to Auschwitz
and executed.

YITSKHOK RUDASHEVSKI–AGE FOURTEEN
(WITH HIS GRANDMOTHER AND TWO COUSINS)
Yitskhok used his diary to record events in the Vilna Ghetto until he
and his family were deported to the Ponar death camp and executed.

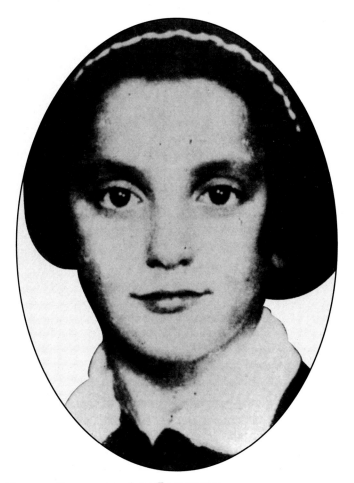

MACHA ROLNIKAS—AGE FOURTEEN
When Macha was forced on the death march from Stutthof concentration camp, she said, "I go on mentally writing my journal in order to feel my powerlessness a bit less and not to think of the torture that is caused by each step."

INA KONSTANTINOVA—
AGE SIXTEEN

*Ina was a partisan saboteur and spy
for the Soviet Union in the fight
against the Germans. She is remembered as a national heroine because
she sacrificed her own life to save
her comrades and because of the
popularity of her diary in Russia.*

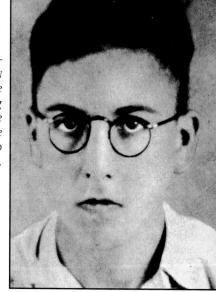

MOSHE FLINKER—
AGE SIXTEEN

*Moshe's diary records the
psychological suffering of a young
Jewish boy who was hiding from the
Nazis in Brussels, Belgium, before
he and his family were deported to
Auschwitz and executed.*

HANNAH SENESH—
AGE SEVENTEEN
Zionist Hannah Senesh was captured
by the Nazis when she parachuted
into Yugoslavia with a band of
Israeli and English partisans. She is
regarded as a national heroine in
Israel, where almost everyone is
familiar with her diary.

SARAH FISHKIN—
AGE SEVENTEEN
This, the only surviving photo of
Sarah Fishkin, shows her with rabbis
and the members of a religious
organization for girls to which she
belonged in Rubzewitz, Poland.

KIM MALTHE-BRUUN—AGE EIGHTEEN
Kim used his diary to write of his love for his friend Hanne and to describe his inner life after the Nazis condemned him to death for partisan activities in Denmark.

COLIN PERRY—AGE EIGHTEEN
An eyewitness to history, Colin recorded everything he could about the London blitz in his diary. He is shown here with Winston Churchill.

JOAN WYNDHAM—AGE EIGHTEEN
*Sixteen years old when the war began in England, Joan kept a
detailed diary of her sexual adventures and misadventures during
the London blitz.*

own supplies, but they are slowly disappearing. What will happen then? The food here stinks. I wonder that anyone can eat it. Gita says that in no time I'll be eating it, too. Perhaps I'll get a parcel soon.

This is the menu for the children's kitchen. Up to sixteen years we get a little better food than the rest.

	LUNCHES	SUPPERS
Monday	Soup, millet	small loaf of bread
Tuesday	Soup, potatoes, turnips	soup
Wednesday	Soup, potatoes, goulash	small loaf of bread
Thursday	Soup, dumplings, gravy	sausage, soup
Friday	Soup, barley	bun
Saturday	Soup, potatoes, turnips	soup
Sunday	Soup, bun with cream sauce	20 grams of margarine, teaspoonful of jam

The menu doesn't look so bad, but it is impossibly cooked and the soups are the same every day. They look like water from washing the floors. B-r-r-r, I never in my life ate soup, and I shan't eat these at all. We have black coffee for breakfast and nothing with it (it's slop).

Tonička and I have made friends. We understand each other very well and we have said that we will have a "commune", meaning that we will keep everything together. Bread, sugar, margarine and parcels from home, even when one gets more than the others. It comes out better that way. We manage to get only one kilogram of bread every three days. They bring it in old hearses pulled by people. Actually, that is the only transportation here. They also carry corpses in them. Sometimes we get mouldy bread and that's bad. We cut off the mouldy part and then we must slice the rest in very thin slices to make it stretch, and it doesn't matter at all that we have to eat dry bread. If only we get enough. Sometimes I'd cut off another slice, but I mustn't. Tonička is a good housewife. I'd just gobble it all down and then the third day I wouldn't have any. Now I've begun to think too much about food. I even eat the disgusting soups sometimes, and only a little while ago I couldn't have imagined it.

I've learned here to appreciate ordinary things that, if we had them when we were still free, we didn't notice at all. Like riding in a bus or a train, or walking freely along the road, to the water, say. Or to go buy ice cream. Such an ordinary thing and it is out of our reach.

Sometimes when I stand on the bastions and below me there is mud and swamp—jumping down would probably mean death. Sometimes it strikes me—would I jump if that would bring the end of the war? I should like to give my life so that it would. I should like to perform some great deed, so that my name would not die out, but I'll not be able to do anything. I know it is stupid, and so I don't tell even Tonička anything about it.

When we go to work we pass normal cottages, where people live a normal life. When will it be granted us to be such people who need not live by regulation? I look through their windows and in the morning their beds are not made up yet. I have a wild desire to climb in and sleep and sleep . . .

Transports are leaving for Poland. Three with 2,500 people in each. Eight girls are going from our room. It's sad. Children of mixed marriages are so far safe from transports; that means that it's probably worse in Poland than it is here. So many old people are going, and orphans must, too. We are arranging "Hilfsdienst," all of us, now. That means helping to pack wherever we are most needed. Mainly old people. The poor things, why don't they leave them in peace? After all, they are about to die and could just as well die here. Yesterday I helped a family with seven children and today one with three children whose mother has tuberculosis.

This is supposed to be a model ghetto, so why do they send people away, especially old people, because it probably wouldn't look nice if some one saw them begging for that disgusting soup? The town is packed, and that also does not make a good impression, either.

The Germans are going to make a film here, so they are up to all sorts of monkeyshines. Sometimes we think it's a joke and it really is funny. To whom will they show us off? Are we something they can brag about? They should be ashamed but probably they don't know how to be. The sidewalks are being scrubbed and wherever there is even a tiny bit of earth they plant flowers. They carried earth to the main square and have made a park, but no one is allowed to go into it. They play music there at noon, too. It sounds nice, but it does not satisfy us and even with the music I am still very homesick. If not more so.

It is rumoured that they are building gas chambers here. People whisper about it and they really are building something mysterious in the fortification catacombs with airtight doors. They say a duck farm. What for? Might it still be gas? I can't believe it. It is too terrible. Never before have I truly admitted the idea of death, and now gas all of a sudden. It's terrible, even if the longed-for end of the war is coming closer. Oh, how stupid I was when I was unhappy over silly little things! For example, that I was unlucky in love, or that I didn't want to get up in the morning. Everything is so petty compared to this thing. Here it is a question of life and we have only one single life. No, it mustn't happen, they can't do it, no one will let them! But why shouldn't they do it? Who prevented them from bringing us here and who will prevent the gas chambers, who—God? I have stopped believing in God, so is this punishment for that? No, it isn't, Tonička and Bertička pray and they would be sent to the gas chambers with me. But I won't give up. I am not a bug, even though I am just as helpless. If something starts, I'll run away. At least I'll try, after all, what could I lose? It would be better to be shot while trying to escape than to be smothered with gas. I'll take Tonička and we'll run away to Litoměřice together. Perhaps someone will take us in there. I know I'm not the only one, but still I'll not give up just like that, without resisting! No, I shan't give up, even if everyone else did, but not I! I want to live, I want to go back home, for after all I've done nothing to anyone, so why should I die?

It's so unjust!

It's interesting that we girls never talk about the gas with each other. It's as if it weren't true if we don't mention it.

Yesterday the girls went to do such unusual work. They had to take urns to the Ohře River and throw them in. For this they each got half a meat paste. And something else strange is going on. On the bastions the Germans are burning their archives. Sometimes a bit of paper flies into our garden and we read it. We are not allowed to pick it up, it's true, and a German soldier is guarding us with a gun, but we are curious, of course. But anyway we can't read much of it. Usually there is just a name and date of birth. They are Jewish names. Obviously the Germans are getting afraid and are trying to smooth over their traces. Why else would they be doing it? It is a good sign ...

Mary Berg (pseudonym)

POLAND ∽ 15 YEARS OLD

Mary Berg, a girl with American citizenship, was living in Poland with her parents at the beginning of the Nazi occupation. Although she alludes to having written in a diary earlier, her published diary begins on her fifteenth birthday, October 10, 1939. A year later, she was imprisoned in the Warsaw Ghetto despite the fact that her mother was not a Jew and was, in fact, an American.

In the ghetto, Mary witnessed and wrote of such horrors that it is almost inconceivable that she could have kept her sanity. But she never stopped recording what the Nazis did to her family, her friends, and her neighbors. Finally, she was informed that she and her mother were to be exchanged for German prisoners and that they would be released from Nazi custody.

Mary Berg's diary is a detailed eyewitness record of the atrocities committed in the Warsaw Ghetto. As such, it is an invaluable historical document. Because the Nazis had searched and looted every inch of the compound for three years, they didn't bother to *search Mary when she was released. She was able to smuggle her huge diary out of the Warsaw Ghetto right under the noses of the Third Reich.*

After being interned with other American citizens for a time in France, Mary and her family eventually were allowed to go to America, where she translated the diary from Polish into English and made arrangements to have it published when she was twenty years old. Only a few libraries in the world contain Mary's diary, which is called Warsaw Ghetto: A Diary. *It was published in New York by L.B. Fischer Publishing Corporation in 1945.*

October 10, 1939

Today I am fifteen years old. I feel very old and lonely, although my family did all they could to make this day a real birthday. They even baked a macaroon cake in my honor, which is a great luxury these days. My father ventured out into the street and returned with a bouquet of Alpine violets. When I saw it I could not help crying.

I have not written my diary for such a long time that I wonder if I shall ever catch up with all that has happened. This is a good moment to resume it. I spend most of my time at home. Everyone is afraid to go out. The Germans are here.

I can hardly believe that only six weeks ago my family and I were at the lovely health resort of Ciechocinek, enjoying a carefree vacation with thousands of other visitors. I had no idea then what was in store for us. I got the first inkling of our future fate on the night of August 29 when the raucous blare of the giant loud-speaker announcing the latest news stopped the crowds of strollers in the streets. The word "war" was repeated in every sentence. Yet most people refused to believe that the danger was real, and the expression of alarm faded on their faces as the voice of the loud-speaker died away.

My father felt differently. He decided that we must return to our home in Lodz. In almost no time our valises stood packed and ready in the middle of the room. Little did we realize that this was only the beginning of several weeks of constant moving about from one place to another.

We caught the last train which took civilian passengers to Lodz. When we arrived we found the city in a state of confusion. A few days later it was the target of severe German bombardments.

We spent most of our time in the cellar of our house. When word came that the Germans had broken through the Polish front lines and were nearing Lodz, panic seized the whole population. At eleven o'clock at night crowds began to stream out of the city in different directions. Less than a week after our arrival from Ciechocinek we packed our necessities and set out once more.

Up to the very gates of the city we were uncertain which direction we should take—toward Warsaw or Brzeziny? Finally, along with most of the other Jews of Lodz, we took the road to Warsaw. Later we learned that the refugees who followed the Polish armies retreating in the direction of Brzeziny had been massacred almost to a man by German planes.

Among the four of us, my mother, my father, my sister, and I, we had three bicycles, which were our most precious possessions. Other refugees who attempted to bring with them things that had been valuable in the life they had left behind were compelled to discard them. As we advanced we found the highway littered with all sorts of objects, from fur coats to cars abandoned because of the lack of gasoline. We had the good luck to acquire another bicycle from a passing peasant for the fantastic sum of two hundred zlotys, and we hoped it would enable us to move together with greater speed. But the roads were jammed, and gradually we were completely engulfed in the slow but steady flow of humanity toward the capital.

Mile after mile it was the same. The fields withered in the terrible heat. The gigantic cloud of dust raised by the vanguard of refugees swept over us, blotting out the horizon and covering our faces and clothes with successive layers of dust. Again and again we flung ourselves into the ditches on the side of the road, our faces buried in the earth, while planes roared in our ears. During the night huge patches of red flared up against the black dome of the sky. The fires of burning cities and villages rose all around us.

When we arrived in Lowicz, the city was one huge conflagration. Burning pieces of wood fell on the heads of the refugees as they forced their way through the streets. Fallen telephone poles barred our path. The sidewalks were cluttered with furniture. Many people were burned in the terrible flames. The odor of scorched human flesh pursued us long after we had left the city.

By September 9 the supply of food we had taken from home was used up. There was nothing whatever to be had along the way. Weak from hunger, my mother fainted on the road. I dropped beside her, sobbing wildly, but she showed no sign of life. In a daze, my father ran ahead to find some water, while my younger sister stood stock-still, as if paralyzed. But it was only a passing spell of weakness.

In Sochaczew we managed to get a few sour pickles and some chocolate cookies that tasted like soap. This was all we had to eat the entire day. Finding a drink of water was almost as difficult as procuring food. All the wells along the way were dried up. Once we found a well filled with murky water, but the villagers warned us not to drink from it because they were sure it had been poisoned by German agents. We hurried on in spite of our parched lips and aching throats.

Suddenly we saw a little blue plume of smoke rising from the chimney of a house at the side of the road. We had found all the other houses along the road deserted, but here was a sign of life. My father rushed in and returned with a huge kettle, but there was a strange expression on his face. In a trembling voice he told us what he had found, and for a while we could not bring ourselves to touch that precious water. . . . He had found the kettle on a stove in which the fire was lit. Near by, on a bed, a man was lying with his face turned to the wall. He seemed to be sleeping peacefully, so my father called out to him several times. But there was no answer. Then he walked over to the sleeping peasant and saw that he was dead. The bed was full of blood. The window panes were peppered with bullet holes.

The kettle which we "inherited" from this murdered peasant became our faithful companion on the long road to Warsaw. As we neared the capital we met the first German prisoners of war walking along the highway, led by Polish soldiers. This sight was encouraging to us, yet the Germans did not seem cast down by their condition. They wore elegant uniforms—they smiled insolently. They knew they would not be prisoners for very long.

We had our first taste of cooked food in Okecie, a suburb of Warsaw. A few soldiers in a deserted building shared their potato soup with us. After four days and nights of seemingly endless traveling we realized for the first time how tired we were. But we had to go on. There was not a moment to lose, for as we left Okecie we saw men and women building barricades with empty streetcars and cobblestones torn up from the streets, in preparation for the siege of the capital.

In Warsaw we found women standing at the doorways of the houses, handing out tea and bread to the refugees who streamed into the capital in unending lines. And as tens of thousands of provincials entered Warsaw in the hope of finding shelter there, thousands of old-time residents of the capital fled to the country.

Relatives in the heart of Warsaw's Jewish quarter gave us a warm and hearty welcome, but constant air attacks drove us to the cellar during most of our stay with them. By September 12 the Germans began to destroy the center of the city. Once again we had to move, this time to seek better protection against the bombs.

The days that followed brought hunger, death, and panic to our people. We could neither eat nor sleep. At first, in a new home on Zielna Street, we knew real comfort. The owners had fled the city, leaving a clean apartment for our use. There was even a maid to give us hot tea, and for the first time since our flight from Lodz we ate a real meal served on a table covered with a white cloth. It included herring, tomatoes, butter, and white bread. To get this bread my father had to stand for hours on a long line in front of a bakery. As he waited there, several German planes suddenly swooped down and strafed the people with machine guns. Instantly the line in front of the bakery dispersed, but one man remained. Disregarding the firing, my father took his place behind him. A moment later the man was hit in the head by a bullet. The entrance to the bakery shop was now free and my father made his purchase.

After this supper we listened to a broadcast in which an American reporter described the Nazi methods of warfare to his American listeners. "I stood in a field and from a distance saw a woman digging potatoes. Beside her was a little child. Suddenly a German plane swooped down, firing at the unarmed woman, who fell at once. The child was not hit. He bent over his fallen mother and wept heart-rendingly. Thus another orphan was added to the many war orphans of Poland. President Roosevelt!" he exclaimed in a deep voice, "I beg of you, help these mothers who are digging potatoes for their children; help these children whose mothers are falling on the peaceful fields; help Poland in her hour of trial!" But no help came. . . .

Our house at 31 Zielna Street was next to the telephone building, which was a target for the German guns throughout the siege. Although struck by many shells, the lofty and solidly built structure was only slightly damaged and the telephone girls remained at their posts. Many houses nearby were destroyed, and again we had to spend our nights in the cellar. Then one of the bombs exploded in the front room of our apartment, and we were forced to return to the crowded home of our relatives.

I shall never forget September 23, the date of the Day of

Atonement in 1939. The Germans deliberately chose that sacred Jewish holiday for an intensive bombardment of the Jewish district. In the midst of this bombardment a strange meteorological phenomenon took place: heavy snow mixed with hail began to fall in the middle of a bright, sunny day. For a while the bombing was interrupted, and the Jews interpreted the snow as a special act of heavenly intervention: even the oldest among them were unable to recall a similar occurrence. But later in the day the enemy made up for lost time with renewed fury.

In spite of the danger, my father and a few other men who lived in our house went to the neighboring synagogue. After a few minutes one of them came running back, his tallith on his head, a prayer book in his hand, and so shaken that for some time he was unable to speak. A bomb had fallen upon the synagogue and many of the worshipers had been killed. Then, to our great joy, my father returned unharmed. White as chalk, and carrying his tallith (prayer shawl) crumpled under his arm, he told us that many of those who only a moment before had been praying at his side had been killed during the service.

That night hundreds of buildings blazed all over the city. Thousands of people were buried alive in the ruins. But ten hours of murderous shelling could not break the resistance of Warsaw. Our people fought with increased stubbornness; even after the government had fled and Marshal Rydz-Smigly had abandoned his troops, men and women, young and old, helped in the defense of the capital. Those who were unarmed dug trenches; young girls organized first-aid squads in the doorways of the houses; Jews and Christians stood shoulder to shoulder and fought for their native land.

On the last night of the siege we sat huddled in a corner of the restaurant below our house. A few elderly Jews chanted psalms in tearful voices. My mother had wrapped us all in thick blankets to protect us from the tiny splinters that filled the air. When she herself stuck out her head for a moment, she was hit on the forehead by a splinter of shrapnel. Her face was covered with blood, but her wound proved to be only a small scratch. We realized that our shelter was a firetrap, so we set out for Kozla Street to find safer quarters with our relatives, stumbling over the mutilated bodies of soldiers and civilians as we walked. We found only the skeleton of a house rising above a huge cellar packed full of people lying on the concrete floor. Somehow or other they made room for us. Beside me lay a little boy convulsed with pain from a wound. When his mother changed his dressing, one could see that a shell fragment was still embedded in his flesh and that gangrene had already set in. A little further on lay a woman whose foot had been torn off by a bomb. No medical aid was available for these people. The stench was unbearable. The corners were crowded with children wailing piteously. The grownups simply sat or lay motionless, with stony faces and vacant eyes. Hours went by. When daybreak came I was struck by the sudden stillness. My ears, accustomed to the crash of unceasing explosions, began to hum. It was the terrifying silence that precedes a great calamity, but I could not imagine anything worse than what we had already been through. Suddenly someone rushed into the cellar with the news that Warsaw had capitulated. No one stirred, but I noticed tears in the eyes of the grownups. I, too, felt them choking in my throat, but my eyes were dry. So all our sacrifices had been in vain. Twenty-seven days after the outbreak of the war, Warsaw, which had held out longer than any other city in Poland, had been forced to surrender.

As we came out of the cellar we saw our ruined city in the clear September sun. Salvage crews were at work removing victims from the wreckage. Those who still showed signs of life were placed on stretchers and carried to the nearest first-aid stations. The dead were heaped upon carts and buried in the nearest empty ground—in the yard of a ruined house or an adjacent square. Soldiers were buried in public parks, and small wooden crosses were placed over their graves.

We returned to our own street. On the pavement lay the carcasses of fallen horses from which people were carving pieces of meat. Some of the horses were still twitching, but the hungry wretches did not notice that; they were cutting the beasts up alive. We found the last place in which we had stayed, our apartment on the Nalewki, intact except for broken window panes. But there was nothing to eat. The janitor invited us to join him in a dinner of duck and rice. Later I learned that this duck was the last swan our janitor had caught in the pond in Krasinski Park. In spite of the fact that this water was polluted by rotting human bodies, we felt no ill effects from that strange meal.

That afternoon a cousin who lived on Sienna Street invited us to share her large apartment, in which she had stored a great deal of food. So we moved once again. It was a nightmarish journey. On all the squares common graves were being dug. Warsaw looked like an enormous cemetery.

Lodz, October 15, 1939

We are again in Lodz. We found our store and our apartment completely looted; the thieves had cut the larger pictures out of their frames. My father is miserable over the loss of the Poussin and the Delacroix he bought in Paris for a considerable sum only a few weeks before the outbreak of the war. We have been here in Lodz for only two days, but we know now that it was a mistake to return here. The Nazis are beginning to intensify their acts of terrorism against the native population, especially the Jews. Last week they set fire to the great synagogue, the pride of the Lodz community. They forbade the Jews to remove the sacred books, and the "shames" or beadle who wanted to save the holy relics was locked up inside the temple and died in the flames. My mother cannot forgive herself for having persuaded my father to bring us back here.

Lodz, November 3, 1939

Almost every day our apartment is visited by German soldiers who, under various pretexts, rob us of our possessions. I feel as if I were in prison. Yet I cannot console myself by looking out of the window, for when I peer from behind the curtain I witness hideous incidents like that which I saw yesterday:

A man with markedly Semitic features was standing quietly on the sidewalk near the curb. A uniformed German approached him and apparently gave him an unreasonable order, for I could see that the poor fellow tried to explain something with an embarrassed expression. Then a few other uniformed Germans came upon the scene and began to beat their victim with rubber truncheons. They called a cab and tried to push him into it, but he resisted vigorously. The Germans then tied his legs together with a rope, attached the end of the rope to the cab from behind, and ordered the driver to start. The unfortunate man's face struck the sharp stones of the pavement, dyeing them red with blood. Then the cab vanished down the street.

Lodz, November 12, 1939

Percy, my mother's younger brother, has returned from Nazi captivity. Only a miracle saved him from death. On the battlefield, seeing the approaching Nazis, and realizing that his unit had surrendered, he decided to commit suicide. As he was in a medical unit he had all sorts of drugs on his person; he swallowed thirty tablets of Veronal and fell asleep. He lay thus on the open field when suddenly a pouring rain began to fall. This awakened him. "I don't know how it happened," he told us, "but I suddenly began to vomit, and spat up almost all of the poison." He was too weak to move, and soon the Germans picked him up and placed him in a prison camp. Next day, with a comrade, he managed to get through the barbed-wire fence and after wandering for a week in the so-called Kampinowska Forest, made his way to Lodz.

Lodz, November 23, 1939

Today Uncle Percy celebrated his wedding in secret. The Gestapo has officially forbidden Jews to marry, but in defiance of their order the number of Jewish marriages is increasing. It goes without saying that all the marriage certificates are antedated. Because of the dangers which surround us, all the engaged couples want to be together. Moreover everyone wonders whether the Nazis will even let him live much longer.

To attend this wedding we slunk one by one like shadows down the few blocks that separated us from the place of the ceremony. A guard stood at the door on the watch for Nazis, so that we could flee through another exit if necessary. The rabbi trembled while reciting the blessing. The slightest rustle on the staircase made us all rush to the door. The general mood was one of terror and apprehension.

April 28, 1940

We have managed to obtain a separate apartment in the same house where we had been sharing rooms. My mother has tacked up her visiting card on the door, with the inscription: "American citizen." This inscription is a wonderful talisman against the German bandits who freely visit all Jewish apartments. As soon as German uniforms come into view at the outer door of our building, our neighbors come begging us to let them in so that they too can benefit from our miraculous sign. Our two little rooms are filled to the brim—for how could we refuse anyone? All of the neighbors tremble with fear, and with a silent prayer on their lips gaze at the two small American flags on the wall.

Jews who possess passports of neutral countries are not compelled to wear arm bands or to do slave labor. No wonder many Jews try to obtain such documents; but not all have the means to buy them or the courage to use them. Two of my friends have acquired papers proving that they are nationals of a South American republic. Thanks to these they can circulate freely in the city. They went boldly to the Gestapo headquarters at the Bruehl Palace to have these papers sealed with a swastika; and the German experts did not realize that they were forged. They can even go to the country to buy food. With such documents they have at least a 90 per cent chance of survival—the other Jews have only a 10 percent chance at most.

November 15, 1940 [Warsaw]

Today the Jewish ghetto was officially established. Jews are forbidden to move outside the boundaries formed by certain streets. There is considerable commotion. Our people are hurrying about nervously in the streets, whispering various rumors, one more fantastic than the other.

Work on the walls—which will be three yards high—has already begun. Jewish masons, supervised by Nazi soldiers, are laying bricks upon bricks. Those who do not work fast enough are lashed by the overseers. It makes me think of the Biblical description of our slavery in Egypt. But where is the Moses who will release us from our new bondage?

At the end of those streets in which the traffic has not been stopped completely there are German sentries. Germans and Poles are allowed to enter the isolated quarter, but they must not carry any parcels. The specter of starvation looms up before us all.

January 4, 1941

The ghetto is covered with deep snow. The cold is terrible and none of the apartments are heated. Wherever I go I find people wrapped up in blankets or huddling under feather beds, that is, if the Germans have not yet taken all these warm things for their own soldiers. The bitter cold makes the Nazi beasts who stand guard near the ghetto entrances even more savage than usual. Just to warm up as they lurch back and forth in the deep snow, they open fire every so often and there are many victims among the passers-by. Other guards who are bored with their duty at the gates arrange entertainments for themselves. For instance, they choose a victim from among the people who chance to go by, order him to throw himself in the snow with his face down, and if he is a Jew who wears a beard, they tear it off together with the skin until the snow is red with blood. When such a Nazi is in a bad mood, his victim may be a Jewish policeman who stands guard with him.

Yesterday I myself saw a Nazi gendarme "exercise" a Jewish policeman near the passage from the Little to the Big Ghetto on Chlodna Street. The young man finally lost his breath, but the Nazi still forced him to fall and rise until he collapsed in a pool of blood. Then someone called for an ambulance, and the Jewish policeman was put on a stretcher and carried away on a hand truck. There are only three ambulance cars for the whole ghetto, and for that reason hand trucks are mostly used. We call them rickshas.

Snow is falling slowly, and the frost draws marvelous flower patterns on the windowpanes. I dream of a sled gliding over the ice, of freedom. Shall I ever be free again? I have become really selfish. For the time being I am still warm and have food, but all around me there is so much misery and starvation that I am beginning to be very unhappy.

June 12, 1941

The ghetto is becoming more and more crowded; there is a constant stream of new refugees. These are Jews from the provinces who have been robbed of all their possessions.

Upon their arrival the scene is always the same: the guard at the gate checks the identity of the refugee, and when he finds out that he is a Jew, gives him a push with the butt of his rifle as a sign that he may enter our Paradise. . . .

These people are ragged and barefoot, with the tragic eyes of those who are starving. Most of them are women and children. They become charges of the community, which sets them up in so-called homes. There they die sooner or later.

I have visited such a refugee home. It is a desolate building. The former walls of the separate rooms have been broken down to form large halls; there are no conveniences; the plumbing has been destroyed. Near the walls are cots made of boards and covered with rags. Here and there lies a dirty red feather bed. On the floor I saw half-naked, unwashed children lying listlessly. In one corner an exquisite little girl of four or five sat crying. I could not refrain from stroking her disheveled blond hair. The child looked at me with her big blue eyes, and said: "I'm hungry."

I was overcome by a feeling of utter shame. I had eaten that day, but I did not have a piece of bread to give to that child. I did not dare look in her eyes, and went away.

During the day the grownups go out to look for work. The children, the sick, and the aged remain lying on their cots. There are people from Lublin, Radom, Lodz, and Piotrkow—from all the provinces. All of them tell terrible tales of rape and mass executions. It is impossible to understand why the Germans allow all these people to settle in the Warsaw ghetto which already contains four hundred thousand Jews.

Mortality is increasing. Starvation alone kills from forty to fifty persons a day. But there are always hundreds of new refugees to take their places. The community is helpless. All the hotels are packed, and hygienic conditions are of the worst. Soap is unobtainable; what is distributed as soap on our ration cards is a gluey mass that falls to pieces the moment it comes into contact with water. It makes one dirty instead of clean.

June 26, 1941

I am writing this in the bomb shelter of our house. I am on night duty, as a member of the home air defense. The Russians are bombing more and more frequently. We are situated in a dangerous spot, close to the main railway station. It is now eleven o'clock. I am sitting near a small carbide lamp. This is the first time since the opening of hostilities between Russia and Germany that I have been able to write. The shock was tremendous. War between Germany and Russia! Who could have hoped it would come so soon!

July 10, 1941

I am full of dire forebodings. During the last few nights, I have had terrible nightmares. I saw Warsaw drowning in blood; together with my sister and my parents, I walked over prostrate corpses. I wanted to flee, but could not, and awoke in a cold sweat, terrified and exhausted. The golden sun and the blue sky only irritate my shaken nerves.

July 29, 1941

The typhus epidemic is raging. Yesterday the number of deaths from this disease exceeded two hundred. The doctors are simply throwing up their hands in despair. There are no medicines, and all the hospitals are overcrowded. New beds are constantly being added in the wards and corridors, but this does not solve the problem, and the number of victims is growing daily.

The hospital at the corner of Leszno and Rymarska Streets has put up a sign in the window of its office reading: "No vacancies." The Berson Children's Hospital on Sienna Street is packed with children of various ages, all of them ill with typhus. The hospital at the corner of Leszno and Zelazna Streets has closed its doors; there is no room for even one more patient.

A few days ago, on Leszno Street, I saw a father carrying a fairly grown-up boy in his arms. Both father and son were dressed in rags. The young patient's face was burning red, and he was raving deliriously. As he approached the corner of Leszno and Zelazna Streets, the man stopped hesitatingly in front of the hospital gate. He remained standing there for a while, apparently wondering what to do. Finally, the unfortunate man laid his sick son down on the steps leading to the hospital office and withdrew several paces. The exhausted boy tossed in convulsions and groaned heavily. Suddenly a nurse in a white apron came out and began to berate the grief-stricken father who stood with lowered head, weeping bitterly. After a while I noticed that the sick boy had ceased tossing, as though he had fallen asleep. His eyes were closed and a look of serene contentment was spread over his face.

A few moments later the weeping father cast a glance at his son. He bent over his child and, sobbing brokenheartedly, stared at his face for a long time, as though trying to discover a trace of life in it. But all was over. Soon a little black cart, a free service to the community, appeared, and the still warm body of the boy was added to several others that had been picked up in adjoining streets. For some time the father gazed at the cart as it moved away. Then he disappeared.

September 20, 1941

The Nazis are victorious. Kiev has fallen. Soon Himmler will be in Moscow. London is suffering severe bombardments. Will the Germans win this war? No, a thousand times no! Why do not the Allies bomb German cities? Why is Berlin still intact? Germany must be wiped off the face of the earth. Such a people should not be allowed to exist. Not only are the uniformed Nazis criminals, but all the Germans, the whole civilian population, which enjoys the fruits of the looting and murders committed by their husbands and fathers.

September 23, 1941

Alas, our apprehensions before the holidays were justified. Only yesterday, on the eve of Rosh Hashana, the Germans summoned the community representatives with Engineer Czerniakow at their head and demanded that they deliver at once five thousand men for the labor camps. The community refused to obey this order. The Germans then broke into the ghetto and organized a real pogrom. The manhunt went on throughout yesterday and this morning, and shooting could be heard from all sides.

I happened to be in the street when the hunt began. I managed to rush into a doorway which was jammed with people, and I waited there for two hours. At a quarter past eight, considering that it takes half an hour to walk from Leszno Street to Sienna Street, I decided to go home in order to arrive before nine, the curfew hour, after which it is forbidden to be in the streets.

At the corner of Leszno and Zelazna Streets, an enormous mass of people stood drawn up in military ranks in front of the labor office. Most of them were young men between eighteen and twenty-five. The Jewish police were forced to see to it that no one ran away. These young men stood with lowered heads as though about to be slaughtered. And actually their prospects are not much better than slaughter. The thousands of men who have been sent to the labor camps thus far have vanished without leaving a trace.

Suddenly the door of a stationery store near which I stood, as if petrified, staring at the group of condemned men, opened, and I felt a hand on my shoulder. It was a Jewish policeman, who quickly dragged me inside.

A moment later, on the very spot where I had been standing, a man fell, struck by a bullet. A lamentation ran through the crowd like an electric current, and reached through the closed door of the stationery store. The fallen man groaned for a while, but was soon taken away in a hand truck. The janitor at once proceeded to scrub the still warm blood from the pavement.

Trembling, I looked at my watch. The curfew hour, the hour of sure death on the ghetto streets, was approaching. Instinctively, I moved toward the exit. But the policeman would not let me go. When I told him how far I lived and that I did not care whether I was shot now or later, he promised to take me home.

I left the store with a few other people who wanted to get home. It was five minutes to nine. The policeman brought me to our doorway, and when I entered our apartment it was thirty minutes past curfew time. My parents had almost given me up for dead and flooded me with a hail of questions. But I was in no condition to answer them, and fell at once on my bed. Even now, as I write these lines, I am still shaken by my experience and I see before me the thousands of young Jews standing like sheep before a slaughterhouse. So many sons, brothers, and husbands have been torn away from their loved ones, whom they may never see again, to whom they will not even be allowed to say farewell.

In a few months the mothers, wives, and sisters of these men will receive official postcards informing them that number such-and-such has died. It is inconceivable that we have the strength to live through it. The Germans are surprised that the Jews in the ghetto do not commit mass suicide, as was the case in Austria after the *Anschluss.* We, too, are surprised that we have managed to endure all these torments. This is the miracle of the ghetto.

The epidemic is taking a terrible toll. Recently the mortality reached five hundred a day. The home of every person who falls ill with typhus is disinfected. The apartments or rooms of those who die of it are practically flooded with disinfectants. The health department of the community is doing everything in its power to fight the epidemic, but the shortage of medicines and hospital space remains the chief cause of the huge mortality, and the Nazis are making it increasingly difficult to organize medical help. There is a widespread belief that the Nazis deliberately contaminated the ghetto with typhus bacilli in order to test methods of bacteriological warfare which they intend to apply against England and Russia. It is said that the community has irrefutable proof of this theory from the world-famous bacteriologists, Jewish professors from France, Belgium, and Holland, who have been deported here by the Nazis. Thus it is no longer a question of inadequate sanitary measures, or the overcrowding in the ghetto. Tomorrow the Nazis may plant their bacilli in the cleanest section of the ghetto, where the sanitary conditions are exemplary.

Few people today are earning their living by doing normal work. Real money can be made only in dishonest deals, but not many people engage in them; most Jews choose to go hungry rather than become tools in the hands of the Nazis.

But sometimes people are compelled to accept this role. If a person is caught committing a minor violation of the laws, such as wearing the arm band in a manner slightly different from that prescribed, he is arrested and tortured. Such a person is often anxious to commit suicide, but has no easy way of doing it. The Germans find their victims among these tortured people whose spirit and body are broken, and confront them with the choice of life or death. Such people lose all power of resistance; they agree to anything, and thus automatically become tools of the Gestapo. Their chief function is informing. The Nazis want to know who owns jewelry or foreign exchange. An informer can never get out of the Nazis' clutches; he must "accomplish" something to pay for the favor of being allowed to live and receive food. And the Nazis keep threatening him with the renewal of the same tortures.

There are a number of such Gestapo agents in the ghetto, but they are not really dangerous, for they are more or less known and, whenever they can, they even warn the prospective victims of the Gestapo against projected house searches. However, there are a few underworld characters who are really dangerous because they take their services for the Gestapo seriously, just as they used to commit crimes in dead earnest.

Even these sad conditions give rise to various bits of gossip and jokes among us, and serve as material for songs and skits that are sung and played in cafés and theaters.

Every day at the Art Café on Leszno Street one can hear songs and satires on the police, the ambulance service, the rickshas, and even the Gestapo, in a veiled fashion. The typhus epidemic itself is the subject of jokes. It is laughter through tears, but it is laughter. This is our only weapon in the ghetto—our people laugh at death and at the Nazi decrees. Humor is the only thing the Nazis cannot understand.

November 22, 1941

Outside, a blizzard is raging and the frost paints designs on the windowpanes. During these terribly cold days, one name is on everyone's lips: Kramsztyk, the man who presides over the distribution of fuel. Alas, the amount of coal and wood the Germans have assigned to the ghetto is so small that it is barely sufficient to heat the official buildings, such as the community administration, the post office, the hospitals, and the schools, so that almost nothing is left for the population at large. On the black market, coal fetches fantastic prices and often cannot be obtained at all.

In the streets, frozen human corpses are an increasingly frequent sight. On Leszno Street in front of the court building, many mothers often sit with children wrapped in rags from which protrude red frostbitten little feet. Sometimes a mother cuddles a child frozen to death, and tries to warm the inanimate little body. Sometimes a child huddles against his mother, thinking that she is asleep and trying to awaken her, while, in fact, she is dead. The number of these homeless mothers and children is growing from day to day. After they have given up their last breath they often remain lying on the street for long hours, for no one bothers about them.

The little coaches of Pinkiert's funeral establishment are constantly busy. When a beggar sees a usable piece of clothing on a dead body, he removes it, covers the nude corpse with an old newspaper, and puts a couple of bricks or stones on the paper to prevent it from being blown away by the wind. On Komitetowa and Grzybowska Streets fewer beggars are seen this year than last; they have simply died off.

Hunger is assuming more and more terrible forms. The prices of foodstuffs are going up. A pound of black bread now costs four zlotys, of white bread, six zlotys. Butter is forty zlotys a pound; sugar, from seven to eight zlotys a pound.

It is not easy to walk in the street with a parcel in one's hand. When a hungry person sees someone with a parcel that looks like food, he follows him and, at an opportune moment, snatches it away, opens it quickly, and proceeds to satisfy his hunger. If the parcel does not contain food, he throws it away. No, these are not thieves; they are just people crazed by hunger.

The Jewish police cannot cope with them. And, indeed, who would have the heart to prosecute such unfortunates?

The hygienic conditions are constantly deteriorating. Most of the sewage pipes are frozen, and in many houses the toilets cannot be used. Human excrement is often thrown out into the street together with the garbage. The carts that used regularly to remove the garbage from the courtyards now come rarely or not at all. For the time being all this filth is disinfected by the cold. But what will happen when the first spring breeze begins to blow? There is serious apprehension that a cholera epidemic will break out to fill our cup of misfortune to the brim.

December 9, 1941

America's entry into the war has inspired the hundreds of thousands of dejected Jews in the ghetto with a new breath of hope. The Nazi guards at the gates have long faces. Some are considerably less insolent, but on others the effect has been exactly opposite and they are more unbearable than ever. Most people believe that the war will not last long now and that the Allies' victory is certain.

February 27, 1942

Shootings have now become very frequent at the ghetto exits. Usually they are perpetrated by some guard who wants to amuse himself. Every day, morning and afternoon, when I go to school, I am not sure whether I will return alive. I have to go past two of the most dangerous German sentry posts: at the corner of Zelazna and Chlodna Streets near the bridge, and at the corner of Krochmalna and Grzybowska Streets. At the latter place there is usually a guard who has been nicknamed "Frankenstein," because of his notorious cruelty. Apparently this soldier cannot go to sleep unless he has a few victims to his credit; he is a real sadist. When I see him from a distance I shudder. He looks like an ape: small and stocky, with a swarthy grimacing face. This morning, on my way to school, as I was approaching the corner of Krochmalna and Grzybowska Streets, I saw his familiar figure, torturing some ricksha driver whose vehicle had passed an inch closer to the exit than the regulations permitted. The unfortunate man lay on the curb in a puddle of blood. A yellowish liquid dripped from his mouth to the pavement. Soon I realized that he was dead, another victim of the German sadist. The blood was so horribly red the sight of it completely shattered me.

April 17, 1942

I am almost hysterical. A little before six o'clock today, the police captain, Hertz, rushed excitedly into our apartment and said: "Please be prepared for anything; at eight o'clock there is going to be a pogrom." Then he tore out without further explanations. The whole ghetto was seized with panic. People hastily closed their stores. There was a rumor that a special *Vernichtungskommando* (destructive squad), the same which had perpetrated the Lublin pogrom, had arrived in Warsaw to organize a massacre here. It was also said that Ukrainians and Lithuanians would now take over the guarding of the ghetto because the Germans were to go to the Russian front.

April 28, 1942

Last night sixty more persons were executed. They were members of the underground, most of them well-to-do people who financed the secret bulletins. Many printers who were suspected of helping to publish the underground papers were also killed. Once again in the morning there were corpses in the streets. One of the victims was the wealthy baker Blajman, the chief backer of an underground newspaper. His brothers, too, were sentenced to die but they managed to escape and are now in hiding.

In our garden everything is green. The young onions are shooting up. We have eaten our first radishes. The tomato plants spread proudly in the sun. The weather is magnificent. The greens and the sun remind us of the beauty of nature that we are forbidden to enjoy. A little garden like ours is therefore very dear to us. The spring this year is extraordinary. A little lilac bush under our window is in full bloom.

May 4, 1942

On the "Aryan" side the population celebrated May 1 and May 3 by a complete boycott of the Nazis. Throughout those days the people tried to avoid taking trolley cars or buying newspapers, for the money goes straight to the Germans. Someone put a wreath of flowers on the tomb of the Unknown Soldier. The people deliberately stayed at home, so that a dead silence prevailed in the city. In the ghetto, too, the mood was somehow different. Although many Poles, poisoned by anti-Semitism, deny that their brothers of the Jewish faith are their co-citizens, the Jews, despite the inhuman treatment to which they are subjected, show their patriotism in every possible way. Recently there has been much talk of the partisan groups fighting in the woods of the Lublin region; there are many Jews among them, who fight like all the others for a common goal. And yet the Polish anti-Semites say, "It's a good thing, let the Jews sit behind their walls. At last Poland will be Jewless."

Some Jews are ashamed to admit that Poland is their fatherland, although they love it, because they remember how often their Polish co-citizens have said to them "Go back to

Palestine, Jew," or how, at the University, the Jewish students were assigned to the "ghetto benches," and were often attacked by Gentile students for no other crime than their Jewish faith. It is a fact that many Gentiles in Warsaw have been infected by Hitler's propaganda. Naturally, there are people who see the error of such ways, but they are afraid to say anything because they would at once be accused of having a Jewish grandfather or grandmother or even of having been bribed by the Jews. Only a few, and these are members of the working-class parties, speak up openly, and these for the most part are fighting in the partisan units. If all the Aryan Poles got together and tried to help the Jews in the ghetto they could do a great deal for us. For instance, they could procure "Aryan" certificates for many Jews, give them shelter in their homes, facilitate their escape over the walls, and so on and so forth. But of course it is easier to throw stones into the ghetto. . . .

It is beginning to be hot, and often, instead of going to school, I take a blanket and a pillow and go to our roof to sunbathe. This practice is widespread in the ghetto; the houses with flat roofs have been transformed into city beaches.

At 20 Chlodna Street the charge for entering the terracelike roof is one zloty fifty groszy. There are folding chairs, cool drinks, and a bird's-eye view of Warsaw. On our own roof I am always alone. It is pleasant to lie there in the sun, where I can see the quarter beyond the wall. The white spires of a church are very near me. They are surrounded by linden branches and the perfume of these lovely trees reaches as far as my roof. Further on there are private houses now used as

German barracks. The air is pure here, and I think of the wide world, of distant lands, of freedom.

July 5, 1942

Fewer and fewer students come to our school; now they are afraid to walk in the streets. The Nazi guard Frankenstein is raging through the ghetto, one day he kills ten persons, another day five ... everyone expects to be his next victim. A few days ago I, too, ceased completely attending school.

Today I boldly removed my arm band. After all, officially I am now an American citizen.

The inhabitants of the street looked at me with curiosity: "That's the girl who is going to America." In this street everyone knows everyone else. Every few minutes people approached me and asked me to note the addresses of their American relatives, and to tell them to do everything possible for their unfortunate kin.

July 22, 1942

Today the Jewish police gathered up all the beggars from the streets and emptied the refugee camps. These unfortunates were locked up in freight cars without food or water. The transports are being sent in the direction of Brzesc, but will they ever reach there? It is doubtful that all these starving people will arrive at their destination alive; they will perish in their sealed cars. A hundred persons are crowded into each car. The Polish prison guard who whispered all these details to us had tears in his eyes. He lives near Stawki Street, and he witnessed horrible scenes of people being driven into cars with whips, just as though they were cattle.

August, 1942

Behind the Pawiak gate we are experiencing all the terror that is abroad in the ghetto. For the last few nights we have been unable to sleep. The noise of the shooting, the cries of despair, are driving us crazy. I have to summon all my strength to write these notes. I have lost count of the days, and I do not know what day it is. But what does it matter? We are here as on a little island amidst an ocean of blood. The whole ghetto is drowning in blood. We literally see fresh human blood, we can smell it. Does the outside world know anything about it? Why does no one come to our aid? I cannot go on living; my strength is exhausted. How long are we going to be kept here to witness all this?

A few days ago, a group of neutrals was taken out of the Pawiak. Apparently the Germans were unable to use them for exchange. I saw from my window several trucks filled with people, and I tried to distinguish familiar faces among them. Some time later, the prison guard came panting to us, and told us that the Jewish citizens of neutral European countries had just been taken to the *Umschlagplatz* to be deported. So our turn may come soon, too. I hope it will be very soon. This waiting is worse than death.

Dr. Janusz Korczak's children's home is empty now. A few days ago we all stood at the window and watched the Germans surround the houses. Rows of children, holding each other by their little hands, began to walk out of the doorway. There were tiny tots of two or three years among them, while the oldest ones were perhaps thirteen. Each child carried a little bundle in his hand. All of them wore white aprons. They walked in ranks of two, calm, and even smiling. They had not the slightest foreboding of their fate. At the end of the procession marched Dr. Korczak, who saw to it that the children did not walk on the sidewalk. Now and then, with fatherly solicitude, he stroked a child on the head or arm, and straightened out the ranks. He wore high boots, with his trousers stuck in them, an alpaca coat, and a navy-blue cap, the so-called Maciejowka cap. He walked with a firm step, and was accompanied by one of the doctors of the children's home, who wore his white smock. This sad procession vanished at the corner of Dzielna and Smocza Streets. They went in the direction of Gesia Street, to the cemetery. At the cemetery all the children were shot. We were also told by our informants that Dr. Korczak was forced to witness the executions, and that he himself was shot afterward.

Thus died one of the purest and noblest men who ever lived. He was the pride of the ghetto. His children's home gave us courage, and all of us gladly gave part of our own scanty means to support the model home organized by this great idealist. He devoted all his life, all his creative work as an educator and writer, to the poor children of Warsaw. Even at the last moment he refused to be separated from them.

The house is empty now, except for the guards who are still cleaning up the rooms of the murdered children.

Yesterday I saw a detachment of Ukrainians and "Shaulists" (Lithuanians) fully armed, with helmets on their heads, running along Dzielna Street. It had been quiet when, all of a sudden, I heard the clatter of boots. The men ran with fixed bayonets, as though to a front-line attack. Those at the end of the detachment held small hatchets in their hands, such as are used to break down the doors of barricaded apartments. These beasts often use hatchets against human beings too. The Lithuanians are the worst of all.

During the last two weeks more than 100,000 people have been deported from the ghetto. The number of those murdered is also very large. Everyone who can is trying to get a job in the German factories of Toebens, Schultz, and Hallmann. Fantastic sums are paid for a labor card.

September 20, 1942

The massacres have aroused the underground leaders to greater resistance. The illegal papers are multiplying and some of them reach us even here in the Pawiak. They are full of good reports from the battle fronts. The Allies are victorious in Egypt, and the Russians are pushing the enemy back at Moscow. The sheets explain the meaning of the deportations and tell of the fate of the deported Jews. The population is summoned to resist with weapons in their hands, and warned against defeatist moods, and against the idea that we are completely helpless before the Nazis. "Let us die like men and not like sheep," ends one proclamation in a paper called *To Arms!*

The situation improved somewhat in the last days of August, and some began to take an optimistic view of the future. But this was only the lull before the storm. On September 3 and 4 the Germans began to blockade the workshops organized by the community. Elite Guards, accompanied by Lithuanians and Ukrainians, entered the shops, and took several dozen people out of each, alleging that they needed skilled workers. These workers, numbering more than a thousand, were led away to Stawki Street and deported to the Treblinki camp.

Now it is generally known that most of the deportees are sent to Treblinki, where they are killed with the help of machines with which the Germans are experimenting for war purposes. But no one knows any details.

October 10, 1942

Today is my birthday. I spent all day on my mattress. Everyone came to congratulate me, but I did not answer. At night my sister managed to snatch three turnips, and we had a real feast to celebrate the occasion.

October 22, 1942

Is this really our last night in the Pawiak? Is it possible that tomorrow we shall leave? Before nightfall we arranged a "farewell dinner" in the men internees' room. We ate turnips, and our representative, Mr. S., made a speech to the twenty-one American citizens. On the table we placed two little American flags that I had kept in my suitcase, as a relic, since the beginning of the war. The mood was one of elation. Noemi W. wore a silk wrapper that looked like an elegant evening gown. She recited and sang songs. I, too, sang several English songs. The attendants watched us and I had the feeling that they envied us.

December 17, 1942

Dita W., one of yesterday's arrivals, told us last night what she had heard about the camp at Treblinki. During her frequent visits to Gestapo headquarters at Aleja Szucha she became acquainted with a German who was an official in this death camp. He did not realize that she was Jewish, and told her with great satisfaction how the deported Jews were being murdered there, assuring her that the Germans would finally "finish off" all the Jews.

At the *Umschlagplatz* the cattle cars are loaded with one hundred and fifty people each, after their floors have been covered with a thick layer of lime. The cars have no windows or other openings. The people lie on top of each other without sufficient air to breathe, and without food or water. The cars are often left for two or three days at the Stawki station. The locked-up people must perform their natural functions in the closed cars and, as a result, the lime dissolves, filling the cars with poisonous fumes. The survivors are unloaded at Treblinki station and divided according to their trades. Shoemakers, tailors, etc., are grouped separately in order to make the victims believe that they are going to be employed in workshops. The real purpose is to make them go to their deaths more obediently. The women are separated from the men.

The actual death house of Treblinki is situated in a thick wood. The people are taken in trucks to buildings where they are ordered to undress completely. Each is given a cake of soap and told that he must bathe before going to the labor camp. The naked people, men, women, and children separately, are led into a bathhouse with a slippery tile floor. They tumble down the moment they enter it. Each small compartment is so filled with people that again they must lie on top of one another. After the bathhouse is entirely filled, strongly concentrated hot steam is let in through the windows. After a few minutes the people begin to choke in horrible pain.

After the execution the dead bodies are carried out by Jews—the youngest and most vigorous are especially chosen by the Nazis for this purpose. Other Jews are compelled to sort out the shoes and clothes of the victims. After each transport the Jews employed to bury the dead or sort their belongings are relieved by others. They are unable to stand this work for more than a week. Most of them lose their minds and are shot. Even the Ukrainian and German personnel are often relieved, because the older German soldiers begin to complain of their tasks. Only the chief German authorities remain the same.

Escape from Treblinki is impossible, yet two young Jews managed to do the impossible. After long wanderings in the woods they arrived in Warsaw and related other details. According to them the Germans employ various gases as well as electricity in certain execution chambers. Because of the enormous number of the murdered, the Germans have constructed a special machine to dig graves.

People who have traveled in trains past Treblinki say that the stench there is so poisonous that they must stop up their nostrils.

After Dita's accounts none of us could sleep.

December 26, 1942

It looks as though our departure is really imminent. The Nazis are making great efforts to impress us favorably. The day before Christmas all the internees' quarters were scrubbed, even the rooms occupied by the Jews. On Christmas Day we had an exceptionally good meal which consisted of a thick pea soup, a portion of sauerkraut, potatoes, and two pounds of bread.

At nine in the evening Commissioner Nikolaus, accompanied by his aides Jopke and Fleck, and three SS men in uniform, entered our room, saluted us, and assured us that we would surely leave in the very near future.

This morning we received a visit from the hangman, Bürckel. He wore his gala uniform and, probably on account of the holiday, did not carry his riding crop. He had had a good dose of liquor and was in an exuberant mood. He approached old Rabbi R., took him by the hand and, shaking with laughter, wished him a merry Christmas. "We Germans can be kind, too!" he snickered as he staggered out of our room.

January 1, 1943

New Year's Eve for me was full of nightmares. I fell asleep and woke up several times, for I was tormented by horrible dreams; I relived all the scenes I had witnessed during these years of war. Again and again the little children of Janusz Korczak's home passed before my eyes. I knew that they were dead and I wondered why they kept smiling and smiling. Each time I fell asleep these children came before me. Then I was awakened by shouts and laughter coming from the direction of the prison yard. The Nazi officials were gaily welcoming the New Year. From time to time I heard the sound of shots, followed again by laughter and the noise of broken glass. Then came roaring drunken voices.

The first day of 1943 is cloudy and snowy. As I write these lines I cannot stop thinking of Dita W.'s stories of Treblinki. I see before me the tiled bathhouses filled with naked people choking in the hot steam. How many of my relatives and friends have perished there? How many young, still unlived lives? I curse the coming of the New Year.

February 27, 1944

At last a date has been set! The exchange will take place in Lisbon on March 5. Wounded American soldiers and civilian internees are scheduled for exchange. But it is not clear yet what the ratio of the exchange will be: five Germans for one American, or vice versa, five Americans for one German. Various rumors are circulating on the subject. The camp administration organizes a new registration every hour; new people are put on the lists, old ones are crossed off. We are all at a terrible pitch of tension and nervousness. Our family was on the first two lists, but now we have been taken off them. My mother is rushing around from one office to another. Only about thirty persons are supposed to go with the first batch, while there are one hundred and fifty candidates for exchange in Vittel. All these shifts and rumors have completely shattered our nerves.

March 3, 1944

A few minutes ago we exchanged all our money for dollars. This has finally reassured us; we really believe we are going to America now. All the men were made to sign a pledge that they would not fight against Germany in any army. When they left the cars to sign this pledge we saw a train with German internees arrive on another track. They have come from America to be exchanged for us. All of us actually pitied these Germans.

March 4, 1944

Our train is now on Spanish territory. At the stations some people greet us with the "V" sign. The poverty of Spain strikes one at once. Ragged children stretch out their hands, begging for a coin. There are many soldiers, especially smartly dressed officers. The civilian population is dressed in rags, and the people have hollow cheeks.

Many of the Germans who escorted us have remained on the French side of the border, and those who still accompany us now are dressed in mufti. With their uniforms they have shed their insolence.

March 5, 1944

We have just crossed the Portuguese border. The uniformed Spanish police have been replaced by Portuguese secret police. We are still in the same train. Here, too, people greet us with "V" signs.

Our train is approaching Lisbon. I can see the sails of various ships. Someone in our car has just shouted the word: "Gripsholm!" This unfamiliar Swedish word means freedom to us.

I was awakened by the sound of the ship's engine. The "Gripsholm" was on the open sea. I went out on deck and breathed in the endless blueness. The blood-drenched earth of Europe was far behind me. The feeling of freedom almost took my breath away.

In the last four years I have not known this feeling. Four years of the black swastika, of barbed wire, ghetto walls, executions, and, above all, terror—terror by day and terror by night. After four years of that nightmare I found it hard to enjoy my freedom at first. I constantly imagined that it was only a dream, that at any moment I would awaken in the Pawiak and once again see the aged men with gray beards, the blooming young girls and proud young men, driven like cattle to the *Umschlagplatz* on Stawki Street to their deaths.

I even fancied sometimes that I heard the cries of the tortured, and the salty smell of the sea suddenly changed into the nauseating, sweetish odor of human blood, which had often entered our windows in the Pawiak.

I had thought that on the ship I would forget the nightmare of the ghetto. But, strangely enough, in the infinity of ocean I constantly saw the bloody streets of Warsaw.

On deck I made friends with American soldiers and fliers who had been shot down on missions over Germany, and who had been exchanged together with us. Some of them had empty hanging sleeves. Others walked on crutches. Two young officers had horribly disfigured faces; others had had their faces burned. One of them had lost both legs, but a smile never left his lips.

I felt close to these Americans, and when I told them about what the Nazis had done in the ghetto they understood me.

Aboard ship I saw the first American film in four years. It was *Yankee Doodle Dandy*. The soldiers and officers had tears in their eyes when they saw it.

By nightfall of March 14 the outline of the American coast began to emerge from the mist. The passengers went out on deck and lined the railings. I was reminded of the Biblical story of the flood, and of Noah's ark, when it finally reached dry land.

All that day I felt completely broken, as though I had to bear the burden of many, many years. I did not take part in the entertainment that night. I lay in a corner of the deck, listening to the sound of the waves that were growing stormier and stormier.

On March 15 our ship approached New York. People who had gone through years of common misfortune began to say farewell to each other. A mood of fraternal affection prevailed among us. On everyone's face there was an expression of restless expectation.

I saw the skyscrapers of New York, but my thoughts were in Warsaw ...

I shall do everything I can to save those who can still be saved, and to avenge those who were so bitterly humiliated in their last moments. And those who were ground into ash, I shall always see them alive. I will tell, I will tell everything, about our sufferings and our struggles and the slaughter of our dearest, and I will demand punishment for the German murderers and their Gretchens in Berlin, Munich, and Nuremberg who enjoyed the fruits of murder, and are still wearing the clothes and shoes of our martyrized people.

Ina Konstantinova

RUSSIA   ∞   *16 YEARS OLD*

*B*efore Nazi Germany attacked the Soviet Union, sixteen-year-old Ina Konstantinova was living a quiet, comfortable life
with her parents and younger sister Renok near the town of Kashin,
northeast of Moscow. She had been keeping a diary for several years,
mostly focusing on her moods, adolescent existential angst, and the
close friendships she had with other girls and boys.

*Then, the night before her sixteenth birthday, in July of
1940, she wrote a melancholy farewell to her childhood and spoke of
death with a question as to whether she would ever reach old age.
The next day Germany bombed Russia, beginning the war in which
Ina would give her life, at age twenty, while serving as a partisan.*

*From the time she first learned that Russia was under
attack, Ina wanted to serve in the combat zone. This is not as unusual
as it may seem since one million women served in the Soviet armed
forces during World War II, the majority of them in active combat.
But Ina chose the riskiest way of fighting the Nazis. She volunteered
as a saboteur and spy in the partisan underground when she was*

*only seventeen years old. This was commonly known to be so danger-
ous that Ina had to "elope" in order to leave her mother and father,
whom she thought might try to prevent her from going.*

*Formerly given to moodiness and restlessness, Ina seemed
to find new meaning and purpose in her life with the partisan movement. She was never happier than when she was swathed in ammunition belts and carrying a submachine gun. Even the deaths of many
of her comrades did not dissuade her from proceeding with her mission
to kill as many Nazis as possible.*

*What follows is a selection of Ina's diary entries and her
letters home to her family. Many of the letters are undated and are
intentionally vague about her whereabouts. What is known for certain
is that on March 4, 1944, the dugout in which Ina and her platoon
of partisan scouts were hiding was surrounded by a detachment of
German soldiers. When she realized that she and her comrades were
trapped, Ina ordered them to leave while she stayed behind to cover
their retreat with submachine gunfire.*

*The next day, the partisans came back to the dugout and found
Ina lying dead under a nearby pine tree. Her friends and fellow partisans
buried her there and carved her initials into the tree. Her remains were later
exhumed and transferred to a cemetery in her hometown of Kashin.*

*For a girl to die in Soviet partisan service was not unique.
What caused Ina to be regarded as a national hero was her writing.
Her parents were instrumental in having her diary and letters published by the Soviet government. From that time on, Ina was held up
as an example for Soviet youth to follow.*

*These excerpts from Ina's diary and letters were taken
from a translation by K. Jean Cottam, Ph.D., published by MA/AH
Publishing in 1984 in Kansas.*

29 July 1940

ON THE LAST DAY OF MY CHILDHOOD

It is painful to give up all that is close and dear to us, especially one's childhood.

I know one thing: the pure, radiant joys—the joys of childhood—are gone forever. Good-bye, my morning. My day, bright but exhausting, has begun. And there, at the end, my old age awaits me. But will I reach it? Better not to experience this evening of life at all. For it brings . . . death.

Good-bye childhood . . . forever.

22 June 1941

Only yesterday everything was so peaceful, so quiet, and today . . . my God!

At noon we heard Molotov's speech broadcasted over the radio: Germany is bombing our nation, and German bombs have fallen on Kiev, Zhitomir, and other Ukrainian cities. The country is endangered. I can't describe my state of mind as I was listening to this speech! I became so agitated that my heart seemed about to jump out. The country is mobilizing; could I continue as before? No! I ought to make myself useful to my Homeland, to the best of my ability, in its hour of need. We must win!

23 June 1941

This is the second day of the war. Only the second day, but these two days were more eventful than the past two years. Our region was placed under martial law. This means that on the streets, too, lights are forbidden after 10:00 p.m. General mobilization has been declared. Our boys have already been called up by the Military Commissariat; soon they will go away.

Papa has already been mobilized, too, but he is still in Kashin. And what about me? If only there was a way of making myself useful at the front! Immediately, without any hesitation, I would then volunteer for service in the combat zone. But . . . what can I do there now? Well, nothing. But my time will come, too.

3 July 1941

Oh, what a night we had today! I'll never, never forget it. I'll start at the beginning. A week ago, I joined a voluntary aid detachment. We train every day from seven to ten. Yesterday, some of us were summoned for duty to the District Committee of the Red Cross. The time was 10:30 p.m. We were issued night passes, bandages, respirators, and medical bags. Then we were sent to the Technical School. Here everything was made ready to receive a trainload of wounded soldiers. Covered trucks and buses stood by; we climbed into them. I found myself among the Technical School kids.

We sat up all night, until 4:00 a.m. Finally, we drove to the train station. The train arrived at 5:30 a.m., and the unloading began. What an experience! I'll never forget the face of an agitated woman, accompanying the wounded, who—with tears in her eyes—almost threw her arms around my neck and kept repeating joyfully: "My dear little sister, have we really arrived? It is so good to see you!"

I'll never forget the blue eyes of a soldier, a mere youngster, semi-closed and suddenly opening up and flashing from an unbearable pain. How he suffered! I'll never forget this dark-haired youth with both legs torn off.

We carried, transported, and guided people.... But what I remember best was the mood of the soldiers. They all believed in victory, all were cheerful. We transported a girl soldier, a Latvian, wounded in one leg. She spoke almost no Russian. There were many wounded civilians, too, mainly from Riga.

No, I could never fully describe what I lived through that night. I was completely tired out. But it didn't matter!

16 July 1941

A terrible misfortune has befallen this country. The Germans are already so near.... They are bombing Leningrad, Mozhaysk. They are advancing toward Moscow....

We are training in a voluntary aid detachment, and are working in a hospital.

How troubled our life has become! There is an airfield near Kashin; aircraft take off from it constantly. Military detachments march along the streets. Field units, antiaircraft guns, and tanks have arrived.

Even the atmosphere has changed somehow. What does the future hold in store for us? I am anxious to finish training, and ... to go to the front. I dream of ... Nazi defeat, of defending our Homeland and making us happy again!

5 August 1941

On 30 July I turned seventeen. Did I foresee a year ago what is happening today? And what lies ahead for me a year from now? If the war has not yet ended by then, I'll definitely go to the front. They are bound to take me by then. Indeed, by then I would already be eighteen.

Every night Moscow is subjected to air raids. The enemy troops are coming closer and closer. How awful! But, never mind, they will soon be stopped.

17 December 1941

We heard good news over the radio again today. The Germans are receiving a sound beating and are on the run. Well, that's splendid! Soon we'll likely hear a communique from the Informburo to the effect that our troops have entered Berlin. What a holiday it would be! I can't wait!

8 April 1942

What luck: I am so glad, glad; I've never felt so good! Today I have been accepted for work behind German lines. I am in heaven! Oh, I am so happy! I'll write about everything, everything later on. I am so glad!

[Undated]

My dear ones, please forgive me!

I know—it was mean on my part to treat you as I did, but it's better this way: under no circumstances could I have withstood Mama's tears. Don't be too upset, don't feel sorry for me, because my fondest, long-standing wish has come true. I am happy! Remember this. Tomorrow, I'll give you all, all the details, and meanwhile I can only tell you that I am going to join a detachment. Papochka, forgive me in the name of everything that is holy, forgive me for what you call my deceiving you. I came to the Regional Committee . . . and it was too late to back out. My dearest and darling family,

only don't you cry and feel sorry for me. After all, this is
how I wish to live my life. This is how I visualize my happiness. Never mind! It'll be so good to see you, and to kiss
you affectionately on my return in the fall.

Lots of love to you all,

Your disobedient Inka.

[Undated]
Hello, my darling Papusya and Mamochka!

Yesterday we left Kalinin and spent the night here, the
place from which I am writing now. We are having a wonderful trip. It is true that the weather is cool, but I've warm
clothing at my disposal. Do you know that my superiors
have even told Colonel-General Konev [the Front commander] about me, and I'll soon go to meet him, because he
wished to see me?

I am flattered; shouldn't I be? Our partisan commanders
want me to stay at their HQ; I would be completely safe
there, but I don't want that. Well, all right, we'll see what
happens when we get there, and in the meantime I am so
well taken care of!

The commander gave me a personal weapon—a pistol
with two clips—and in Toropets I am to receive a submachine gun (a German one), which I've already learned to use.
On the whole, during these past few days I learned so many
new things, so many interesting things, that I'll never forget
this time of my life.

We passed through places destroyed and scarred by the
Germans. Oh, what horrors I have seen! So much destruction,
so many tragedies they have caused; we must repay them

for all this! My dear ones, if you had seen all that I did, you too would have come with me to join the detachment. Such interesting work awaits me there! Oh, I am so happy!

Ina.

[Undated]
Hello, my dear ones!

I am writing this letter to you from the village of Kun'ya, where we arrived yesterday evening; this is the last day of my stay in Soviet-held land until I return after the victory. Tomorrow we'll cross over "there." Don't worry, I'll be completely safe.

I have found my niche; here I am among friends. I am at peace with myself, and I'll definitely return victorious, but should something happen to me—believe me, I'll die honorably. This is how we all feel. Already many hardships have to be endured, but you should see me, running about carrying out assignments; I have been detailed as the duty person, and I cook dinner, so that you wouldn't recognize me. I sleep very little; I am terribly sunburnt, my face is weatherbeaten and perhaps coarsened a bit, but it doesn't matter.

Besides, I eat very well. So I am not likely to lose any weight.

In short, "life is beautiful and wonderful!" Today the Germans carried out as many as four air raids against our village. The bombing was awful, and their machine guns gave us a good thrashing. The bombs exploded about 70 meters from us, and bullets whistled literally above our heads (I lay in a ditch). But you see—I survived. Consequently, nothing will ever happen to me; I believe this wholeheartedly. From now on, for some time I won't be able to write to you directly, but don't worry; you'll be informed about me by a man who will keep in touch with you.

23 June 1942

I haven't written for a long time. So much has happened! I was not mistaken: this copy-book will see a great deal.

I particularly remember the events of 19 June. At night a large punitive detachment approached our village very, very close. The exchange of fire continued throughout the night. In the morning, when we woke up, villages burned all around us. Soon the first casualty was brought to me. My hands were covered with blood. Then I took this seriously wounded man to a doctor, 6 kilometers away. When I returned, we had to execute a certain village elder, a collaborator. We went to get him; we read him the sentence and led him to the place of execution. I felt awful.

In the evening, about eleven, just as I was getting ready to go to bed, another wounded man was brought in. Again I dressed his wounds, and again had to deliver him to a doctor. And the weather was terrible; it was cold, dark, raining, and windy! I dressed warm and we went. My sick man instantly froze; I had to give him at first my raincape and then my jacket. I had only a blouse on, and was terribly chilled. On the way, the cart broke down and I fixed it, and then we got lost. In short, it took us four hours to get to our destination. I barely had the time to warm up a bit when I had to start back. I returned in the morning; I had quite a night!

8 July 1942

Hello, my dear Papochka, Mamusen'ka, and Renok!

My life is unchanged, that is, I feel remarkably well. Only

don't get the idea that I am saying this just to reassure you. No, in fact, I am very satisfied with my current life.

From the very first day I became a partisan I forgot what it's like to be in a bad mood. The minute I appear crestfallen, our commanders and girls begin to joke, laugh, and cheer me up; in no time I again feel well.

Actually we have fun all the time. Especially in the evenings, when the entire staff, the eight of us, gather at the home base. Everyone tells a story of some kind and makes jokes; we giggle and go to sleep very, very late. By and large, work and leisure leave us no time for moping.

28 July 1942
My dear ones, my darlings!

Well, so we are going away in a half hour. Everything, absolutely everything, has been gathered, checked, and prepared. If you could only see me now—with field service marching order! There are machine-gun belts around my waist and a carbine is slung over my shoulder. I am also carrying a kit-bag, cartridge pouches and grenades, and in my pockets I've a Walther and a field dressing. I am wearing a big, turtleneck wool sweater and a jacket; I find this outfit most comfortable. We are saying good-bye to our Kupuy, and to the dear places that we have become so accustomed to. We are saying good-bye to our native land. We are about to go behind enemy lines for two months. And then to you, home. Don't expect any more mail from me, unless something happens to me; only then you'll get a letter or, more accurately, a message will then be transmitted by radio to the Front HQ and the HQ, in turn, will communicate with you.

But this isn't likely to happen. I'll return soon, in one piece, alive and well.

[Undated]
Hello, my own dearest darlings!

I don't know how to begin. Well, all right; first of all, I am alive and well, and feel wonderful. It is only three days since I returned from behind German lines. Again, I had a bit of an experience. Again, I was caught. This time I fell straight into German clutches. I didn't expect it would all end so well, but, obviously, I returned unharmed. I've lived through so much. . . . Honestly, I thought I might go gray. I'll tell you everything when we meet. I am now detached from the Brigade, on our territory and among our people. I nearly went crazy with joy after I crossed the front line and when I saw our people!

In a few days, I'll probably go back "there."

Don't worry about me. I am deeply convinced that nothing will happen to me, and that I'll soon come home on leave. Probably, in a few days, I'll receive many, many letters from you. This would make me so happy!

I feel remarkably well. After all, I am a hundred times happier than all the girls back home—dancing and supposedly having fun—because during these difficult times I too am useful to my Homeland which needs me, and not for nothing I am a Soviet person. Even if I were to go hungry, fall into Nazi clutches, and walk barefooted hundreds of kilometers—still I would be very rich, for I've the sense of true satisfaction. Well, my dear ones, lots of love and kisses to you.

Your Ina.

24 August 1942
My darling Mamusen'ka!

A few days ago, I received the first letter from you.

If you only knew how infinitely happy I was! How I cried over it! As if the two and a half months during which I heard nothing from you didn't happen. You wrote it on 6 August.

I now lead the kind of life I dreamed of: a soldier's life— active and for real. It is true that I am awfully sorry it is coming to an end. That is, not my life, but this kind of life. I am doing quite well, apparently. The command appreciates my service; I have been serving in a reconnaissance platoon from the beginning, and am now an expert scout. I carry a submachine gun and a pistol, and I ride Mashka, a nice, fiery, little mare. In no respect am I inferior to the boys; in fact, on the contrary, the commander often singles me out as an example to follow.

My personal score now stands at fifteen Germans killed.

I'll soon go to Moscow to study. Consequently, it is not unlikely that we'll soon see each other.

Meanwhile, lots of love and kisses to you.

Your Ina.

Moshe Flinker

BELGIUM ∞ *16 YEARS OLD*

Moshe Flinker was a Jewish boy whose family fled
the Dutch city of The Hague in 1942, when the Nazis began to intern
all the Jews of Holland in concentration camps. Moshe, his mother,
father, five sisters, and a brother all crossed into Belgium and went
into hiding in a small apartment in Brussels. Belgium was also under
Nazi attack, but the family felt that they would be safer there than
in Holland.

Even though fear confined the large family to their apartment, they managed rather well until a Jewish informant reported
them to the Gestapo. On Passover eve in 1944, the entire family was
arrested and sent to Auschwitz, where Moshe and his parents were
murdered by the Nazis. All of his siblings survived, and after the
liberation, when his sisters returned to the apartment in Brussels in
which the family had been living, they found the diary Moshe had
been keeping since November of 1942, when he was sixteen.

Moshe began his diary with an explanation of why he

261

was writing. "It is because I hate being idle that I have begun this diary," he said. Unable to attend school and only rarely able to leave the family apartment, Moshe's life mostly consisted of reading and writing.

Although his native language was Dutch, Moshe chose to write his diary entirely in Hebrew, one of eight languages that he had studied. This choice of Hebrew was reflective of how deeply he yearned for a homeland where he could be of service to his fellow Jews. For him, the "safety" of Brussels was almost unbearable because he felt tremendous guilt about how much easier his life was than that of the majority of his people. He longed to be sharing the suffering of the Jews of Eastern Europe. It is ironic, and doubly tragic, that he, who had endured years of guilt for living "too well," finally lost his life in the Auschwitz crematorium.

Moshe's diary was first published in Hebrew in 1958, and then in English in 1965, by Yad Vashem in Israel.

December 22, 1942, Morning

Last Friday afternoon, as I was about to finish my Arabic studies, my father came in and told me that he had some bad news. He had heard that many Jews were dying in the East, and that a hundred thousand had already been killed. When I heard this, my heart stood still and I was speechless with pain and shock. I had been fearing this for a long time, but I had hoped against hope that they really had taken the Jews for forced labour and that therefore they would have to feed, clothe and house them enough to keep them alive. Now my last hopes have been dashed.

December 28, 1942

This morning it snowed for the first time this winter; the snow froze hard. I think the temperature was nine degrees below zero. I felt the cold when I had to leave the house to go and fetch potatoes—about ninety pounds—and suddenly I thought again, even more sharply than before, of the fate of my brethren in the East. I am always thinking of them, I never forget them all day. I silently pray for the salvation which does not seem to want to come, and I hope that it will speedily arrive, that God will have mercy on His people, who are in so terrible a plight.

January 7, 1943

Last night my parents and I were sitting around the table. It was almost midnight. Suddenly we heard the bell: we all shuddered. We thought that the moment had come for us to be deported. The fear arose mostly because a couple of days ago the inhabitants of Brussels were forbidden to go out after nine o'clock. The reason for this is that on December 31 three German soldiers were killed. Had it not been for this curfew it could have been some man who was lost and was ringing at our door. My mother had already put her shoes on to go to the door, but my father said to wait until they ring once more. But the bell did not ring again. Thank heaven it all passed quietly. Only the fear remained, and all day long my parents have been very nervous. They can't stand the slightest noise, and the smallest thing bothers them.

This small event showed me how much we fear deportation. Although so far everything has passed peacefully, that little ring of the bell was able to disturb our lives profoundly and fill our hearts with fear.

As I have noted, the inhabitants of Brussels are forced to be off the streets by nine o'clock. But that is not the only punishment the Germans have inflicted on them. They must also give the Germans ten thousand bicycles, and all the bars and places of entertainment, such as cinemas, etc., must be closed until their proprietors get permission to reopen them.

February 12, 1943

During recent days an emptiness has formed inside me. Nothing motivates me to do anything or write anything, and no new ideas enter my mind; everything is as if asleep. Although I do not know from where this emptiness has come, I can feel it with my whole body. When I pray I feel as if I am praying to the wall and am not heard at all, and there is a voice inside me that says: "What are you praying for? The Lord does not hear you." A few times already there has flashed into my mind the verse which I think I heard on *Simhat Torah*: "And the spirit of Thy holiness do not take from him." Yes, I think that the holy spark which I always felt within me has been taken from me, and here I am, without spirit, without thought, without anything, and all I have is my miserable body. I don't know what I will do.

March 9, 1943

What shall I do? The emptiness has spread within me and now fills me completely. For a few days now, no new thought or idea has come to me. I have tried various measures and nothing has helped. I tried going to bed very late, and went to bed at three, but nothing changed. For two weeks I have reduced my daily meals from three to one, but this, too, has been to no avail. Maybe these things will yet help, but so far I am completely in the grip of this nothing-ness, this lack of will and thought. I have tried to find a reason for all of this, but I have been unable to settle on anything for sure. Maybe it is due to the fact that I am living a life of peace and quiet while my brothers are in a situation so bad that God alone knows its full horror. Maybe this void will disappear soon; there are some signs of this, but I cannot be sure.

Lately I feel so lonely, so barren—a feeling I have never had before. I feel myself so far from all my brothers, from everything nationally Jewish. And all that I see that reminds me of Jewish things I embrace and clasp to my heart with a love that I never before felt. Thus I found in the Hebrew library a Palestine school almanac. I had already seen it there a few months ago and taken it home, but then I did not feel so barren as I feel now. A few days ago I again took it from the library and read it in a spirit entirely different from the first time. It now seemed like a letter to me, as a sign of life of the rest of my people. I love it so much that I can hardly bring myself to return it to the library. The name of the almanac is "My Homeland." How many times have I not said this word to myself in the last week, and each time it comes into my mind I am filled with yearning for it, and my soul longs for my country that I have loved—and still love— so much. Even before the war my heart longed for my home-land, the Land of Israel, but now this love and yearning have greatly increased. For it is only now that I feel how much we need a country in which we could live in peace as every people lives in its country.

April 7, 1943

I used to laugh when someone would tell me or when I would read in a book that some persons have a great need to pour out their hearts to a friend. I always would tell myself that I, at least, have no need for such things and that it is only a manifestation of a kind of soft-heartedness that I have always despised. In those days I used to say that if, at rare intervals, I should ever feel the need to pour out my heart I would pour it out to myself. But from then until now I find myself completely changed. I didn't know then what it was to live without knowing anyone even a little, without having anyone, to be as lonely as if one were in a desert. Oh, how I wish I could see some of my old friends; how my soul longs to talk with my friend Finkel.

All day long, thoughts of my people never leave my mind, not even for a minute. They are with me everywhere, whether I am standing or sitting, eating or talking, or whatever I am doing. I try so hard to deprive myself of the numerous pleasures that are to be found all around. I walk in the street and the sun is burning hot and I am covered with perspiration, and then I think of going for a swim—immediately afterward I remember where my people are and then I cannot even dream of going swimming; or I pass a pastry shop and I see in the window some attractive, delicious-looking cream-cakes and I am just about to enter the shop—and then the situation of my brothers flashes across my mind and my desires are destroyed, and I am overcome with shame for having forgotten their plight. But there is yet another place where I am continually brought in mind of them for wholly different reasons than those which I have noted and which brings me completely different thoughts than those I have mentioned. That place is school.

Lately I have been going to school, on the suggestion of my father, to learn typing and shorthand. I have been attending this school for about two months. I get there at nine in the morning and sit and pound the typewriter; then some girls who also study there enter and they are full of laughter, joy, and gaiety. And already, this sight—I mean seeing these impudent girls, laughing and gay at a time when the girls of my people are wretched and have not known the happiness these girls enjoy—excites in me jealousy and hatred for them. But that is not all. When they sit down and I hear them tell each other where they were the night before, what movie they saw, who their boyfriends are, or what love letters they have received, then because of my great jealousy as I remember our people, I am on the verge of tears. At such times I don't think so much of the physical affliction of my people as of their spiritual anguish, which may well be greater than their physical pain. I know full well how bitter it is when children have nothing to eat and when their parents can give them nothing—but how much more bitter it is when the entire youth of a nation is sad, when its young girls no longer laugh and its young men are melancholy. It is at such moments, that I feel a burning love for my poor people which, because of my not being involved physically, makes me more aware than ever of its troubles.

What are the real spiritual values of these boys and girls, who may well be regarded as a typical sample of high-school youth. While such terrible events are going on, while millions of young people are being plucked in the bud, while millions more risk their lives for the sake of ideas, whether correct or

distorted but at least with the honest and consecrated inten-
tion of ensuring the world a better future—at the same time
these boys and girls sit here and by their expressions you
would never guess that anything had happened in the world
or that lawlessness and violence are the order of the day.
Shallow youth, with neither ideas nor ideals, without any
kind of content whatever, really completely worthless.

I was suddenly aroused from my thoughts by quite an
unexpected question. I saw that the fellow who had been the
cause of my coming here had made good use of the time in
talking with the girls, and had suddenly asked them their
first names. They had immediately supplied them, and so
came to ask my first name, which until then I hadn't mentioned. The difficulty is that, though I am named after a man
compared with whom all these people are as nothing, yet
this name identifies me as a member of a certain group of
people who are hated everywhere. Therefore, I never give
people my right name. In this case, then, I answered their
question by repeating it: "Yes, my name," and still sunk in
thought said "My name is Harry." Yes, Harry. And as I said
that, it seemed to me that I lost merit. Before these terrible
times I would never have dreamed of hiding the smallest
detail of my origin and give the impression that I was
ashamed of it. However, times change. But it was not this
that depressed me so much as the surroundings and atmosphere in which the incident occurred. They had served as a
standard to which I had tried to adjust my own values.

My inner vacuum, moreover, is giving rise to all kinds of
thoughts, which are expressing themselves in strange desires.
For in life one cannot be neutral, neither positive nor negative; if one has nothing positive, then all sorts of negative

tendencies appear unhindered. So now all day long I do nothing but search for some positive content for my life, so as not to be entirely lost. In every single thing I hope to find a meaning which will fill me and satisfy me, but it is as if I heard a voice inside me always saying: "You are deceiving yourself if you think this is of value for you; it can at best fill only part of your spiritual void." This has been my situation for quite some time; I am lost and seek in vain, for meaning, for control, for purpose.

[Undated]

What shall I think? What shall I do?—two things which are interrelated very closely. What use is thought without action, or action without thought? In the beginning there was action and then came thought. Now I need action. It has been a long time since I have done anything except think. Thought after thought, and no action comes from any of this. Now I can think no more. What good is all my thinking without action? I am not alone in this world. I almost feel as if I don't have the right to think further before I have done something. It is as if a voice within me were saying "You have no right to think while your body is at rest." But what can I do? I am hemmed in on all sides, like a bird in a cage. Where should I go? Where should I turn? Here is my beloved people, who are in infinite anguish now, my dearest people, my brothers and sisters, who are closer to me than I am to myself. Every day that I am idle I feel pain inside of me. At a time when so many are suffering, I do nothing, and even my rations are not reduced. I do not deny my body the slightest pleasure—not because I do not wish to, or because I am unable, but because it will do no good. I am here in Brussels like any other Belgian, and my people are over there in their place of suffering which is worse than slavery. Therefore it would be useless to deny myself some food, or washing, or indulge in other mortifications. For the whole difference is one of location. I am here and my brothers are there, and no mortification and no deprivation will bring me nearer to them. What is to be done? After endless thought I have come to the decision that the only place where I could be of any use to my people is in our faraway, dear, and beloved country. Only there shall I be able to achieve my object of helping my people, which is my only wish and my life-long aspiration. I decided this a long time ago, but until now I have not achieved even the slightest part of what took me such a long time to figure out. I have already tried a few things, but none of them helped. There are always my parents, who by their excessive watchfulness hinder my every act and accomplishment. Thus I am imprisoned on all sides, and time is ceaselessly running out, and I can do nothing. O Lord, save me, fortify me, and encourage me. Prepare me for Thy will, which is my only desire. Thy will is mine, my Lord. Hear my prayer!

[Undated]

I am sitting facing the sun. Soon it will set; it is nearing the horizon. It is as red as blood, as if it were a bleeding wound. From where does it get so much blood? For days there has been a red sun, but this is not hard to understand. Is it not sufficient to weep, in these days of anguish? Suffering stares at me as on every side and in every direction, and still further troubles appear before your eyes. Here a man and woman, both over seventy, are taken away. There you meet a Jew who has been hiding and has no money to live, and elsewhere you meet a Jew whose fortune has gone because he invested it in dollars, which for some unknown reason have become worthless. Trouble never ends ... And every time I meet a child of my people I ask myself: "Moshe, what are you doing for him?" I feel responsible for every single pain. I ask myself whether I am still participating in the troubles of my people, or whether I have withdrawn completely from them.

Some three or four months ago I would have had no trouble at all in answering these questions, because then I was attached to my brothers with all the fibres of my heart and soul, but now all has changed. From the moment I became empty, I have felt as if all this no longer concerns me. I feel as if I were dead.

Joan Wyndham

ENGLAND ∞ 16 YEARS OLD

When the Germans began bombing England, Joan was a very sophisticated sixteen-year-old living in London in an untraditional family headed by her mother and her mother's friend Sidonie. Even as bombs started to explode nearby, Joan simply could not take the war seriously. She viewed it as a colorful backdrop that added poignancy to the accounts she wrote in her diary of her various romantic adventures.

Joan's focus on her sexual awakening may leave some readers wondering where her heart was at a time when the fate of Europe hung in the balance. Like Colin Perry, the other English diarist in this book, Joan was not easily moved by danger, death, and the destruction of her country. It wasn't until people she knew were killed and houses all around where she was living were bombed to oblivion that she began to realize that the war was not a play put on for her amusement. At that point, Joan volunteered to fight in the Women's Armed Services. Her diary, which she called Love Lessons:

A Wartime Diary, *was published in 1985 in England, Canada, and the United States. It leaves off with her entry into basic training.*

Joan survived the war and continued writing. In 1992, another book she wrote, Anything Once, *was published in England.*

Tuesday, 22nd August 1939
Orchard Close, Ramsbury

It's very hot this August, the hottest summer I can remember for years. There's thunder in the air which gives me a headache. I wish the rain would come to cool everything down.

Spending the hols with Granny is really quite an experience. The service is incredible, with everything done for you. I wish I could have seen the head housemaid's face when she unpacked my case, and found a grubby suspender belt and my signed photo of John Gielgud in *Hamlet*—not to mention a paperback of Casanova's *Amours.*

At dinner there is a sort of changing of the guards ceremony between courses—and when I asked for some aspirin for my headache, the butler brought them on a silver salver!

Granny is a bit of a bore, always chasing me to wash my hands and wear a dress—but luckily she's in bed a lot of the time, wearing a chin-strap and a little circle of tin pressed into the middle of her forehead to keep the wrinkles at bay—it's hard work being an ageing beauty.

The nicest person here is Aunt Bunch—Mummy says she takes drugs and goes around with Negroes, but I don't care, I really like her. I am in love with Harold the butler, and

Macrae who looks after the horses. He is like a brown monkey and smells of wet ferns. Granny says Macrae hasn't had a bath within living memory.

I'm writing this in the music room, feeling quite sick with excitement, waiting for Daddy Dick to arrive—I don't know why everybody calls him that, as if I had a choice of other, more suitable daddies. Unfortunately all I have is DD, maddening, self-centred and never there. I suppose he'll be late as usual, although it's nearly a year since he last saw me.

LATER

DD finally arrived in a very expensive-looking car called an Alvis, and we drove out for a cream tea in Marlborough. His face is tanned and he wears a blue shirt with a red tie. He looks much better now he has stopped drinking. The tea was supposed to be a kind of treat, to make up for neglecting me for so long. He seemed unusually friendly and interested, and asked me about Mummy and whether she was OK. I said yes, but we could do with a bit more money if he could spare it, which he jolly well ought to, considering what his paintings fetch nowadays.

'And how is the exotic Sidonie?' he went on, very sarcastic because he can't stand her. 'Still painting her face white and going to Mass every morning?' I don't know why he should be so down on her, Mummy's jolly lucky to have someone to look after her and love her—it can't be much fun being divorced at twenty-three.

The clotted cream and scones arrived and we laid into them. 'We're both rather greedy aren't we?' Daddy observed. 'It's strange how like me you are, in spite of our hardly ever seeing each other. I wonder how you'd have turned out if you'd been brought up by me instead of by two religious ladies.'

'Just like Aunt Bunch I expect,' I said, 'getting drunk and rushing around after drugs and Negroes.' Which he seemed to think was rather funny.

On the way back I could see the speedometer touch 82. I thought the wind would blow my head off. We listened to the wireless after dinner and heard Chamberlain say we would stand by Poland against Hitler, even if it meant war.

Thursday, 24th [August]

A blazing hot day, just right for the treasure hunt. I was winning—I knew the last clue must mean the sundial in the rose garden. Suddenly I saw Granny almost running across the lawn, a letter in her hand, and while I was distracted Daddy pounced on the prize. He's such a cheat. The letter was from Mummy, saying I must go back to London right away—it looks as if war is inevitable.

I read it out and no one seemed to know what to say. Daddy opened his prize, a box of chocolates, and handed it round. I chewed a caramel slowly, feeling the sun on my face and smelling the roses. I thought, 'What a bore!' It was terrible saying goodbye to Daddy and Bunch, and lovely Harold and Macrae.

Friday, 25th [August]
Milborne Grove

Home on the morning train, to the smell and roar of London, and the hot dusty Fulham Road. Nothing felt any different, only our house looked curiously shabby and small after the grandeur of Orchard Close, as if it had shrunk during the holidays.

There was Mummy, desperately worried, and Sid in that awful mauve smock that clashes with her red hair, her face even whiter than usual. Cook was in bed suffering from nerves so there was no lunch, only cold meat and pickles. After we'd eaten it Sid took us up to the little altar on the landing outside her room. She lit the candles, and we all prayed aloud to Our Lady for peace. All I could think about was getting back to RADA—we have our holiday play to rehearse, *Hedda Gabler* in German, produced by the lovely Dorothea Alexander on whom I have a slight crush.

Sid looked terribly shocked when I told her. 'A *German* play! You don't mean you're still going on with it now?' I lost my temper and said, 'What on earth does war have to do with art or the theatre?' I admire Sidonie but she does frighten me—her saintliness tends to give me guilt.

Wednesday, 30th [August]

Rehearsed all day in D's room in Swiss Cottage. Bare yellow walls and a piano—afterwards everyone was talking about arty subjects, Verlaine, Toulouse Lautrec, Baudelaire, and so on, except for Anton who was deeply preoccupied with the question of whether girls are nicer to kiss with or without lipstick. Nobody talks about Hitler. It is absolutely taboo. Dorothea's father was killed in Vienna a few weeks ago and anyway we want to forget about it if possible. It wasn't till someone put on the wireless at nine that she finally lost control of herself and went off into a kind of silent, stony, twitching hysteria. I am becoming more and more infatuated with her.

After dinner we went for a walk on Hampstead Heath thinking it might be the last time we would enjoy the full moon with untroubled minds. The moonlight made the grass a silvery grey and the dew was falling, wetting our feet. I became aware that I am passionately in love with her, in the rather unreal way I do fall for people. She is so sweet, so clever and so exciting, and ten years older than me. We climbed the hill that looks over Highgate and lay in deck chairs at the top, smoking in the moonlight.

'But I thought you were going to teach me to cry,' I said in dismay.

'You won't need any teaching soon,' she replied sadly and took me to her bank where she drew out all her worldly possessions—£127. Then we bought some pimentos and went home and stuffed them for lunch. There was no more talk of the play—that is finished. RADA is closing down.

After lunch the rest of the actors came in to say goodbye. Because we didn't want to think of the war we talked of the really important things in life like Bach, Mozart and Beethoven. Anton loves music almost as much as girls.

He put the Brahms violin concerto on the gramophone and we listened like people drugged. On the top note of the cadenza, a note as ethereal as air, the newsboys began to shout. We heard their voices far away, raucous, impersonal and frightening. As they came nearer we could just hear two words, 'Hitler' and 'Poland'. There are going to be hardly any buses tomorrow, owing to the children being evacuated, so we thought we'd better say goodbye and get it over with. Also I knew my mother would be worrying about me if I stayed out late.

I said goodbye to Anton and Dorothea. She kissed me on

the cheek. I went out before we both became too emotional for comfort.

Friday, 1st September

The posters say 'HITLER INVADES POLAND'. Everywhere children are waiting in expectant noisy herds, but the mothers are quiet, grey and some of them are crying. Passing a side street I saw a Punch and Judy show playing to an empty road. Everything tilted at a slightly grotesque angle, like a surrealist film. Mummy and Sid went to church so I sat in my room and got completely drunk for the first time in my life—on rum. It was a very nice experience indeed. I no longer cared a damn what happened to anybody.

I rang up Dorothea: 'I'm completely drunk.'

'That's right, so are we.'

'Goodbye and good luck.'

'Goodbye, darling.' Everything now is goodbye and good luck.

Later on Mummy and Sid came back from the Servite church with Alfred and Bertie. Alfred is the one I like best of all Sidonie's friends. He's tall and lean and wears dark blue shirts, and has a gigantic appetite for treacle pudding. I love his calm, deep, drawling voice and the way he shakes with silent laughter, the sound coming through his nose and not his mouth. On the other hand his room-mate Bertie is pretty awful, sensuous-looking and plump, with a girlish face.

After dinner Alfred played Debussy, his long thin fingers trailing over the keys, while Bertie crouched on the window-seat listening.

'It's a drug of course,' Alfred said as he finished 'La Cathédrale Engloutie', and I heard Bertie's velvet murmur, 'How heavenly drugs are!'

Saturday, 2nd [September]

Awful news: they are planning to close the theatres! I rushed straight off to the New to see John and Edith Evans for the last time doing *The Importance*. Sat in the gallery. People in the street seemed really quite cheerful, and all the people in the gallery queue were talking to each other, which is unusual for the English!

When I got home Mummy and Sid were absolutely furious with me for going to the theatre. They seemed to think it was a dreadfully frivolous thing to do at such a time.

Sunday, 3rd [September]

This morning war was declared by the Prime Minister over the radio.

Five minutes after the National Anthem, while we were still sitting around feeling rather sick, the air-raid warning went. For a moment we didn't believe our ears—we hadn't had time even to realise we were at war—then we went down to our gas room and began damping the blankets with pails of water.

When the room was ready we went and sat on the front doorstep waiting for the first gun. The balloon barrage looked too lovely in the sun against the blue sky, like iridescent silver fish swimming in blue water. After a bit the all-clear sounded. We heard afterwards that it had all been a mistake.

Monday, 27th [May, 1940]

The Germans are in Calais. I don't seem to be able to react or to feel anything. I don't know what's real any more. I don't think I'm real or that this life is real. Before this last winter everything seemed real, but since then I seem to have been dreaming. I wanted to mix with artists so I rented a studio, and because of the studio I'm pretending to be an artist, when I don't even know what painting means. Ever since then I've been listening to people talking a new language, filth and blasphemy, and heard myself talking it too. I see myself acting like a tart, and men hurting me and sponging on me and trying to make love, and asking if they can pee in my sink, and telling me to take my clothes off and I really don't know whether I'm awake or asleep.

The bombs, which I know must come, hardly enter my fringe of consciousness. Bombs and death are real, and I and all the other artists around here are only concerned with unreality. We live in a dream, and it may be desperate but it's not dull.

Monday, 17th [June]

After an hilarious lunch at the café, with Jo doing imitations of Mussolini, I came home to find my mother as white as a sheet and telephoning wildly. She said, 'France has surrendered—you'd better leave London tonight! Granny isn't well, so you can't go there, but your Aunt Lalla says she'll have you. I'll take you down tomorrow.'

I fought tooth and nail but it wasn't any good—a lot of balls about being young and having your life before you—if London's going to be destroyed I'd rather stay with it as long as possible and go on working and being with my friends until we're all blown up. But my mother, who has no stamina, and is terrified of staying in London herself—*she* is staying on and sending *me* away, so that she won't have to worry about me!

Friday, 30th [August]

Tonight when I went round to the studio just for a check-up, I was surprised to hear the door-bell ring. It was Rupert, who seemed to have something on his mind. After some casual conversation he suddenly said, 'Oh by the way, I was looking through my pockets for some money this morning and I found half a crown in my dressing-gown, so determined to prove my manly powers, I leapt on to my bicycle and went to the chemist down the road and bought *three* contraceptive apparatuses! ". . . The cheapest you've got and be quick before I change my mind!" I cried. . . . There was a pause. 'So what do you think about that, eh Joanie?'

I thought it was very funny and rolled on the floor laughing. 'Oh dear, dear,' I thought to myself. 'What a funny life.' . . .

Saturday night, 7th [September]

The tempo's speeding up, tonight the blitz started.

About nine, Sid and I were looking through the top-floor window when we saw four bombs fall on Kensington High Street—flash, boom!—and sparks and debris shot into the air four times in quick succession. The sky over by the docks was red as if it were an enormous sunset.

MIDNIGHT

Well here I sit in the air-raid shelter with screaming bombs falling right and left, and Sir John Squire, roaring tight, sitting opposite me next to his Scotch Presbyterian cook. Squire's breath fills the shelter and the cook looks as if she's going to be sick. Sid is reading Maxim Gorky and I'm trying to write this diary, though I can't see very well as there is only a storm lantern. Squire keeps on saying he wants to read Wodehouse's *Uncle Fred in Springtime* once more before he dies.

The bombs are lovely, I think it is all thrilling. Nevertheless, as the opposite of death is life, I think I shall get seduced by Rupert tomorrow. Rowena has promised to go to a chemist's with me and ask for Volpar Gels, just in case the French thingummy isn't foolproof.

Another bomb, quite near this time. Squire's leapt to his feet and is making for the exit. 'I want some cigarettes. I'm going to the pub—'

'Oh no you're not,' says Sid, clutching his arm. 'You're not leaving this shelter until the all-clear goes!'

'Maam,' says Squire, evading her with dignity, 'I am!' He climbs over her, remarking indistinctly that he has never stepped over a lady before, and disappears into the shell-scarred night, walking with difficulty.

Monday, 9th [September]

None of us slept Saturday night. The all-clear went at five a.m. All clear for my lovely Rupert, I thought. I'm really in a very nice state of mind over him. I went up and lay on my bed for a bit but didn't sleep.

At nine I got up, put on my new black and white trousers that make me look like a cross between Oscar Wilde and a Christy Minstrel, and a pale green jersey. I looked and felt as if I'd slept for hours. The papers said—500 planes over London, 400 dead, 1,400 injured, the docks ablaze.

As it was Sunday, we all went to church—funny how devout people look after an air-raid, but all I noticed was that the priests stood in a line of decreasing height—you could have walked upstairs on their heads. I felt most undevout, and my stomach rumbled.

The studio—one o'clock. Rupert rang the bell. Went to De Cock's and bought beef rissoles and Campbell's tomato soup for lunch. The rissoles are very nice if you dunk them in the soup and eat it all together.

After lunch we lay down and tried to sleep, but there was another air-raid. Then Rupert finally put his hand under my jersey, took hold of my right breast and said, 'Do you still want to be seduced?'

'Yes,' I said.

'Shall we go over to number 34 and go to bed properly?'

I knew then that my hour was upon me, and said in a panic, 'Oh, must we go right now—today?'

'Yes I think so—don't you? Unfortunately, we'll have to do it right under Prudey's nose—she's hopping mad to know whether I've done the deed or not. You realise she's the village gossip and it'll be all over Fulham and Chelsea once she finds out?'

'Can't be helped, provided my mother doesn't hear about it! You go on and I'll follow. Leave the door on the latch.'

Rupert went.

'Well, well, well,' I said, looking at myself in the glass. 'Farewell, a long farewell to my virginity.' I lit a cigarette and powdered my nose. Then I slunk over to number 34, where I found Rupert playing Spanish records to keep his courage up. He had moved the bed into the back room and drawn the curtains, but it was still pretty light.

'Come on,' he said, 'let's get on with it before I change my mind!'

I stood on one side of the vast bed and felt like a block of ice.

Rupert slipped off his clothes, and I suddenly realised he looked terribly funny in the nude and began laughing helplessly. . . .

. . . 'Take your clothes off.'

'You turn over and go to sleep, then I will.'

'Shy and virginal Joanie!' Rupert chuckled, turning his back on me.

I took the opportunity to slip out of my things and was under the bed-clothes in a jiffy.

'I'm not really shy,' I lied. 'It's just that this sort of thing doesn't happen to me every day and I feel a bit peculiar.'

'What, never been in bed with a naked man before?'

'No of course I haven't.' Well I was now, and very queer it felt too, as if I was about to undergo an operation. . . .

. . . After that, for a short time we were lying together like one person, panting and sobbing in unison and . . . my eyes were tight shut. When I came to again and opened my eyes I could see his face pressed against mine, covered in beads of sweat, and heard him making pleased exhausted sorts of noises and saying, 'Hello Joanie! Did you have an orgasm?'

Gosh, I thought, is it all over? Is that all it is? I didn't even know it had happened yet.

'No,' I said, rather puzzled, 'and what's more I think I'm

still a virgin. I mean, what about all the blood and everything that you read about in books?'

'Well,' Rupert said, 'it's most peculiar. There doesn't seem to be anything there—it felt exactly like sleeping with a non-virgin. There I was, expecting terrific mountains and obstacles and there wasn't anything at all!'

We examined the sheets for signs of gore but there weren't any.

'Of *course*, I've got it. Perhaps I did it to myself with a Tampax!'

He looked at me in amazement. 'My dear girl, didn't you know virgins can't use Tampax?'

'But I've used them for years!'

'Oh my God!' Rupert said. 'All the fuss and the drama and the toing and froing, and half the men in Chelsea and Fulham turning pale at the thought of seducing you, and what were you? A fraud! Not a virgin at all!'

'Swear you won't tell anybody,' I begged, 'Particularly Jo. I could never hold my head up again.'

After we had stopped laughing, Rupert turned his back to me and dozed off. I leant on one elbow and lay looking at his bare brown shoulders. I looked at the pink sheets and the afternoon light filtering through the thin brown curtains, and the engravings over the mantelpiece, *Minerva visiting the Muses*, and *The Birth of Bacchus*, all brown and fly-specked, and I thought, 'Well that's done, and I'm glad it's over! If that's really all there is to it I'd rather have a good smoke or go to the pictures.'

'What are you meditating on so lugubriously?' Rupert asked, waking up and turning towards me.

'Whether shrimps make good mothers,' I replied coldly.

'Disappointed, eh? Well most girls don't like it the first time—cheer up Joanie, let's have some tea.'

I got up and walked across the room naked, without any embarrassment now that I'd got it over with. After I'd made the tea, we took it out on to the roof, and Rupert lay beside me on the striped mattress. He could see that I was still looking depressed, so he explained to me that people like us with a certain amount of intelligence find it difficult to lose our identities—we watch ourselves making love instead of losing ourselves in it. What we need is a kind of yoga in reverse, to give matter control over mind.

Wednesday, 11th [September]

About eleven o'clock we were all in the shelter drinking rum out of teacups. It had been quite a noisy night and we thought the rum might make us go to sleep.

Suddenly there was a flash of light and a sound like the crack of doom. The concrete shelter shook in the earth like a ship at sea and the storm lantern swung out. I didn't know it then, but that was *the* bomb—our bomb! And if I could have seen Rupert at that moment I certainly wouldn't have slept another wink. At it was, I didn't know anything about it till old Squire came round before breakfast and said they'd hit Redcliffe Road. I hurtled into my clothes and together we set off to see what they'd hit. I could see that my house was standing, but it looked as if the last houses in the row had gone. I said, 'My boyfriend lives at 34.'

'Thirty-four?' Squire asked. 'Number 28, 29, 30, 31, 32, 33—oh dear, it looks as if it's 34 they've hit!'

I hope I may never live through such a moment again. I turned faint and sick and my head buzzed. There was the green door with the three bells, and after that two flights of stairs leading up to doors that opened on to nowhere. Below the stairs I could make out the splintered remnants of broken-down floors, Prudey's gum tree wedged upside down with its leaves moving in the breeze, and the bed I was seduced on hanging out over the street with three foot of solid mortar where Rupert's head should have been. Leonard's studio was completely gone.

I rushed up to a warden and said, 'Where are all the people from that house?'

'Couldn't say miss, no bodies though, at least none that I've seen.'

Old Squire was properly sympathetic and reassuring but I was shaking all over and couldn't get my words out. Choking back my sobs I ran down the street to my studio to see if Rupert might have gone there after the bomb. When I arrived I found I'd locked the door and hadn't got the key, but outside on the landing was deposited one guitar in a dented and dusty case, one un-neutered male ginger cat in a basket, very cross, and one gas mask inscribed 'RUPERT CHARLES AUSTIN DARROW, STILL LIVING BY THE GRACE OF HIS OWN INGENUITY'.

Arcana came out in her nightdress and said, 'Your friend came round with these in the middle of the night. He'd just been blown up, it was most extraordinary, he seemed to treat the whole thing as a joke. I couldn't believe him at first, he looked so cheerful.'

Thank you God, I thought, thank you for saving Rupert.

I carried Henry Miller home in his basket and was upstairs doing my hair when I heard someone talking to my mother in the hall. Coming to the top of the stairs I saw Rupert, covered in dust, his shoes broken at the toes and his hair smoothed down with a wet brush, smiling at my mother with suave green eyes and talking very calmly. I let out a yell, ran downstairs and put my arms around him.

'I thought you were dead!' I cried, overcome with relief at seeing him again. 'How were you saved?'

'By the skin of my teeth actually! I happened to go down to the shelter to borrow sixpence off Leonard for the meter when the bomb went off. Prudey was saved because she spent the night at the Players Theatre, sleeping on the floor.'

Mummy made Rupert a cup of tea, and I could see her giving him the once-over, then we went back to Redcliffe Road to see what we could salvage. Everyone there was wildly excited and talking to everyone else, the way they do when there's a crisis. An Irish policeman tried to stop us, saying, 'Don't you go near there miss, there's a one thousand pound unexploded bomb in Cathcart Road, and when it goes off Gawd help this street!' God help it, and us too! I thought, striding into the ruins. While we were scrabbling around some bombers flew over, and R stood in the middle of the road with a striped cushion on top of his head, screaming 'Go away, naughty bombskles' and pointing his gun-stick at them. After we'd rescued his bicycle we made up four bundles and carried them back to my studio, clothes, bedding and two suitcases of Prudey's things, including her precious novel and her Helena Rubinstein Apple Blossom Skin Fragrance. There was also a tin of pilchards hanging from the roof of Prudey's studio so we knocked it down with a broom and took it home for lunch.

Rupert's first thought was for his damned guitar. 'A little out of tune but otherwise uninjured,' he murmured and sat down on the piled-up bedding to play the Grenadinos as if nothing had happened. 'See how steady my hands are,' he boasted. 'I feel like a Spanish refugee playing amid the ruins of Barcelona!'

He was still strumming away when the bell rang, and there on my doorstep was Squirrel, looking very small and worried in yellow corduroy dungarees and a camel-hair coat, asking if Rupert was there. (He's quite right—she does look dreadful in yellow!) My hackles rose at the sight of her, but very politely I asked her to come up, in the calm icy voice of the female in possession. R had to go off to the Labour Exchange to try and get compensation, so I moved some dirty shirts so as to give her a place to sit.

'I guess Rupert had better sleep at my place tonight,' says Squirrel.

'Oh no, he can quite easily make up a bed here,' I reply sweetly. I mean *really*, she may be his mistress, but there's no need to buzz around as if she owned him!

Finally Rupert returned and settled the whole thing by saying he'd sleep at Jo's, and meanwhile he'd leave all his stuff in my studio and diddle the Government by telling them he'd taken an unfurnished room! Triumph! My eyes darted flames at Squirrel. He'd even given the Post Office *my* number as his official address and all. 'What exciting times we live in,' said R, and went off to diddle the Labour Exchange for some more money. Still no sign of Prudey.

I wandered home through the shattered streets. It's getting cold now, the autumn leaves starting to fall and a sharp wind blowing round the fallen houses. Six shops in the Fulham Road have been gutted.

Wednesday, 25th [September]

By this morning I had worked myself up into such a state of passion over the absent Rupert—I hadn't seen him for a week—that I didn't know what to do with myself. All morning at the post I was thinking about him and wondering how much longer I could bear life without him.

On the way home I saw seventeen German planes in arrow formation cutting through the blue sky, with hundreds of shells bursting around them. The guns were so loud I took shelter in the door of the Servite church. As I was cowering there I heard a yell—'Woo hoo! Joanie!'—and there was old R lurching down the street with a cheery smile on his face, completely ignoring the guns.

We brewed coffee on the oil stove, while I sat on the edge of his chair with my arms round his neck. He looked around the studio appreciatively. 'Gosh, you have cleaned the place up—you know this studio's quite classy now. It used to be a howling wilderness where Jo and his cronies painted—now he'd damn well have to take his boots off before coming in! Would you say your artistic career has come to a grinding halt? I don't seem to see the usual dreadful paintings around.'

I explained that what with the bombs and working at the first-aid post I really didn't have time for art any more.

'All the more time for looking after Rooples,' he chortled with satisfaction. I choked down my happiness and got lunch ready. Rupert had bought minute steak—it took the whole of his meat ration. I hadn't had any for weeks. He set about frying the onions and I sat watching him, marvelling more and more at his extraordinary physical charm. Why the handsomest man in Chelsea and Fulham should want to sit around my dump frying onions is more than I can fathom.

Old Madame Arcana has got her eye on him too; every time I go to the lavatory she comes up in her yellow-striped Arabian coat with the dove on her shoulder, and makes passes at him until I pull the chain—then she shoots into the centre of the room and pretends she came up to borrow a smoke.

Boy, what a steak! And what onions!

After we had eaten he wanted to lie down with me but I resisted, and we crashed down together on to the sofa, most undignified.

'Now this here Heloise,' Rupert said reprovingly, sitting on my stomach, 'she used to *glide* down to Abelard's couch— in fact she spent most of her time doing it, clad only in a loose-bodied gown and carrying a lamp. Now let's see *you* glide down to me, Joanie, ten stone or no ten stone.' Looking v. intense, I glided. 'You know I think I almost missed you,' R said.

After that we quit being funny and made love very seriously, and I was filled with peace and delight. You can't write about sensuality mingled with tenderness and pity, it just becomes maudlin or goes bad on you in some way—so call it love and leave it at that, one of the few transcendent and satisfying things left in this bloody awful life.

Saturday, 12th [October]

Decided I'd better go to Confession—after all Rupert hadn't poked me for nearly two weeks, and I thought maybe he never would again, which is as near as I'll ever get to a firm purpose of amendment, so I'd better go while the going's good.

I was petrified and started straight off with the bit about making love to get it over with—my first mortal sin! I could almost hear Father Corato's hair rising on his scalp. He could hardly wait for me to finish before launching his attack.

'And er—how many times have you—ah—have you—'

I thought, oh God the record's stuck, but just then he got a brainwave, and called it 'committed this sin'.

'Oh,' I said cheerfully, 'only twice, and we used birth control once, and he's *not* married!'

After that I was given a long talk on preserving my chastity in future, to which I replied rather unconvincingly that I'd do my best. I have an awful feeling he *can* recognise my voice! He jolly well should do, he's been to supper enough times. Finally I got *fifty* (!) Hail Marys right off, and staggered out feeling distinctly chastened.

Monday, 14th [October]

Unexpected visitation to the studio by Mummy, who found a very domestic scene. Me on one side of the fire darning Rupert's socks, he opposite practising his guitar, the birds singing and the dinner bubbling on the oil stove, just as if we were married. I really don't know what she imagines our relationship is! I don't think that she believes I'm his mistress, but Sid does. She's fanatical. She didn't speak to me for days when she first began to suspect it. She went all pale and sour and awful for weeks, as if she was ill, and wouldn't come near me or touch me. She told Mummy I was leading a filthy life and she was just blinding herself to it.

R acted very sweetly with Mama and I think she likes him

and feels a bit motherly towards him. He could make anyone like him.

After she went I told Rupert about my going to Confession, and he was furious. 'Chastity!' he bellowed. 'What do you mean, preserve your chastity? You've lost it haven't you? Damn it all girl, you can't pull a fast one on God like that!'

I tried explaining about absolution and penances. 'Christ,' Rupert said, 'that stuff's only for half-wits! What happens if you sleep with me again, and again after that? Do you get excommunicated or something? Anyway what's the problem, are you afraid to die unshriven?'

'I'm afraid to die in mortal sin. I'm afraid of going to hell.'

At this Rupert could no longer restrain himself—his amazed laughter nearly choked him. 'Hell? This is fantastic! Oh you funny little girl, you really *are* a funny little girl—why, you're a museum piece!'

I slapped his face hard.

He didn't say a word but just lay there, breathing as if he were asleep, his back turned to me. It was as if all contact, mental and physical, were cut off between us. I went cold with misery, I felt so helpless and so frightened by this frigid immobility. It lasted for hours or seemed to, and then suddenly he turned towards me, and took me in his arms. He pulled the rug up over our shoulders, and we went to sleep together in mutual warmth and amity.

When we woke it was late afternoon. We leant out of the window and saw it had turned to a lovely evening with an enormous double rainbow over Redcliffe Road. We could see three bombed houses to the left and two to the right, plus a church with the steeple blown off, four air-raid shelters, several piles of broken glass and wreckage, barrage balloons overhead and this amazingly lovely rainbow stretching from one end of the street to the other with a fainter repetition above it.

As we were admiring it we heard the sound of marching soldiers in the distance. Redcliffe Road heard it, and pricked up its ears. The soldiers swung out of Cathcart Road with pipes and drums in front, and it was the first time I'd seen soldiers marching since the war began. It seemed to make it all more real. Old grannies were coming out of their cellars, weeping and wringing their hands for joy in the streets.

Tuesday night, 15th [October]

This is certainly hell and no mistake. Hardly a minute's pause between each load of bombs and each one sounding as if it's going to hit our house. Gosh, it's awful; this is the heaviest bombing we've had since the war began, the absolute poetry of destruction. I sit in the shelter in my new navy-blue siren suit, reciting Rupert Brooke—'If I should die think only this of me/That there's some corner of the Fulham Road—'.

Wednesday, 16th [October]

When we emerged into the Fulham Road this morning there didn't seem to be much of it left—they'd certainly buggered it up! The whole place was a shambles like the last days of Pompeii, with shop windows shattered and their goods destroyed, the road thick with glass and the air with dust. Tulley's has been burnt out and there are two houses down in Limerston Street. People still digging for the bodies. Huge crater outside the tobacconist with a burst water main spouting in it. Poor old Redcliffe Road has lost another two houses, three bodies in the wreckage and my skylight broken.

As I approached number 48 there was a huge explosion and the time bomb finally went off behind 37; black smoke hung in the air and everyone ran as big bits of masonry hurtled towards us. The studio looked very dirty with bits of glass everywhere.

Went off to see if Rupert had been hurt but met him half way—all that was wrong with him was a chill in his stomach, which he'd caught last week from leaping naked out of bed and putting out a firebomb in his mother's garden by peeing on it. He was wearing his famous black overcoat that he used to impress clients with when he was in advertising. It hangs down to the pavement like a box all round him and has such huge padded shoulders that old ladies in buses turn pale when they lean up against him and half of him collapses.

While he was rather unwillingly patching up my skylight, Madame Arcana came up, pale and ghastly after the night's terrors, and said she hadn't been able to sleep because she had gone to bed in her stays, and when she had finally dozed off she dreamt that Aleister Crowley was trying to rape her, and woke up in a cold sweat just as the time bomb went off.

Sunday, 20th [October]

Arrived home from night duty to find Milborne Grove wrecked. Eight bombs had fallen within the Boltons alone; one, three doors away from our house. Our windows and shutters had been blown in, the doors jammed, and half the tree on the front lawn had fallen through the drawing-room window. While we were working on the house, collecting up broken glass etc., who should ride up to the wreckage on his bicycle but Rupert.

'Hello,' he yelled up at the window. 'Are you all right? I expected to find corpses!'

I ran out completely forgetting about my rage, and began talking cheerfully about the bomb. Then I suddenly remembered and snapped out, 'I thought you'd gone to the country!'

Alas for my suspicions! His ma had put him off till Monday, so there was no row after all—v. disappointing.

My new plum corduroy coat has arrived from Harrods, very smart! Luckily my bedroom hasn't been destroyed by the bomb so I could try it on.

We went for some beer to a little pub near Dovehouse Street, very warm and cheery, then wandered round the Fulham Road looking for a cake shop but couldn't find a single one; they'd all been blown up!

'No more custard tarts,' I told Rupert. He came and sat on my lap and put his head on my shoulder and said, 'You rock me to sleep like my old nanny used to do, very comforting.' I bounced him gently up and down and sang him 'Rock a Bye Baby'.

Friday, 25th [October]

Workmen still clearing the rubble out of our house in Milborne Grove. Had a lovely day at the studio; made colossal stew while R practised his guitar and played me his new farruca. Suddenly he hit a discord, clutched his stomach and said, 'Oh, I've got an awful pain just here—do you think the meat was off?'

'You've probably got wind,' I said.

'No, it's not that, I've been feeling a bit peculiar lately. Not quite myself you know. Do you believe in premonitions? I feel the way I did just before the house was blown up.'

Saturday, 26th [October]

Thetis came to lunch. She's hoping to go to Bermuda with the Censorship, lucky bastard. The room was looking very nice and lived-in, stew on the fire, guitar music lying around, Rupert's boots on the floor, and beside the typewriter a poem by Rupert ... with a note from the cleaning lady scribbled on the back—'Mr Darrow, you owe me three shillings, could you let me have it before this evening as I am relying on it'!

Everything seemed so normal, and I felt at peace with the world. 'Come on Teta,' I said, 'let's go and try to find a cake shop that's open.' As we went downstairs I saw there was a big yellowish envelope in the letterbox. I pulled it out and saw 'R. C. A. Darrow, On His Majesty's Service'.

'Oh Teta! Do you think he's been called up?' I tore it open and the nightmare sprang. 'Report for Military Service— Royal Navy—and from thence to His Majesty's training ship *Raleigh*—7th November.'

'Oh no!' I cried, 'I can't bear it.' And I sat down on the linoleum because my knees had given way.

Thetis looked surprised. I didn't know you cared for him so much,' she said.

I kept thinking, 'I must get away from here and join the WAAFs or the WRAFs or something, or go to Bermuda with Thetis, anything to get away from London.' I looked at myself in the hall mirror. I was wearing a pale blue hat with a pink feather and my plum corduroy coat and I thought, 'What a mockery, I ought to be wearing sackcloth.'

About six o'clock, after Thetis had gone and it was getting dark, there was the familiar sound of someone tearing up the stairs. I jumped to my feet and Rupert came in wrapped in his huge black overcoat, glowing with the cold. I put out both my hands and said, 'I've got bad news for you. You've been called up!'

'*Called up?* Where? When? How soon? What for?' He seized the paper from my hands, glaring in horror at the four shilling postal order for his train to Plymouth. I could almost see how sick he was feeling. He dropped the forms on the floor and looked at me despairingly. 'You see what this means, don't you? I'm done for, finished, it's all over! I'm trapped—*worse than school!*—and for the next two or three years probably! And you *never* get leave—oh Joanie!'

'Oh Rupert!' He sat on my lap and we rocked together in misery.

'Do you think I'll get killed?' he asked. 'Do you think they'll let me practise my guitar?'

I tried to reassure him on both points. Horrible pictures were now racing through Rupert's mind of himself wielding a marline-spike or clambering aloft to the crow's nest. 'It's getting late,' I said, at last. 'We'd better go.'

We stood up feeling awkward, and Rupert's fear filled the room. He put his head clumsily against mine and our lips met. He had never kissed me standing up before. It is the only one of his kisses I shall ever remember properly.

'Do you really think it will be all right?' he asked, like an apprehensive child.

'Of course it will,' I said. 'Come on, I've got to go.'

There was no moon. The road was swept by a cold wind

and cats prowled like coyotes around glistening piles of wreckage.

'Do you remember how cheery this road used to be?' Rupert asked. 'Pianos tinkling day and night, guitars on hot roofs, people on balconies taking tea under striped awnings, hundreds of typewriters tapping, thousands of paintbrushes squeaking—why, it must have been one of the jolliest streets in London! It'll never be like that again.'

Two lighted shops at the end of the street reminded me of Christmas. 'Oh God,' I thought. 'Christmas alone.' Christmas is always the worst time at home, with pictures in the magazines of parties that I never get asked to.

'Maybe I'll be drowned,' said Rupert as we walked slowly down the street. 'And I'll meet Gerhardt floating around in mid-Atlantic, and me and Gerhardt and the fishes will all have a lovely Christmas together. Darling Joanie—will you come and rescue me when I'm in wicked old hell? Will you save me from the devil?'

'Of course I will.'

'And we'll get on a bwoomstick and wide and wide through the twees, wicked old devil hot in pursuit?'

Hutchinson's was warm and bright, so we went in to buy cigarettes and while we were there the siren went for the evening blitz. The guns began in the distance.

'Oh dear,' Rupert said, 'what are we going to do? There's nothing we *can* do. Only ten days! It's like the last week of the hols.'

'Never mind,' I said, 'remember you're serving your country.'

'Yes, like *Elizabeth and Essex*.'

He left me and I ran back through nightmare streets, cold

and dark and the guns going, past a time bomb barrier, running into ropes that held me back like spiders' webs, and treading on broken glass that cracked horribly underfoot and made my heart jump.

Thursday, 31st [October]

Mummy is suspicious, because I haven't had the curse for two months.

'You're either anaemic or pregnant,' she said, 'and I mean to find out which. So she's taking me to a doctor. She keeps on asking me if I'm still a virgin or whether there's any cause to believe I'm going to have a baby. She's really put the fear of God into me—it's not so much the thought of having a baby, it's the ghastly maternal fuss that would attend such an occurrence.

Saturday, 2nd [November]

While I am still lying in bed, Mummy comes in and says in would-be normal tones, 'The doctor will see you on Tuesday. It's over two months now, isn't it? I do hope you're not pregnant—how terrible it must be for a girl who *has* slipped up when she misses her curse for two months! Just think of the agony she must go through!' She can be a very cruel woman sometimes. I wondered if she was deliberately torturing me.

Couldn't eat breakfast. Was Sid looking at me strangely? Funnily enough I hadn't given much thought to this pregnancy thing till now, but all at once I began to feel more and more certain that I was in for it, that it was true, that nothing could stop it. I was buggered and bitched.

I broke out in a cold sweat and tore back to the studio.

There I found a bottle of quinine pills left behind by Prudey, and I remembered how she told me the girls in Redcliffe Road used to take them when their curse was late. It said 'Take one or more as directed'. So I took six, swallowing them with water.

Sitting now at the switchboard I feel queer, giddy and remote. If I hold out my hand it shakes and I can't feel my fingers much, they're all cotton-woolly. Oh dear God, get me out of this, never no more, I promise! It's not the baby, it's the home fuss that worries me. Sid *must know* by now—I couldn't face her, that would be too much. Wish my fingers didn't miss the holes when I dial. Wonder how soon it will show. I tried looking it up in books where girls have babies, but they never give accurate dates. Why did this have to happen to me?

Sunday, 3rd [November]

When I went over in the morning Rupert was sitting at the table writing to his ma and listening to Beethoven on the wireless. 'God,' he said as I came in, 'what a bad writer Beethoven was!' he seemed very cheery. 'The great problem facing me now,' he went on, 'is how to become an officer, preferably an admiral, as soon as possible. I'm concentrating all my guile and cunning to that end.'

I was just wondering how to break the bad news when Prudey called in, full of bounce and go. She has acquired a new image, her hair combed straight down like an intellectual, calling everybody darling this and darling that, much to R's disgust. He thinks she has gone off terribly since she began living with the Baron.

'And how are you, darling?' she asked, turning to me. 'You look a bit pale and tired.'

I took a deep breath and pulled my shabby old coat around me. 'Yes I suppose I do—Mummy thinks I'm pregnant.'

I watched Rupert's face change from cheerful cynical amazement to blank horror.

'What?' he shouted, as the realisation hit him.

'Yes,' I said calmly. 'I haven't had the curse for two months.'

'Haven't had the curse for two months! Then you *are* pregnant! Oh my God, I feel sick and ill!'

Prudey prowled around shaking with laughter. 'Oh, how exciting, I *am* glad I called on you this morning! Have a cigarette, darling. Now do be careful, won't you, and don't let Rupert throw you down the stairs.'

'I can't stand this, one staggering shock after another. The whole world seems to have turned upside down since Saturday. I'm in a cold sweat,' he went on, wiping his brow with the back of his hand. 'Prudey for God's sake leave us alone.'

After she'd gone I waited for Rupert to say something.

'Thank God I'm going to the Navy on Wednesday,' he said finally. 'How long have you thought this might be happening?'

'Oh, off and on for a month.'

'Why the hell didn't you tell me before?'

'I thought it might have made you lugubrious.'

'Yes but then I could have taken you to a doctor straight away and it could all have been settled by now. Christ almighty, I shall be in the Navy and I won't be able to manage things. You *must* have an abortion, and pretty damned quick too.'

'But I don't want an abortion,' I said.

'What do you mean you don't want one? What *do* you want?'

'Well, if all else fails, I'll have the child.'

'You're crazy, you don't know what you're saying! Do you realise what an illegitimate child means? No man will marry you, they hate illegitimate children, and the child will always feel ashamed and inferior.'

'Never mind. I told you I've always wanted a child. If it feels inferior then it's a fool. I won't have an abortion. The Catholic Church forbids them.'

'I always knew the Catholic Church would get me in the end. Now listen Joanie, I know it's all very strong-minded of you, but just be practical for a minute—nice girls like you don't have bastards and I certainly can't stand the idea of marriage. The responsibility would give me the most awful claustrophobia. On the other hand, I'm a kindly chap, not cut out to be a betrayer of young maidens and all that, not my *métier* at all.

'Oh God I'm going to kill myself, I can't cope, my brain's buzzing! I don't think I've ever felt so lugubrious before in all my life. Has your curse ever stopped before?'

'Never for so long. Perhaps you'd better throw me down-stairs after all.'

I didn't mention the quinine I'd taken in a moment of panic although I was feeling dreadfully ill. 'Please,' I said, 'this is like a scene in a play, I keep on wanting to laugh— let's go and have some lunch.'

Monday morning, 4th [November]

Still a terrible pain in my stomach. Could the quinine be working? It feels like—yes it must be!

LATER

I could feel the blood coming out. I dashed into the bathroom, fell on my knees, thanking God again and again.

After Mass I ran to the telephone and phoned Rupert. 'Darling,' I said, 'I've got the curse!'

Rupert's voice was completely unemotional. 'Oh have you? Well that's a relief. You working this morning? OK, I'll be round in half an hour.'

I suppose my nature must be very uncontrolled, for I would like to have fallen on his neck and cried with relief, but with Rupert it's not possible. He sheathes himself in icy calm after coming through any stress. In fact he came in without saying anything about it. The most he would offer after ten minutes of triviality was, 'What a bloody awful hour to ring me up—I was asleep! As a matter of fact,' he went on, 'I made a few plans last night. If all else failed I was going to have you kidnapped and forcibly aborted. I actually rang up Billy Bolitho and he said it was quite easy. He'd give me something that would bring your curse back in two days and cost me exactly five bob. I told him you wouldn't take it so he promised to give it to me in powder form so I could mix it surreptitiously into your food.'

I didn't tell him about the quinine because I felt rather guilty about it already. Had I been pregnant? Had the quinine worked, and if so, is it as big a sin as an abortion? I suppose I will never know. In any case both Rupert and I dropped the subject and he'll probably never mention it again.

Sunday, 9th [March, 1941]

Last night the raid was bad—it was the night they hit the Café de Paris, where Yurka and I danced.

I felt dreadful about it; the bomb fell on the band killing them all except the drummer—gentle, magnetic Snakehips Johnson with his thin elegant face and his joyous rhythm— the best swing band in London gone.

They were dancing to 'Oh Johnny' when the bomb fell. The couples on the floor, killed by the blast, stood for some seconds as if they were still dancing, just leaning a little— then fell, heaped on top of one another.

Today I masturbated for the first time. It came about almost involuntarily. I was thinking about Rupert and when it became unbearable my thoughts started to turn themselves into acts and soon I found a way to bring it about. I was crying out loud with short, hoarse gasps.

God, I thought, coming to myself again and lying back exhausted, what a dreadful business, what am I coming to? I really mustn't let it happen again.

Monday, 24th [March]

Letter from the WAAFs at last. They order me to report immediately to Victory House for my medical and end, 'Yours sincerely, Commandant in charge of WAAF recruiting. PS. Do not come when your period is in progress.'

Tuesday, 25th [March]

Ten a.m. Victory House.

Was interviewed by glamorous officer called Pearson, the

first WAAF to be decorated for gallantry. She was charming to me, asked how long I'd been an art student and whether I'd enjoyed it and so on. Then she put me down for special duties which are very hush-hush—map-plotting and so on—and sent me in for my medical to see whether my eyes were good enough.

After sitting in a vast room full of girls all shaking with nerves, one or two with suitcases and in tears, I was sent by a corporal into an inner room and made to sign a paper saying I had never suffered from fits, bed-wetting, suppurations of the ears, St Vitus's dance, or venereal disease. I wrote 'no, no, no' till my hand was exhausted but noticed my neighbour, earnest and sweating, giving each item her full consideration, with pen poised doubtfully over sleeping sickness.

I finished the list and was pushed into another room, weighed, measured—' 'at orf, coat orf, be'ind that screen'—and wrapped in a dirty towel while my hair was searched for nits.

The next stop was a canvas booth with partitions, where a bored and weary woman murmured without opening her eyes, 'Please pass water for me, dearie,' and handed me a bottle. I managed to oblige her after a strenuous effort, poured the result into a UD milk bottle and marched back through the crowded room carrying it in front of me with some embarrassment. Horrified mutterings from the girls who were waiting. 'Cor! Look wot they make you do!'

'Looks orlright to me!' said the lady who'd first seen me, holding it up to the light, then, turning on me again, 'Dress orf, undies orf, be'ind *that* screen!' There I was confronted by a lesbian-looking doctor, completely hung around with stethoscopes. 'Undress!' she said in a deep bass voice.

'Completely?' I asked nervously.

'Completely!'

She then punched and pummelled me, listened to my heart, hit my reflexes with so much force that my foot shot up and nearly knocked her out and finally said, 'Well, you seem pretty fit,' and then with biting scorn, 'And what brought you in then? Mr Bevin?'

'Not at all,' I said huffily, 'I just got sick of my job. I was at the first-aid post and there didn't seem enough to do.'

Finally, after someone had stuck tubes down my ears and blown down them, I had the dreaded eye test. Of course I couldn't see a thing on the chart without my glasses, but I fooled them because I had learnt lots of it off by heart while waiting my turn.

So I was passed, registered as fit for special duties, and told to be ready for call-up in five to six weeks' time.

Bought some Maltesers and went to the Forum to see Peter Lorre in *Island of Doomed Men*. Wish I could write about important things instead of the nonsense that I do. Sometimes I feel the significance of what is going on in the world, but even then I can't put it into words. This war is probably the biggest thing that's happened in history, one half of the world trying to destroy the other. Nothing will ever be the same again— we are gradually reaching starvation point as rationing becomes stricter. Civilians, for the first time, are living under fire. We are expecting the invasion in the spring, poor Rupert's going to sea and may be killed, bombs fall every night and so on, but I don't feel any different to what I did in peacetime, except that I'm a bit happier.

Thursday, 3rd [April]

Letter from Rupert. Amazed and impressed to hear that I am now a member of the Armed Forces—and of my own free will! He says he's going to be posted to Canada but he's waiting for his ship.

Last week he went on manoeuvres and spent most of his time in the crow's nest, covered in icicles with only his nose sticking out of his balaclava. He says for the most part the sea always looks the same—no trees and no cake shops. Poor Rooples.

Hannah Senesh

*H*annah began her diary in 1934 at age thirteen in Budapest, Hungary. She lived with her mother and older brother George, her father having died when she was only six. By the time she was sixteen, she was so passionately devoted to the ideals of Zionism that the majority of her writing focused on her hopes of moving to Israel. When she turned eighteen, she convinced her mother to let her go and she was just about to leave when World War II began. Her desire to live in the Jewish homeland was so strong that she continued on with her pilgrimage despite the danger of her voyage.

This kind of courage in the face of personal danger was characteristic of Hannah. In the relative safety of kibbutzim, where she lived for several years, Hannah heard what was happening to the Jews of Eastern Europe and determined that she would help them, no matter what. She volunteered as a parachutist with the English partisan underground. Her mission was to drop into Yugoslavia and then

make her way to Hungary to help save the Jews from Nazi
extermination.

She survived the parachute drop but was captured by the
Nazis when she tried to cross the border into Hungary. She was
tortured for months and then executed in Budapest in November of
1944. Eventually her body was taken to Israel, where she was buried
with the highest military honors. She became a national heroine whose
poems and diary nearly everyone in Israel has read.

Hannah was seventeen when she wrote the first passages
excerpted here. She continued her writing even after she became a
partisan parachutist, sometimes in the form of letters, sometimes poetry, until very near the time she was captured by the Nazis. One of
the last things she wrote was "Blessed Is the Match," a poem that
schoolchildren memorize in Israel.

Hannah's diary and letters were first published in Hebrew
in 1945, and then in English in 1966. Hannah Senesh: Her Life
and Diary *is in print and available from Schocken Books.*

September 17, 1938

We're living through indescribably tense days. The question is: Will there be war? The mobilization going on in various countries doesn't fill one with a great deal of confidence.
No recent news concerning the discussions of Hitler and
Chamberlain. The entire world is united in fearful suspense.
I, for one, feel a numbing indifference because of all this
waiting. The situation changes from minute to minute. Even
the *idea* there may be war is abominable enough.

From my point of view, I'm glad George is in France,

though Mother is extremely worried about him. Of course this is understandable. The devil take the Sudeten Germans and all the other Germans, along with their Führer. One feels better saying these things. Why is it necessary to ruin the world, turn it topsy-turvy, when everything could be so pleasant? Or is that impossible? Is it contrary to the nature of man?

October 1, 1938

It is the Saturday before the Day of Atonement. I should have gone to synagogue, but instead I wrote a poem, and now I would rather attempt some self-analysis in my diary.

I don't quite know where to begin. That I made many errors this past year (though I don't feel I actually sinned) I know. Errors against God, righteousness, people, and above all, against Mother, and even against myself. I know I have many mistakes to answer for, and see them all clearly in my mind's eye. But I find myself incapable of enumerating them, of writing them all down. Perhaps deep down I'm afraid that someday someone might read what I have written. And I am really incapable of 'confessing'.

I would like to be as good as possible to Mother, to wear my Jewishness with pride, to be well thought of in my class at school, and I would very much like always to be able to believe and trust in God. There are times I cannot, and at such times I attempt to force myself to believe completely, firmly, with total certainty.

October 27, 1938

I don't know whether I've already mentioned that I've become a Zionist. This word stands for a tremendous number of things. To me it means, in short, that I now consciously and strongly feel I am a Jew, and am proud of it. My primary aim is to go to Palestine, to work for it. Of course this did not develop from one day to the next; it was a somewhat gradual development. There was first talk of it about three years ago, and at that time I vehemently attacked the Zionist Movement. Since then people, events, times, have all brought me closer to the idea, and I am immeasurably happy that I've found this ideal, that I now feel firm ground under my feet, and can see a definite goal towards which it is really worth striving. I am going to start learning Hebrew, and I'll attend one of the youth groups. In short, I'm really going to knuckle down properly. I've become a different person, and it's a very good feeling.

One needs something to believe in, something for which one can have whole-hearted enthusiasm. One needs to feel that one's life has meaning, that one is needed in this world. Zionism fulfils all this for me. One hears a good many arguments against the Movement, but this doesn't matter. I believe in it, and that's the important thing.

I'm convinced Zionism is Jewry's solution to its problems, and that the outstanding work being done in Palestine is not in vain.

November 12, 1938

I have so much to write about I don't even know where to begin. We have got back the upper part of Northern Hungary. From the 2nd of November until the 10th the joyous and enthusiastic entry of Hungarian troops took place from Komárom to Kassa. We had no school, and thanks to the radio we too felt involved in the entry. And this morning the four senior classes, in groups of ten, attended a special holiday sitting of Parliament which was very interesting. But I must honestly state that to me the road I am now following in the Zionist Movement means far more, both emotionally and spiritually.

I am learning Hebrew, reading about Palestine, and am also reading Szechenyi's *Peoples of the East*, a brilliant book which gives fundamental facts concerning the lives of all the people of the world. On the whole, I'm reading considerably more, and about far more serious subjects than hitherto.

I am determinedly and purposefully preparing for life in Palestine. And although I confess that in many respects it's painful to tear myself from my Hungarian sentiments, I must do so in my own interest, and the interests of Jewry. Our two-thousand-year history justifies us, the present compels us, the future gives us confidence. Whoever is aware of his Jewishness cannot continue with his eyes shut. As yet, our aims are not entirely definite nor am I sure what profession I'll choose. But I don't want to work only for myself and in my own interests, but for the mutual good of Jewish aims. Perhaps these are but the vague and confused thoughts and fantasies of youth, but I think I will have the fortitude, strength and ability to realize these dreams.

Mother is having difficulty accepting the idea that I will eventually emigrate, but because she is completely unselfish she won't place obstacles in my way. Naturally I would be so happy if she came too. The three of us must not be torn apart, must not go three different ways.

George is well, and we are always eagerly awaiting news from him. Recently he won a ping-pong tournament in Lyon;

his picture was even in the papers there. We were so pleased for him.

December 11, 1938

It's nine o'clock in the morning but I'm the only one up—surrounded by paper streamers and an untidy mess. Yesterday I finally had my 'evening'—or whatever one can call it, as it was 6:30 in the morning by the time I got to bed. Whether it was a successful party I can't say. I would be pleased to state it was, but to me the entire thing was, somehow, a disappointment. Perhaps one of the contributing factors was that I, personally, didn't enjoy myself very much. By this I mean there was no one with whom I spent any great length of time, or who really interested me. But there is something else: the times. And above all, my ideological point of view has so vastly changed since last year that I could not help but consider the affair frivolous, empty, and in a certain measure quite unnecessary at a time such as we're now going through.

There were nearly thirty people here, and only a few among them seriously interested me. I kept thinking how nice it would have been to have put all the money the party cost into the collection box of the Keren Kayemet. Oh, dear, I would like best of all to go to Palestine now. I would be glad to forfeit my graduation, everything. I don't know what has happened to me, but I just can't live here any longer, can't stand my old group of friends, studying, or any of the things with which I've been familiar up till now.

I don't know how I'm going to bear the next half year. I would never have believed that I would spend my senior year this way. I see I haven't written anything at all about the party, but I just can't. A ship is leaving today with a great many Hungarian Jews aboard. I so wish I could have gone with them. I don't understand how I could have lived this way for so long.

March 10, 1939
Perhaps I don't exaggerate if I write that the only thing I'm committed to, in which I believe, is Zionism. Everything connected with it, no matter how remotely, interests me. I can barely think of anything else. I am not afraid of being one-sided. Until now I have had to cast my sights in many directions. Now I have the right to look only in one direction—the direction of Jewry, Palestine and our future.

I am sending off my application to the Nahalal Girls' Farm. If only they'll accept me!

July 21, 1939
I've got it, I've got it—the certificate! I'm filled with joy and happiness! I don't know what to write; I can't believe it. I read and re-read the letter bearing the good news, now I can't find words to express what I feel. I have no feeling other than overwhelming happiness. But I can understand that Mother can't see the matter as I do; she is filled with conflicting emotions, and is really very brave. I won't ever forget her sacrifice. Not many mothers would behave as she is behaving.

I have to be in Palestine by the end of September. I still don't know when I'll leave. I won't write any more now, but there is one more thing I would like to say to everyone, to all those who helped me, to God, to my mother: Thank you!

Yesterday we went to Pécs. It was a beautiful day, very

pleasant. But I can't write about the trip because it is nothing compared to what happened today.

September 8, 1939

Much has happened, but I have had neither the time nor the desire to write about it. The war we feared has begun. It broke out over the matter of Danzig and the Polish Corridor. Danzig itself is a small place, and while its population is actually German, all of Poland—and finally all Europe—is in danger. If they had really wanted to they could have preserved the peace. But they didn't want to—so there is now war between Germany and Poland. The Germans have already captured a large part of Poland, and France and England, Poland's allies, have entered the war. There is nothing they can do as yet to be of any real help, but they're standing by, arms at the ready. Italy is still neutral, as are Hungary and many other countries. They are all aware that war nowadays will cause more destruction than ever before, and they are doing everything to prevent it. That is politics.

As for our private lives, George is in France, and Mother doesn't know whether he should return to Hungary, or stay there. We are still at peace, and France is at war. But who knows whether Hungary will participate or not; to be a Hungarian soldier now is not a particularly pleasant thing. And who knows what will happen to foreigners in France? Our situation is difficult, and we can't decide.

And now for myself. I received the certificate, and yesterday I also received the visa. I long to leave already, even though a sea journey now is not particularly safe.

Nahalal Agricultural School
Palestine
September 23, 1939

Today I must write in Hungarian as there are such an endless number of things to write about, so many impressions to record, that I can't possibly cope with them all in Hebrew as yet.

I would like to be able to clearly express today, on Yom Kippur, the Day of Atonement, all that I want to say. I would like to be able to record what these first days in Palestine mean to me. Because I have been here four days.

Yesterday, on Yom Kippur Eve, I was very low. I mean spiritually. I made an accounting of what I had left behind, and what I had found here, and I didn't know whether the move would prove worthwhile. For a moment I lost sight of the goal. I deliberately let myself go because once in a while one must completely relax from all one's tensions and from being constantly on guard. It felt good to let go, to cry for once. But even behind the tears I felt I had done the right thing. This is where my life's ambition—I might even say my vocation—binds me; because I would like to feel that by being here I am fulfilling a mission, not just vegetating. Here almost every life is the fulfilment of a mission.

I am in Nahalal, in Eretz. I am home.

The being 'home' does not refer to school. After all, I have been here only two days, and haven't become a part of the regular life yet. But the entire country's atmosphere, the people—all of them so friendly—one feels as if one had always lived here. And in a way this is true since, after all, I've always lived among Jews. But not among such free, industrious, calm, and, I think contented Jews. I know I still see things idealistically, and I know there will be difficult days.

To write a stage-by-stage account of the two-day, exciting train journey, the five-day voyage on the *Bessarabia* (a Roumanian ship), of the inexplicably pleasant experience of disembarking in Tel-Aviv and Haifa and of being among Jewish porters and officials, and what this means to a person ... to write about Haifa, Beth Olim, the Krausz family, where I went on the recommendation of Art Thieben, and where I found a most warm welcome ... to write of the drive by bus to the Emek and of the arrival at the school ... somehow or other I can not write any of this now. But everything is beautiful, everything is good, and I am happy that I'm able to be here. I would like George to come as soon as possible. And then Mother.

May 14, 1940

I was sitting, studying a notebook on general agriculture, when suddenly I was struck by the realization of how cut off I am from the world. How can I have the patience to study and prepare for an exam while the greatest war in history is raging in Europe? We are witnessing, in general, times which will determine the fate of man. The European war is engulfing vast areas, and fear that it will spread to our land is understandable. The entire world is gripped by tension. Germany grows mightier daily. And with the entire world on the edge of an abyss it is difficult to deal with minor problems, even more difficult to believe that personal problems are of any importance.

June 17, 1940

The Germans are on the threshold of Paris. Perhaps today the city will fall. Paris and France, and the entire world. What is going to become of us? All I ask is, how long? Because that Hitler must fall, I don't doubt. But how long has he been given? Fifteen years, like Napoleon? How history repeats itself. Napoleon's career, life, battles; but a 20th-century German version turns everything into inexpressible horror.

Italy has also 'stepped into the war', one hears a thousand times over. Due to this the immediate danger has increased here also. We are preparing as much as possible. If we are still alive 10–15 years from now perhaps we will know why this is happening. Or perhaps it will take a hundred years before this life becomes history.

June 29, 1940

France, George, my mother ...? It's difficult to say what hurts most as the days pass. France has negotiated a shameful peace. It has actually ceased to exist.

Communications with George have been cut off completely. His certificate arrived too late. I've no idea where he is now. But I'm still hopeful; perhaps he'll still come; perhaps he'll still be able to leave. I study the face of every young man, secretly hopeful. ... Oh, how awful it is to feel that I'm to blame, that I'm responsible for matters, in so far as they concern George. On the other hand, I know that in times like these, during a war, no one is to blame. It is impossible to judge, to decide whether it is best to be here or elsewhere.

And Mother ... I can imagine her spending sleepless nights, getting up in the morning worried, searching the newspapers, waiting for the post, locking all her worries and sadness in her heart because she is much too noble to burden others with her worries. And I, thousands of miles away, cannot sit beside her, smooth her creased brow, calm her, share the worries.

I'm working in the field, gathering hay, reaching—or imagining I'm reaching—my goals. And my goals are, I think, worthy—even beautiful. But does one have the right to long for what is distant, and give up what is close at hand? The only possible way I can answer this question is by saying that I would not have been able to continue living the life I led in Hungary. I would have been miserable. Each of us must find his own way, his own place and calling, even though the entire world is on fire, even though everything is in turmoil. No, I can't look for explanations, reasons. The 'aye' and the 'nay' storm within me, the one contradicting the other.

November 2, 1940

I dream and plan as if there was nothing happening in the world, as if there was no war, no destruction, as if thousands upon thousands were not being killed daily; as if Germany, England, Italy, and Greece were not destroying each other. Only in our little country—which is also in danger and may yet find itself in the centre of hostilities—is there an illusion of peace and quiet. And I'm sitting here, thinking of the future. And what do I think about my personal future?

One of my most beautiful plans is to be a poultry farming instructor, to travel from one farm to another, to visit settlements, to advise and to assist, to organize, to introduce record-keeping, to develop this branch of the economy. In the evenings I would conduct brief seminars for kibbutz members, teach them the important facets of the trade. And at the same time I would get to know the people, their way of life, and would be able to travel about the country.

My other plan is to instruct (seems I only want to teach) children in some sort of school. Perhaps in the institute at Shfeya, or in a regional agricultural school. The old dream is to combine agricultural work with child guidance and teaching.

My third plan—a plan I consider only rarely—has nothing to do with agriculture or children, but with writing. (As I write this the *Unfinished Symphony* is being played on the radio downstairs.) I want to write books, or plays, or I don't know what. Sometimes I think I have talent, and that it's sinful to waste or neglect it. Sometimes I think that if I really do have talent I'll eventually write without worrying about it, that if I feel the need of self-expression, the urge to write, I'll write. The important thing is to have a command of the language. I've made considerable progress during this first year in the Land, but I must do better.

April 12, 1941

Why am I so lonely? Not long ago I strolled through the Moshav one evening. It was a fabulous, starry night. Small lights glittered in the lanes, and in the middle of the wide road. Sounds of music, songs, conversation, and laughter came from all around; and far, far in the distance I heard the barking of dogs. The houses seemed so distant; only the stars were near.

Suddenly I was gripped by fear. Where is life leading me? Will I always go on alone in the night, looking at the sparkling stars, thinking they are close? Will I be unable to hear the songs . . . the songs and the laughter around me? Will I fail to turn off the lonely road in order to enter the little houses? What must I choose? The weak lights, filtering through the chinks in the houses, or the distant light of the stars? Worst of all, when I'm among the stars I long for the small lights, and when I find my way into one of the little houses my soul yearns for the heavenly bodies. I'm filled with discontent, hesitancy, insecurity, anxiety, lack of confidence.

Sometimes I feel I am an emissary who has been entrusted with a mission. What this mission is—is not clear to me. (After all, everyone has a mission in life.) I feel I have a duty towards others, as if I were obligated to them. At times this appears to be all sheer nonsense, and I wonder why all this individual effort . . . and why particularly me?

April 23, 1941

Yugoslavia has fallen. In Greece the British and Greeks are retreating. The fighting in Libya is heavy, and the results still uncertain. And Palestine is deadlocked in weakness, misunderstanding and lack of purpose. Everyone is discussing politics; everyone is positive the front is getting closer. But no one dares ask, What will happen if the Germans come here? The words are meaningless—on paper. But if we close our eyes and listen only to our hearts, we hear the pounding of fear. I'm not afraid for my life. It's dear to me, but there are things I hold more dear. Whether I want to or not, I must imagine what the fate of the land will be if it has to confront Germany. I'm afraid to look into the depth of the abyss, but I'm convinced that despite our lack of weapons and preparedness, we won't surrender without resisting strongly.

Half a million people can face up to a force, no matter how greatly it is armed. And I'm sure Britain will help us—or, to be more exact—will do all it can on its own behalf. And I continue to believe in a British victory.

But will there still be an Eretz? Will it be able to survive? It's dreadful to contemplate the possibility of its end at close hand. And though everyone wants to be hopeful, to reassure himself, deep within is submerged the thought . . . perhaps . . . And no man has come along yet with the ability to unite the people and to stop, even for a moment, the inter-party conflicts. There is no one to say, 'Enough!' No one to whom they will listen. I feel a deep sense of responsibility: perhaps I ought to say the word! But this is not my job. I don't have the opportunity to do so, or the knowledge. But even if I had the courage to rise up and speak, they wouldn't listen to me. Who and what am I to assume such a task? I can't do this, of course. But to do nothing, merely to look on from afar—that I can't do either. As if in a nightmare, I would like to scream, but no voice comes from my throat; I'd like to run, but my legs lack the strength. I can't come to terms with the thought that everything must be lost, destroyed, without us having the slightest say or influence on the course of things.

I want to believe that the catastrophe won't come to pass. But if it does, I hope we'll face it with honour. And if we can't hold out, that we will fall honourably.

May 17, 1941

There is a certain feeling of transition in our lives now. We plan something and add: 'If meanwhile . . .' and don't finish the sentence. Everyone understands. I don't think about dying, in any sense, though objectively speaking the possibility is very close. But I feel I still have a lot to do in this life, and that I cannot die before doing it all. Obviously everyone feels this way, particularly the young people who have already met death, and those who will yet meet it during this dreadful war. Our entire young country, filled with love and the will to live, feels this way.

June 14, 1941

Greece has fallen, and so has Crete. The war is now raging in Egypt and Syria. The British army marched into Syria three days ago, so the war is now virtually on our doorstep. Haifa was bombed for two nights. We went outside and listened to the bombs exploding, and the firing. Today we heard that Tel Aviv was bombed last night too, leaving many dead and wounded. The city is defenceless, an easy prey. It looks now as if the war is starting here.

At times one wants to view things from a longer range, from an historical rather than a fatalistic point of view, to seek explanations for things that can't be explained.

Look, let me draw a picture of a fruit orchard: an orchard of people. Saplings and full-grown trees, good trees and bad trees. They have blossomed, yielded fruit; winter has come and their leaves have fallen. The gardener comes and sees their dry, stunted branches. He thinks of the spring, and mercilessly trims and prunes, thereby strengthening them.

An ancient tree stands in the middle of the orchard, its trunk thick, its roots and branches spreading over and under the orchard. Its branches have dried up, the earth's life-giving moisture is unable to reach it. The gardener's eye notes that its roots are still vigorous, its trunk healthy. It's a noble tree, still able to yield fruit. But it must be more carefully pruned and tended than the other trees. He unhesitatingly cuts off the thick branches, and the pruning hook leaves fresh, golden wounds.

Will the tree survive? Look! In place of the amputated branches new ones are budding. A small twig appears near the roots, with fresh, full buds containing the hope of renewed life. Does the pruning hook snip it off too? Is it possible the gardener will fail to recognize the new life under the grey bark? And should the unseeing hand trim it off . . . will the Tree of Israel ever blossom again?

July 19, 1941

AGED TWENTY

They haven't started pruning yet. At least not for the time being. The pruning hook has turned towards Russia where the fiercest battles since the beginning of the war are now raging. Germany attacked Russia about two weeks ago, and swiftly captured Russian Poland, as well as a good part of Finland, and has begun advancing towards the interior of Russia. According to newspaper and radio reports, the Nazis are now encountering strong Russian opposition. Everyone knows the results of this struggle will be decisive to the future of the world, thus the suspense is enormous. The bombings have become frequent here too, and it's a miracle there have been so few casualties.

Yesterday I received a telegram from Mother which came via Turkey, and I gather she is frightened and worried about me. It's awful to think that while I'm living a normal, comfortable, peaceful life Mother is worried sick, envisioning me in all sorts of frightful situations, allowing herself no peace. I'm conscience-stricken that I have it so good and easy here while others are suffering, and feel I ought to do something—something exerting, demanding—to justify my existence.

Ness Tziyona: September 21, 1941

It's the eve of Rosh Hashana, the Jewish New Year. Two years have already passed since I left home. Two years away from my mother, my home; from my brother I've been away three years; and I've lived two years in the Land. If I could, I would write a few words to my Mother. I have so much to tell her. It's hard to know what I'd talk to her about were we to meet now. I would tell her about these years, about my dreams, my plans, my anxieties. I would tell her how I felt yesterday: I was so desperately depressed that I cried. I felt I was faced with two possibilities: to seek personal happiness and shut my eyes to all the faults in my surroundings, or else to invest my efforts in the difficult and devastating war for the things I deem good and proper.

But I don't think the decision is up to me. I feel hidden traits within me will determine my course, even though all the hardship and suffering it will entail are clear to me. But I wonder whether I have the strength and the ability to achieve what I want. I also wonder if what I want will be the right thing?

Dear God, if You've kindled a fire in my heart, allow me to burn that which should be burned in my house—the House of Israel. And as You've given me an all-seeing eye, and an all-hearing ear, give me, as well, the strength to scourge, to caress, to uplift. And grant that these words be not empty phrases, but a credo for my life. Towards what am I aiming? Towards all that which is best in the world, and of which there is a spark within me.

So much for myself. Now what can I say about the world around me—the world that is virtually destroying itself? Or about the tens of thousands of people perishing daily? How shall I grieve for them on the eve of Rosh Hashana? About the suffering, the pain; the injustice . . . what can I say, and to whom? *He* knows—thus there is nothing for me to say on this solemn evening.

Do I believe in God? I don't know. For me He is more a symbol and expression of the moral forces in which I believe. Despite everything, I believe the world was created for good.

August 22, 1942

AGED TWENTY-ONE

'I'm well, only my hair has turned a bit grey,' Mother writes. It is obvious between the lines why her hair has turned grey. How long will all this go on? The mask of comedy she wears, and those dear to her so far away? Sometimes I feel a need to recite the Yom Kippur confession: I have sinned, I have robbed, I have lied, I have offended—all these sins combined, and all against one person. I've never longed for her the way I long for her now. I'm so overwhelmed with this need for her at times, and with the constant fear that I'll never see her again. I wonder, can I bear it?

Caesarea: January 8, 1943

I've had a shattering week. I was suddenly struck by the idea of going to Hungary. I feel I must be there during these days in order to help organize youth emigration, and also to get my mother out. Although I'm quite aware how absurd the idea is, it still seems both feasible and necessary to me, so I'll get to work on it and carry it through.

Caesarea: February 22, 1943

How strangely things work out. On January 8 I wrote a few words about the sudden idea that struck me. A few days ago a man from Kibbutz Maagan, a member of the Palmach, visited the kibbutz and we chatted a while. In the course of the conversation he told me that a Palmach unit was being organized to do—exactly what I felt then I wanted to do. I was truly astounded. The *identical* idea!

My answer, of course, was that I'm absolutely ready. It's still only in the planning stage, but he promised to bring the matter up before the enlistment committee since he considers me admirably suited for the mission.

The entire plan may miscarry, and I may receive a brief notification informing me the matter will be postponed, or that I don't qualify. But I think I have the capabilities necessary for just this assignment, and I'll fight for it with all my might.

I can't sleep at night because of the scenes I envisage: how I'll conduct myself in this or that situation . . . how I'll notify Mother of my arrival . . . how I'll organize the Jewish Youth. Everything is still indefinite. We'll see what the future brings . . .

May 29, 1943

I'm waiting to be called. I can't think of anything else. I don't think there is any outer, noticeable change in me. I do my daily work as usual, but sometimes feel as if I'm seeing things from a distance. I look at everything from one point of view only: is it, or is it not necessary for my mission? I don't want to meet people. It'll be easier to leave if I don't. No. That's a lie. Now, more than ever, I'd like someone who is close to me.

There are some things one can't express. One tends to confuse them and believe that as long as one doesn't find expression for them they don't exist. I pray for only one thing: that the period of waiting will not be too long, and that I can see action soon. As for the rest—I'm afraid of nothing. I'm totally self-confident, ready for anything.

June 12, 1943

The settlement decided to allow me to enlist. I'll soon be leaving for instruction.

September 19, 1943

I arrived in the Land four years ago. Immigrant House; Haifa. Everything was new, everything beautiful, everything a world of the future. Only one figure takes me back to the past; my mother at the railway station. Four years. I never would have believed the distance between us could ever be so great, so deep. Had I known ... Or perhaps I knew but didn't dare admit it.

There's no sense to all this accounting. I'm now in Bet Ruthenberg, a splendid mansion, spending a month at a Working Youth Seminar. Before that, I was at another course. After this—I don't really know. Am I satisfied? It's hard to say. I spent two years in Nahalal, after that almost two years at Sdot-Yam and Caesarea. Many struggles, and considerable satisfaction, but always loneliness. No friends, no girlfriends, but for Miryam.

And now I stand before a new assignment again, one that demands great preparation for a difficult and responsible mission. Again a sense of transition coupled with strong emotions, aspirations, tensions. And the everlasting aloneness. Now it's clearer to me than ever that this has nothing to do with outside factors. There's a certain peculiarity within me, and a lack of sociability which keeps me away from people. This is especially difficult where it concerns men.

At times I think I love, or could love, someone. But ... There are many objective 'buts' in the way, and I lack the courage to overcome them. Meanwhile there are a few men who love me, and I'm thinking of Moshe in particular ... about whom I can say only good things. And yet, I can't love him. All right, at least my heart is far from breaking. But even so, there is something which terrifies me: I am twenty-two years old, and I don't know how to be happy.

I wear a placid mask, and at times I say to myself, What is this? Is this how my life is going to unfold? It's no longer an external matter, but something within me. I have no complaints about life, really. I'm satisfied. I can't imagine a state in which I would be more content. On the contrary. And the assignment which lies ahead draws me on. But I forget to laugh—to really laugh, heartily, as I once could with George while wrestling on the couch until we rolled off onto the floor—laughing about nothing but the joy of living, of being young and alive. Are hardship and loneliness to blame for the lack of that particular kind of joy? Or do I bear this sorrow from the time when—at the age of seven or eight—I stood beside my father's grave and began to write poems about the hardships in life? I feel I'm just chattering. However, this is necessary too. Amid essays, speeches, and silences, it's good to converse sometimes, even if only with oneself.

January 11, 1944
   This week I leave for Egypt. I'm a soldier. Concerning the circumstances of my enlistment, and my feelings in connection with it, and with all that led up to it, I don't want to write.
   I want to believe that what I've done, and will do, are right. Time will tell the rest.

Sarah Fishkin

POLAND ∽ 17 YEARS OLD

*S*arah's family was living in Rubzewitz, in northeast-ern Poland, when the Germans bombed the town in 1941 and began mass executions of the Jews. Six years before, when Sarah was eleven, she had begun writing a diary in which she expressed her innermost feelings. After the German invasion, she continued her writing, de-scribing the feelings of the Jewish population as a whole.

There were few details of everyday life in Sarah's writing after the German occupation. Rather, her diary depicted how she saw the suffering of her people reflected in the natural world. For the most part, it was an elegy for the lost hopes and dreams of the Jews.

When Sarah was eighteen her family was torn apart. The Nazis buried her youngest brother and sister alive in a pit along with most of the young children of their village. Her father and younger brother Jacob were deported to a different death camp from Camp Dwortz, where she, her mother, and her Aunt Rachel were sent. When Sarah was deported she had to leave her precious diary behind in Rubzewitz.

Sarah's mother died due to the inhuman conditions in Camp Dwortz. Her Aunt Rachel saved her life and her children's by building a hiding place within the death camp into which she crawled during the camp's liquidation. She had tried to convince Sarah to hide with them, but Sarah chose to be with the majority of the inmates in the camp who were executed just prior to liberation.

Sarah's younger brother Jacob survived the death camp to which he had been sent, and many years later he found his only surviving relative, Aunt Rachel, living in Germany and in possession of Sarah's diary. After she escaped from Camp Dwortz, she had joined a partisan unit, and eventually she returned to the family's hometown of Rubzewitz. Although there was very little left of the town or the family's home, she found Sarah's diary in the rubble and took it with her to Germany. When Jacob was reunited with his Aunt Rachel, she entrusted his sister's diary to him.

Jacob has treasured and preserved Sarah's diary for almost fifty years. In keeping with a request that she made in her diary that it should be published when the people of the world were most in danger of denying and forgetting the annihilation of the Jews, Jacob has not accepted previous offers to publish Sarah's work. He had the diary translated into English some years back and then waited for the time when the younger generations seemed not to know the meaning of the Holocaust.

Now, thanks to Jacob and his diligence in following his sister's wishes, a portion of Sarah's diary finally appears in print to remind us all of the unimaginable horror of the Holocaust.

Sunday, 22nd June 1941
Today the war between the Russians and the Germans began.

Monday, 23rd June 1941

The moment has now arrived to make a person look for a way to save his own life, to hide from the bombs which may be coming in the very near future. Many leave their homes. They ride off without a destination. One looks the end of life squarely in the eye: the bullet could hit soon. Still, the desire to spite Fate and go on living is very strong: one wants to see what the end will look like when it does arrive.

Wednesday, 25th June 1941

Today the Germans entered our city and captured it. A short time passed quietly, then suddenly a German aircraft came rushing in and commenced a bombardment of the city. We were afraid to remain indoors any longer and went out to an orchard where we waited calmly for Death to approach. It is terrible when the bullets are flying about overhead and it seems that at any moment one of them will strike and put an end to our young lives.

Shortly after the bombing and strafing of the city begin, we suddenly notice a large army of Germans approaching us on the road we are traveling. All thoughts of staying alive become shrouded in great sadness. I feel in my heart the desire to perish together with my family, to end my young life beside my parents ...

But how much more cheerful one's heart grows when our lives are spared and we are commanded to leave the place where we are! We go, although we do so with great hopelessness, and stop some distance away. From afar we can see the city engulfed in terrible flames, great clouds of smoke obscuring the light of the sun, which keeps shining on as if to say that all this has nothing to do with it, neither pains nor moves it. Human labor and sweat are being consumed in the flames. Innocent people, their lives stopped by bullets fired by a deliberate barbaric hand, drop in the streets. It is so painful to watch. The same kind of end awaits everyone.

Thursday, 24th July 1941

It is difficult to believe that the good times are gone, that our moments of joy, the hours of studying and enjoying ourselves are past, that I must give up forever my thoughts of future goals and the fantasies I hoped to see realized. I would never have believed that it would all disappear so soon, be cut down, burned out, orphaned in so short a time. Emptiness and desolation, saddened aching hearts, are our present constant companions. There seems to be no future for the Jewish population.

For the Jew the light of day is covered with a thick veil: his road is overgrown with tall wild grasses. Every horizon upon which his eye rests is stained with the tears of lost children searching for their mothers in the dense woods. Convulsed with sobbing until their little souls expired, the youngsters are now lifeless, at eternal rest. Only the quivering trees know of their death and will later on bear witness about the sacrifice of these little ones.

No human heart can remain untouched and unpained by all this. It is beyond human endurance to see so much trouble and so much suffering experienced. It is painful to see people tortured by people until life is ended. Where is human conscience, to demand the truth, to cry out?

"Man, what are you doing? Consider! Hold back your raging hand, the wild nature that prompts you to beat the Jew merely because he is a Jew!"

But this torturer is not a human being. And the Jew must turn his back and become accepting of all. For one cannot and dare not resist.

And G-d looks on and sees it all, sees how innocent people are cut down who never did any harm, not even to a fly, for they understood that it, too, has a desire for life. Such people are being killed by a shot from a gun in the heavy hand of a human with animal instincts, with the nature of a wolf.

3rd August 1941

We seem now to have reached the end of everything. But one wants to live. One craves more of youth and joy. However, the present time presents little other than tragic pictures, all of them mirrored in the eyes of thousands, of millions of individuals. One's sole thought is to survive this painful, oppressive time and to see something better before one's eyes.

Wednesday, 20th August 1941

The days are now shorter, the nights longer. The grain is being harvested from the fields. Every morning we must report to the work-assignment place. Whether it is to labor on the roads, near the bridges, or elsewhere, everything has the self-same purpose: to torment the Jew, to oppress him more and more.

I took my diary in hand. I turned the previously filled pages in the hope of tempering the effect of my present hardships, for we are tortured daily as though we were slaves like those in Egypt long ago.

Rosh Hashana, Monday, 22nd September 1941

In these stormy times questions about today, about the day one is living, are uppermost. All secondary problems are erased from daily life. A person's mind becomes impaired, far from beautiful thoughts. One goal is dominant: to maintain life.

In the life of today there is one road, and on it two pictures keep alternating before my eyes: death ... life.... For a moment I seem dead, but the thought comes that I am still alive.

Another season of cold is coming on to replace the lovely warm summer days which were a comfort to the suffering people. The fields and gardens were filled with good things and one could be outdoors and sleep under the clear, starlit sky. And now that too is gone and the warmth has disappeared along with the good days. For some, hunger adds to the general sense of apprehension and insecurity. At times, however, you hope and you lend courage to each other.

Wednesday, 1st October 1941. Yom Kippur

We awaited the day of Yom Kippur with much sadness and prayer to G-d. It is a day different from all others. It is concerned with charting a good and pleasurable year. How sad and broken are the many tens of thousands of hearts being poured out before G-d, hearts that find no comfort in the present heavy darkness. They dream of something better in their lifetime, but if that is not to come, they wish for their dismal life to end as soon as possible.

All about is shattered, destroyed and burned. All is obstructed by fresh graves, a virtual cemetery. Dark, menacing clouds cover everything. The entire surroundings are weeping and crying out ...

Sunday, 26th October 1941

It is difficult to be alive and to survive in these dark, oppressive times. As one listens to the accounts of the wild, barbaric deeds of those man-eating Hitlerites in the city of Koidanov, not far from us, one shudders and is pervaded by deathly fear. With what deep sighs we hear the accounts of the kind of death man suffers at the hands of men! On a lovely morning, as the sun was just beginning to rise, a death-presaging black cloud suddenly appeared. When all the Jews of the city had been gathered together, when the long graves had been dug and prepared and stood open before the eyes of the mothers, fathers and little children, they looked at them wide-eyed, not knowing what was about to happen in the ensuing moments. Then were heard pain-filled sobs and farewells to one's children.

Some sought ways to hide. From the hiding places, too, they were led to the slaughter. The thousands of people who fell are now at rest. The long graves have been closed again, but the earth will not rest. One can see it heave, as if to say:

Dig away the covering and let out these people who have just fallen, whose blood will not be still and finds no peace in the earth.

It is difficult to listen to these accounts of tragic actual events. Our own end could be the same on any coming day. May the one G-d preserve us from such harm and may He bring death to the attackers who quell their wild feelings with the blood of thousands of human beings.

Kim Malthe-Bruun

DENMARK ∽ 18 YEARS OLD

*K*im was an eighteen-year-old Danish boy who began
his diary in 1941, when he left school and signed on as a merchant
seaman. He had just fallen in love with a girl he called Hanne, and
it was really for her that he did most of his writing.

When he docked at various ports in Europe and saw what
the Nazis were doing to Jews, he was deeply troubled and eventually
decided that he must do something to help stop the oppression. In
September of 1944, he left the life he had loved at sea and joined the
partisan underground.

He and his compatriots were arrested by the Nazis in
1945 for their partisan activities and sentenced to death. From his
prison cell, Kim kept his diary going in the form of letters to his
mother, Hanne, and a friend named Nitte. He was executed in April
of 1945, just one month before the end of the war. After liberation, a
portion of his diary was found hidden in the walls of the Copenhagen
prison in which he had been tortured and murdered.

The diary was edited by his mother and published ten years after his death, in 1955. The explanatory notes between the diary entries were written by Kim's mother.

Danzig: 18 May 1941
Dearest Hanne,

I've just arrived here. The weather is marvelous—hardly a breeze, not a cloud in the sky. But it's maddening to see the Germans parading around here. They even come on board.

I'm lying on the big hatch cover as I write this and I'm in a perfect spot to see everything that's going on.

At midnight on Thursday, May 15, my thoughts went out to you, but I was sad because I couldn't be with you on your birthday. But just the same I was with you all that day, Hanne. . . . Rarely have I been so happy and so sad at the same time. As I paced up and down on the lookout for mines, I thought of you and felt warm all over. . . . I could see your mother congratulating you on your birthday and I was there when you opened your presents. I was also around in the afternoon when you had invited a few friends in for a cup of chocolate and I trailed you until you were again in your bed when the day passed in review before your eyes. I hoped so much that you would also be thinking of me. When you had fallen asleep, I kept on watching over you until 4 o'clock the next morning. I was off duty during the next four hours and admit that I slept like a top. You can imagine, my darling, all the plans and thoughts that went through my head during this time—plans and thoughts that I won't go into right now, perhaps later.

We still don't know where we go after we leave here, but as usual I'm hoping that it will be Copenhagen or its vicinity.

I was interrupted. A big German submarine passed us at a distance of not more than twelve feet. It was one of the biggest ones on its way to its mission of destruction on the open seas. You can't imagine the horror of seeing one of those "coffins" and all the anguish of the women and children crying as they run along the quay. The Germans themselves are the cause of all this misery, but it's a terrible thing to see just the same.

Sweetheart, here I am again. I went ashore to look around. The destruction is unbelievable: shell holes everywhere and trees stripped of their bark and ruined. In the woods about three minutes' walk from here is a small barracks completely shot to pieces. The bullet holes aren't even three feet apart. The battle of Poland was a catastrophe and what an unspeakable horror that the Germans should be the victors! Around here we almost go out of our minds at the thought of the Germans—in fact, everything German. When I see how they treat their prisoners of war, I could slit their throats, every last one of them.

This place, as well as Stettin, has an aviation school and as a result the sky is filled with all sorts of planes. They certainly manage to look impressive, but we curse them because they are German and keep hoping that they'll crash, which unfortunately hasn't happened until now—at least not while we were watching.

Tomorrow I have watch, but I still have to work with the

others, so I'll probably be dead by tomorrow night. It's amazing how little sleep I can get along on when necessary. Several times we've worked around the clock without being too knocked out. But when I finally do bunk down, I sleep like a log and am not too pleased at having to get up again after a few hours. Hanne, do you know that when I lie down I dream wonderfully about you until I fall asleep? It's like the times when I have watch on a clear moonlit night—I feel as if I could fly and my dreams take off on such flights of fancy that it would be impossible to hold on to them in full daylight. How I wish that you could live through a night like this with me at sea! Then you would understand what I mean.

You should have seen what we saw this morning—a big cart loaded with stone to which Polish prisoners were harnessed! Behind them came two Germans with bayonets. We were all beside ourselves with fury and disgust at the display of such brutality, and at that moment I could have murdered any German. This made me think of how the Danish peasants used to behave in times past and I asked myself what sort of progress in human behavior we have to show in the year 1941.

Danzig: 19 May 1941

Hello, my darling. I'm just about dead, but I still want to write a few words to you. Today we were told that we're going to Vejle, which was an awful disappointment to me. My shipmates are thrilled to pieces because rumor has it that the girls there are very pretty. But what does that matter to me when my girl doesn't live in Vejle? From there we will probably go on to Aabo, Finland. It will be a great relief to get out of Germany, which is rotten to the core, although it will be terrible to be away from you for so long. But this will only make me twice as happy to see you when I do come home.

Sunday, 25 May 1941

The wildest rumors are going around here that the Germans have sunk a whole lot of English warships—big ones, that America has officially entered the war and that the Germans are about to attack Russia. The tension is growing by the hour. The Germans have planted a double row of mines outside the port and in here they have gathered together several fleet units. It looks as if we'll be right in the middle of the line of fire when the war against Russia is launched. According to what the German soldiers say, all relations with the Russians are broken off and they are only waiting for the shooting to start. I can't swear to the truth of these rumors because as a matter of principle I don't talk to the Germans except when I try to tell them how stupid and futile their policy is and how little hope there is for them.

I'm sure that something will break tonight because there has been a wild buzzing of planes overhead, the like of which I've never seen. This time they seem to have a purpose and are not just playing around as before. Lots of them have left and only a few have arrived. They have been taking off most of the night, one after another, all heading toward the south. If the lid blows off now, it will certainly be interesting to have been on the spot, but "interesting" won't be the word for it if we're still here when the shooting starts.

11 June 1941

If you only knew how I felt after I had read your letters! They showed you to be what you are—sincere and genuine, with no pretense, no glib phrases, just the plain truth. This is to me of infinitely more worth than any declaration of love.

I have bad news. We are leaving Vejle for Finland (Pernavik) and from there to Bandholm and Naestved, so unfortunately you and I won't be seeing each other for some time. "Unfortunately" isn't the word to describe the pain I feel, but if this is our destiny we have to accept it.

Finland: 27 June 1941
Dearest Hanne,

I can't, or rather I'm not permitted to write much, and nothing about where we are. We are continually on the move to avoid you know what. Please write even if you don't hear from me. I've written a letter to you which you probably won't get because I wrote a lot of things which I shouldn't have. It's "hot" here and getting "hotter" all the time, but the gods just have to help me get back to you. I can't bear the thought of being separated from you and don't know how I'll get through the time that lies ahead. Please do something for me. Call Mother—you don't need to tell her how bad things look, but only that we may be here for months, perhaps until the war is over.

Pernavik: 1 July 1941
Darling, I wasn't able to get this letter off to you. All hell has broken loose. The Russians launch their bombing attacks as many as ten times a day, and every time they seem close we have to run for the woods to seek shelter behind the rocks. Things couldn't be much worse, but I haven't felt afraid of dying a single time.

Lübeck: 7 March 1944

Tonight I've been talking to an Austrian saloon-keeper. He was burning up with hatred for the Germans. He put his face close to mine and the whites of his eyes showed as he gave vent to all his indignation. He trembled with rage and seemed for once to be able to let himself go. But it was quite a shock to see how humble he became when another guard passed by.

The town is covered with posters—all telling the same story. One depicts a railway station crowded with happy Germans, taken from above. Over the picture lies the heavy shadow of a man in a big coat, and underneath is printed in large letters. "The enemy is listening." Two of the posters preach economy, and I'll never be able to forget the last one. It shows an ugly face reflected in a hand mirror, looking very much like a rat and with a loathsome expression over his features. Almost in relief is an angular, semitic nose and the caption under the poster reads: "Look at yourself in the mirror. Are you a Jew or aren't you?" How rotten all of these people must be in order not to react violently to this. The Germans are like a ripe fruit that has been damaged and now the rottenness has come to the surface.

Vasa: 7 August 1944

Tonight the cook and I have been discussing the Germans, and the punishment that ought to be given them. That fellow is really a Dane to be proud of. He was sick at heart at the thought of all the Germans who would be shot. He felt that punishment ought to be given in such a way that they would be fully aware that it was a punishment. He pointed out how futile it would be to shoot them down without reason at the moment when they would be rejoicing at the thought of going home after five years in military service. Who would have the heart to put a gun against his chest and pull the trigger while they're retreating?

I maintained that this is what most people would do, and that I had heard people talk in dead earnest about sterilizing the whole German people. He shook his head sadly and said, "Then we might as well tie a rope around our necks and hang ourselves, because there would be no further reason to live among men."

Toward the end of September Kim left the ship to work in the resistance movement.

Hellerup: 28 November 1944
Dear Nitte,

This is an extraordinary time we're living in, and it has brought forth many extraordinary people. It's almost beyond my grasp. But I do know that there is no other time in which I would prefer to have lived than the one we are now going through. Everything is trembling and the agony which is part of every birth is everywhere. Never has the world been exposed to such suffering, but never has the feeling of life been as strong or as intense as now. I'm living a fantastic life among fantastic people, and it is through this that I have come close to them. And because true feelings are always exposed when nerves are on edge, I'm getting to know people in a different way than I ever did before.

I used to look at the world through the eyes of a dreamer, and to me it's always had a special glow. Every night I went to sleep with a smile on my lips and a smile in my heart, and every morning I woke up rested and filled with wonder at the life to which I was born.

Now at night I fall into a heavy sleep, taking with me all that is on my mind. But when I wake up, it isn't because I can't sleep any longer, but because something tells me that I have work to do. It is only the present that counts. I feel that I must always follow my inner convictions, always be prepared for the unexpected, always be ready to spring into action. You know what this is like, living for the moment only and with our lives at stake. The group with which I'm working has completely accepted this.

Hellerup: 3 December 1944
Dear Nitte,

I think that I will go through a big change when I can withdraw from people and be myself again. I can't explain why or how, but I feel as if I've lost something among people that I could see, understand and feel when I was alone.

The more I live among city people, the more I realize the tremendously important role that the peace and the stillness of nature play in our development. Something is lost when you live too much among other people, the way you do in a city. The ideas and thoughts of others penetrate you, and you get so caught up in them that you are no longer able to feel or understand what is taking place in your own life.

On December 19, 1944, Kim was caught in an apartment on Classen Street, together with two friends. He was unarmed and carrying his own identification papers.

Two days later the first letter from Kim arrived, accompanied by a familiar form letter:

Persons who are inmates of the Vestre Prison, German Police Section, may only send and receive one letter consisting of twenty lines every two weeks. All letters must contain the prisoner's full name and birth date and must be legible. A visitor's permit may be obtained fourteen days from the date of arrest and should be addressed to the Danish Red Cross, Amaliegade 18, Copenhagen. Only one visit per month is permitted, and only one visitor is allowed. A direct appeal to the Police will be useless.

Parcels containing clothing and toilet articles can be left at the prison every other Thursday between 12 and 7. No special permission is required, but it must be done in alphabetical order as follows: Thursday 12/7/44 from A–K and Thursday 12/14/44 from L–O, etc. The parcels may not contain letters or food. Tobacco and reading material may not be added without written authorization.

Severe measures will be taken against anyone violating these rules. Address: German Police Section, Vestre Prison, Copenhagen V.

Vestre Prison, German Section, Cell 252:
21 December 1944
Dearest Mother,

Everything is just fine, and I'm getting adjusted to my new life much better than I had expected. This is certainly a great change, with entirely new impressions, but there is undoubtedly a lot to be learned from it all. Many times during the past two days I've thought of how wonderful it was to live at home with you and enjoy all the things that home has to give. I've also been hoping that you are feeling as calm and confident as I am. There are so many things which you can see and understand only after being separated from others. I share this cell with five other fellows, and we have lively discussions about everything under the sun. I've received permission to read and smoke, so I'd be very grateful if you would send me some tobacco and reading matter. Please don't worry. I'll be back home again before long.

I wish you all a Merry Christmas and a very Happy New Year. Please don't let the thought of me spoil your holidays. I assure you that the most difficult thing for me are my worries about you.

Thanks for the package and your greetings.

Vestre Prison: January 1945 [smuggled out]
Dearest Mother,

You ask if I want anything. There is only one thing: to get out of here. Otherwise I don't need anything. You know that I've always been able to get along on very little.

Thank you for what you said in your letter. It's meant a great deal to me. Your calmness and your wisdom make me very happy. You say that I've fulfilled all your expectations. I'm afraid that all of you see me in some sort of rosy light and forget to look at the facts. You forget that my daily life has prepared me for hardships much worse than the ones I've been exposed to here. Therefore you must realize that none of all the things that are so tough on the others—the food, the bed, the confinement, the questioning, have affected me in the least. I wouldn't have missed this experience for anything. Don't forget either that adventure is in my blood, and at the time of my arrest I was more excited at the thought of the experiences that were ahead of me than anything else. Neither the Gestapo nor anyone else has frightened me in the least. It's the primitive ones who are the most interesting. When they took me to the Shell Building for questioning I thought that I felt the way an animal trainer must feel when he enters a cage of wild animals. The trainer probably has a sort of affection for the animals, even if he knows that some of them are mangy and have to be destroyed. I've never been afraid of dogs, although I know that you have to proceed with caution when dealing with wild ones.

Until now I haven't been harmed. I had to take my clothes off, but that was all. The man standing beside me looked as if he were about to spring on me, but each time I ignored him without being directly impolite and started to talk to his colleague. Only once did we confront each other, and I realized what would happen if he lost control of himself. I calmly asked him, "Are you afraid?" Never have I seen a more astounded look on anyone's face. Then he flew into a rage but had to check himself because I had turned toward the other fellow, who was apparently his superior. After that he didn't flare up quite so much and did his job with a little less zest.

Vestre Prison [smuggled out]
Dear Nitte,

It was wonderful to hear from you, and this seemed to confirm the bond that exists between us. I feel so close to you, and it made me so happy to know that you feel the same way. I want to try to think about it, try to feel and understand what it is which fills us both, I in my cell and you at Loendal. But in our relationship, it's your life that has been affected—not so much mine. I have you in Loendal, Hanne at her studies, Mother in her office, while you have lost me behind a fog of conjectures—prison, cell, confinement, questioning—behind a lot of barriers which it seems impossible to penetrate, and which make it so hard for your imagination to follow me in my thoughts and feelings and to see what my life is like. But I haven't changed at all and could just as well be sitting beside you at Loendal at this moment. It's strange that you never felt too far away from me when I was in Finland or some other far-off place, but that you do now when only a locked door separates us.

Nothing happens. I'm sitting here behind four walls and a locked door and nothing happens. I keep on saying that I live in the present and I do, but in the same way as the winter crops do. They sleep peacefully under their protective covering of warm earth, waiting for the warm summer which must come before an abundant harvest can be reaped. Behind these four solid walls a wonderful feeling of peace has come over me. Nothing can happen here, in any case nothing too surprising, and that gives me a sense of drowsiness in my hibernation.

Vestre Prison: 21 January 1945 [smuggled out]
Dearest Hanne,

I've just been lying here and thinking about what a marvelous girl you really are. There are so many things in you that I appreciate and love when I've been separated from you for a while. You're so delightedly unconcerned about all the things which occupy most people. I can't help thinking about how wonderful you were at the time of my arrest. I think you were completely calm inside.

A lot of things have happened to me while I've been here which don't happen to everybody. Don't be angry with me, but if I don't manage to get out of here I would like to be sent to Germany, first to Froeslev to get to know the life there, and then to Germany to see the collapse of the Reich inside its borders. It's going to be enormously interesting. Have faith in me. I don't think that there are many as well-equipped to get through it as I am.

I've always felt that there is a reason for everything and that this chain of events is leading me some place. I feel this more strongly now than ever before. I'd feel cheated if I didn't get out of here either to see the end of the occupation and the people wild with joy here at home or else see the tragedy and breakdown in Germany.

I'm not quite sure how you stand on this, but I think you feel as I do that our lives follow lines which are not accidental and that what happens to us is always for our greatest good.

One change has taken place in me since I've been here. Before I always had a strong desire to criticize you, to change you so that you would be on the same wavelength as I happened to be. I don't feel this way at all any more, and my sense of peace and confidence in our relationship is stronger than before. You radiate so much calm and light that I don't even miss you, but I wouldn't be without you for anything in the world. I wouldn't be myself any longer if I didn't have you.

I'd give a lot to know if I'm leaving for Froeslev tonight or if it isn't a false alarm as so often before. In any case I should think that I would be leaving here soon, since my case is closed.

I must say that up to the present time I've been very lucky to have the chance to live a life so full of change and movement with so many new impressions. It's really wonderful to be alive. I still don't know what death is like, but it would seem to me that it's the high point of our lives. I can't help thinking of this when I see how nervous the Gestapo and the collaborators are when they go into town. But I'm a bit different from them just the same.

On February 5 Kim was sent to the camp at Froeslev together with some other prisoners. In the meantime the Gestapo had obtained new evidence against him. Upon his arrival at Froeslev his name was called out and he was placed in solitary confinement. Three or four days later he was sent back to Vestre Prison.

When they were clearing out the prison after the German capitulation, one of the resistance fighters found a letter which Kim had received from Nitte toward the end of February. On the back of this letter he wrote the following, probably to give vent to his feelings, never thinking that it would ever be read. The entire sheet was covered with microscopic writing, possibly continued elsewhere or was to be continued, because "as you" was squeezed in the lower right-hand corner of the page. At any rate, the rest has never been found. From witnesses inside the prison we know that Kim was brought back to the cell unconscious, after having been tortured.

3 March 1945

Yesterday I was sitting at the table. I looked at my hands in amazement. They were trembling. I thought about it for a moment. There are some things which produce a purely physical reaction. Suddenly, as I was sitting here, I was possessed by the desire to draw something. I got up and started to sketch on the wall. I was fascinated and became more and more absorbed. Under my hand suddenly appeared a farmer, standing by a barbed-wire fence. I sat down, got up and made some changes, sat down again and felt much better. This was much better than anything I'd ever done before. All day I worked on it. There were so many things which I couldn't make come out the way I wanted them to. I studied it, stretched my imagination to the utmost and was suddenly completely exhausted. I erased all of it and since then even the idea of drawing makes me sick.

I've been thinking about this strange experience a good deal. Right afterwards I had such a wonderful feeling of relief, a sense of having won a victory and such intense happiness that I felt quite numb. It seemed as if body and soul became separated, one in a wild and soaring freedom beyond the reach of the world, and the other doubled up in a horrible cramp which held it to the earth. I suddenly realized how terrifically strong I am (but perhaps I only tried to talk myself into this). When the body and soul rejoined forces, it was as if all the joys of the world were right there for me. But it was as with so many stimulants; when the effect wore off the reaction set in. I saw that my hands were shaking, something had given inside. It was as if there had been a short circuit in the roots of my heart which drained it of all strength. I was like a man hungry for pleasure and consumed by desire. But still I was calm and in better spirits than ever before.

Although I feel no fear, my heart beats faster every time someone stops outside my door. It's a physical reaction.

Strange, but I didn't feel any resentment or hatred at all. Something happened to my body, which is only the body of an adolescent, and it reacted as such, but my mind was elsewhere. It was aware of the small creatures who were busying themselves with my body, but it was in a world of its own and too engrossed to pay much attention to them.

I've learned something by being alone. It is as if I'd reached rock bottom in myself, which usually can't be seen for all the layers of egotism, conceit, love, and all the ups and downs of daily life. It is this which makes me feel as if I'd had a short circuit within me. When I'm with other people, their interests, their conversation, act as a balm, covering the rock bottom in myself with a warm compress. When I'm alone, it is as if layers of skin were being scraped away. Your mind is not at ease, you can't concentrate on reading, the spirit as well as the body must keep on pacing up and down. I suddenly understood what insanity must be, but I knew that this was like everything else which has happened to me, and in a couple of days I'll be myself again.

21 March, 1945
My dearest little love,

On Wednesday, February 21st, at midnight I was sent to Police Headquarters for questioning, and on Wednesday, the 28th, I was sent back to Vestre. On Thursday I was placed in solitary confinement and forbidden to write letters. I was only allowed to go to the toilet morning and night with a guard when there was no one in the corridors. My food was brought by the soldiers. I was happy to be alone in my cell.

I took off all my clothes and had a good wash and it gave me such a sense of freedom. That night I slept in a bed with sheets and a mattress.

I did some thinking and meditating, and the days passed very pleasantly. I had opened my window, and the sun was shining. I could smell spring in the air, the grass shooting out of the ground, the moist earth. I could hear the birds singing, and such a big streak of sunshine came in through the bars that I could sit on the bench and let it warm my face.

On Monday, March 5, I was transferred to Police Headquarters and put in Detention. On Wednesday they allowed me to receive my blanket.

Have been in the following cells: December 19, 1944 to February 2, 1945, in 252; from the same day at 8 o'clock, in 585 (dark cell); February 7 to 11, Froeslev. From February 12 to March 1 occupied the following cells in Vestre: 286, 284, 282, 276, 270. From March 1 to 5 in 586. Was then transferred to Police Headquarters: March 5 to 12, cell 50, March 12 to—? cell 37.

Twice I've been waiting in the cells of the Shell Building to be questioned so I think that I've been living a rather varied cell life. The cell I had when I sat in Detention was on the small side—6 feet, 3 inches by 4 feet—with a small bench and a table. I walked up and down—one and a half paces in each direction; twenty-four hours and all alike, only broken by the opening of the door when two slices of rye bread were handed to me. This was a real event. In the toilet they allowed me to wash, and it was wonderful. Then I paced up and down again, very much surprised that I didn't suffer. I thought of the days spent in solitary confinement and how rewarding they had been. I had the sun, the blue sky, and once in a while a little white cloud, and if I really made an effort I could see a plowed field, grass, people, and lots of other fascinating things. I could smell the earth and feel the coming of spring. It made me choke up inside and I felt very happy. All this had such a sound and soothing effect on my mind.

They say that the Shell Building was bombed yesterday and this upset me very much. Your school is so close by. Something could have happened to you, you might even have been killed, and here I sit writing to you not knowing if you're alive or if you will ever read this.

I've caught lice, but I hope that I've gotten rid of them again. I had an awful lot of bites, and the itching almost drove me mad. Today I examined my clothes, which haven't been off my back for three weeks since I sleep on the floor with only a blanket over me. There were masses of eggs and lice. But now I've washed myself and my clothes so I hope this is the end of it.

I'm kept going by one thought: that nothing is impossible no matter how black things look at the moment. There are millions of possibilities which can't be foreseen, and no situation exists which can't be completely changed in a moment.

27 March 1945

When I went up for questioning, or perhaps when I was already there, I said to myself all of a sudden, "If you could only come out in the woods with me as woodcutters, away from everything, even if only for a short time, a change would come about in you—perhaps not a permanent change because you are made of different material—but so that you would see and feel, for a little while at least, how profound life is and how rich is the world around you which you refuse to understand.

Vestre Prison German Section, Cell 411:
4 April 1945
My own little darling,

Today I was taken before the military tribunal and condemned to death. What a terrible blow this is for a little girl of twenty! I've been given permission to write this farewell letter, but what shall I write? How shall I formulate my swan song? Time is short and there is so much to say.

What is the final and most precious thing I can give you? What do I possess that I can leave you as a parting gift so that in spite of your loss you will smile and go on living and developing?

We sailed on a stormy sea, we met in the trusting way of playing children and we loved each other. We still love each other and always will, but one day a storm separated us. I went aground while you were washed up on shore, and you are going to continue living in a new world. I don't expect you to forget me. Why should you forget something so beautiful as that which existed between us? But you mustn't become a slave to this memory. You must keep on going with the same easy and graceful approach to life as before and twice as happy because on your way Life gave you one of its greatest gifts. Free yourself—let this greatest of joys be everything to you, let it shine brighter and clearer than anything else, but let it be only one of your most treasured memories. Don't let it blind you and keep you from seeing all the wonderful things life has in store for you. Don't be unhappy, my dearest one. You must mature and grow rich in inner resources. Do you understand this, my beloved?

You will live on and you will have other beautiful adventures, but promise me—this you owe to everything I have lived for—that never will the thought of me come between you and Life. Remember, I will continue to live in your heart, but the part of me which remains there should be sound and natural and mustn't take up too much room. Gradually as bigger and more important things appear, I shall glide into the background and be a tiny speck of the soil out of which your happiness and your development will keep on growing.

Now you are heartbroken and this is what is known as sorrow, but Hanne, look beyond this. All of us are going to die and it isn't for us to judge whether my going a little earlier is good or bad.

I keep on thinking about Socrates. Read him and you will find Plato expressing what I feel at this moment. My love for you is without bounds, but not more so now than before. It's not a love which causes me pain. This is the way it is, and I want you to understand it. There is something inside me alive and growing—an inspiration, a love—call it what you like; something which I still haven't been able to define. Now I'm going to die and I still don't know if I have started a little flame in another being, a flame which will survive me. But still, my mind is at rest because I've seen the richness and abundance of nature. No one takes notice if a few seeds are trampled under and die. When I see all the riches that still live on, why should I despair?

Lift up your head, my most precious love, and look! The sea is still blue, the sea which I loved and which has enveloped us both. Now you will live for the two of us. I am gone and what remains is not a memory which will make you into a woman like S., but mold you into a woman living and warm, mature and happy. This does not mean that you are to try to rise above sorrow, because then you will become rigid and assume a saintly attitude with regard to your faith in me and in yourself, and you will lose what I most loved in you—that you are first and last and always a woman.

Remember—and I swear this is true—that all sorrow gradually turns into happiness. But few are those who admit it when the time comes. They cloak themselves in mourning; habits makes them think that it is sorrow, and so they continue to cloak themselves in it. The truth is that after suffering comes maturity and after this maturity the fruits are gathered.

You see, Hanne, one day you will meet the man who will be your husband. The thought of me will flash through you, and you will perhaps deep down have a vague, uneasy feeling that you are betraying me or something in you which is pure and sacred. Lift up your head once more, Hanne, look straight into my eyes which are smiling at you and you will understand that the only way to betray me is by not completely following your natural instincts. When you see him, let your heart go out to meet him—not to drown your sorrow but because you truly love him. You will be very, very happy because you now have a base on which feelings still unknown to you will nurture.

Greet Nitte for me. I've thought of writing her but don't know if I'll have the time. I seem to feel as if I could do more for you because all that is life to me is now concentrated on you. I would like to breathe into you all the life that is in me, so that it can go on and as little as possible of it go to waste. This is the way I was made.

Yours, but not for always.

Vestre Prison German Section, Cell 411:
4 April 1945
Dearest Mother,

Today I went before the military tribunal together with Joergen, Niels and Ludwig. We were condemned to die. I know that you're strong and that you will be able to take this. But listen to me, Mother. It isn't enough that you are able to take it. You must also understand it. I'm not of importance and will soon be forgotten, but the ideas, the life, the inspiration which filled me will live on. You will find them everywhere—in the new green of spring, in people you will meet on your way, in a loving smile. Perhaps you will also find what was of value to me, you will love it and you won't forget me. I would have liked to grow and mature, but I will still live in your hearts and you will live on because you know that I am in front of you on the road and not behind, as you had perhaps thought at first. You know what has always been my greatest wish and what I thought I would become. Mother dear, come with me on my journey. Don't stop at the last stage of my life, but instead stop at some of the preceding ones and you may find something which will be of value to the girl I love and to you, Mother.

Colin Perry

ENGLAND ❦ 18 YEARS OLD

*A*n eighteen-year-old office boy living with his parents and brother Judd in a suburb of London when the blitz began, Colin Perry saw the war as an opportunity to launch a writing career. Fancying himself an eyewitness to history, he set out to record everything he possibly could in his journal with the hopes that one day it would be published.

Colin wrote so much that even though he kept his war diary only from March to November of 1940, there was still enough material to comprise a full-length book. Thirty-two years later, Colin's dream of publication became a reality when his diary was published as Boy in the Blitz by London publisher Leo Cooper Ltd., in 1972.

By no means content to limit himself to portraits of his home life, Colin recklessly ignored air raid warnings as he bicycled through the streets of London gathering news for his diary. He barged across police lines and refused to take shelter even though commanded to by the wardens. Binoculars in one hand and his notebook in the *other, Colin was ever at the ready to race his bicycle to the highest hill for close-up views of balloons, parachutists, and bombers.*

Proclaiming that he never felt fear during any of his exploits, Colin seemed impervious to the emotional impact of the war. He said he regarded it with "curiosity" and "indifference." However, after several months of nearly nightly bombings, he began to see that the war was a dreadful reality that was crushing the life out of his country and causing tremendous suffering for his friends and neighbors. When he was face to face with mangled bodies and death, Colin came to the conclusion that all the dogfights—and the sweat, toil, and blood Churchill had warned of—did not equal glory. "A new Perry," as he called himself, began to feel compassion for the suffering people of London.

In November of 1940, Colin left off writing his diary when he was accepted by the Merchant Marine. He signed on as ship's writer aboard H.M.T. Strathallan and sailed from England for "destination unknown."

After the war, Colin Perry became a certified public accountant, married, and had two children. He is still living in England. His diary is available from the author in a self-published paperback edition.

London: Monday, 17 June, 1940

France has capitulated. Britain is alone.

Is it better to die, if die we must, as an Empire and foremost world power, fighting to the last drop of our blood, or now, immediately, lay down arms and not hold our country and breed in lunacy of death for the sake of tradition? If our

Government realize the situation is hopeless, is it right that they should risk the appalling loss of life which must result if we pursue or struggle to end this Nazi tyranny? Condemn him to hell who is responsible for bringing Britain to the verge of her existence—Britain whom we love, and whom our ancestors placed into the leadership of the world.

12 July

Oh boy, oh boy, *Oh Boy!*

Just back from lunch and you can guess the reason for my jubilation. Or can you? Yep, you're right. It's the 'Girl in the ABC'—tra la lah la . . . I am full of the joys of Spring, tra lah.

We caught one another's eye . . . she looked, just dead straight ahead . . . at me (of course) and I—well I did the same as her. A glimmer of a smile flickered round her face.

There you are. The ice cracked slightly, ever so slight, and I can hardly wait until Monday lunch-time. We each appreciated the other's amusement, of that I am sure. Well now I do know, come hither go thither, I am resolved to speak to her—sooner, or later.

It was a tremendous sensation—her smile. It somehow warmed 'the cockles of my English heart,' and I hope I warmed hers, bless her heart. Tra lah lah . . .

17 July

Tonight we in our proud Island prepare ourselves for the word that the invader has commenced his attack. The air-raid wardens have passed information round that the Military at Tolworth will tonight throw up a smoke-screen, which will spread and envelop the whole Metropolis, blot out vital objectives, and generally throw invading hordes into confusion. At any moment—now, as I write this—the attack may commence. We are waiting with calm fortitude for the inevitable. Air-raids, massed murder, total devastation of beautiful buildings: the unknown: and gas, too, maybe, to poison our food and pollute our water. All these evil possibilities confront the people of England, now. We have witnessed countries torn to shreds by this Moloch of our age. We, alone, await his onslaught, calm, confident, determined.

Despite all this, which but a year ago would have sounded fantastic, my ordinary life continues. And today it is not the war which occupies the whole of my inner mind, but 'the Girl in the ABC.' I am callous about the war business. Certainly not in any degree scared or anxious. I am intensely interested. *Britain at Bay*, the film I have just seen, makes me want to join the army tomorrow. It showed our fair Kentish fields, the pleasant Surrey woodlands, the broad moors of Devon and Cornwall to the wild bracken of Scotland; from the smelly City to the remotest village hamlet—this is the 'front-line'; this is where we stand to defend our right with all our might. Somehow it is magnificent and terrible in one.

15 August (evening)

Overhead a hum of aircraft became audible, and I looked upwards into the slowly setting sun thinking to see a 'Security Patrol'; then I saw three whirling 'planes, and Alan yelled, 'Look! see them, it's a German!' and by God it was. I tore hell for leather to the top of our block of flats, and standing on the window-sill of the hall-landing I looked out over Surrey. Yes, thunder alive, there over Croydon were a pack of 'planes, so tiny and practically invisible in the haze,

and—by God! the Hun was bombing Croydon Airport. I
yelled down to Mother, roused the Court, 'Look, Croydon's
being dive-bombed' and I rushed to commandeer my excel-
lent vantage point. Machine-guns rattled over the still air,
and there, only a few miles away bombs commenced to drop.
At last, the war was here! At last I was seeing some excitement. Anti-aircraft guns threw a dark ring around the darting
'planes, Spitfires and Hurricanes roared to battle. A terrific
cloud of smoke ascended from the town; two more fires,
obviously slight, rose on the wind. Boy this was IT!

I munched an apple and went out armed with my enviable
story. I didn't get far though, for a whine, fluctuating, grew
from afar to a sudden deafening crescendo. Only the air-raid
sirens. Hell, they were a bit behind time, the damn raid was
over. Least I was convinced it was, and it happened I was
proved right. Still people were not to know that, and all the
milling throngs calmly drifted to their nearest shelter. The
wail died away, and the roads, practically deserted, made
way for a police car speeding along the Upper Tooting Road
at something like 80 mph complete with a whirring, piercing
siren. Just like G-men on the films, I thought. The wardens
efficiently took up their action stations, and I, well I still sat
munching my apple on the steps, thinking well at last a bit
of excitement had hit the everyday routine. My one regret
was I had to be an onlooker; boy, if only I had been in one
of those Spitfires—oh Hell! those 'planes got me; I must be
a pilot!

Well, I hardly imagined that my journal would ever bear
such an interesting story. I would mention that I was absolutely the first person in the whole of our district to spot the
raiders and definitely the first by far to witness the actual

bombardment. Naturally, all the papers will be hot on the trail. By God why on earth didn't I phone to the *Express* an eye witness view of the bombing? Hells bells I might have got my name in the paper. Ah, well, it's too late now.

Sunday, 18 August

We had just settled down to a delightful dinner—chicken, marrow, peas, new potatoes and baked potatoes, stuffing and gravy, when the air-raid sirens started. Dad and Alan both took their dinners down the shelter. I, only dressed in pants and singlet, took some four minutes to dress, and hugging my brief case I too toddled off down. Aircraft were roaring overhead, and I didn't have time to survey the scene. However, having deposited my belongings safely below ground, I came up to the surface. I went across to No. 1 block to the top floor, and sure enough Croydon once again was in smoke. A big fire also showed in the Wimbledon direction. Putney too appeared to have been hit, but it may have been a factory chimney. As I was looking out I heard a terrific roar approaching, and being from the north I could not see anything from where I stood, so I ran into the court, to the shelter, where everyone was busily scanning the sky. Then I shouted—first again—some 30 or 40 enemy bombers, accompanied by fighters, were sweeping in a direct line for Croydon. They were indeed very near us. It presented an amazing spectacle, like a swarm of bees surrounding their queen; fascinating, most certainly. A puff of smoke and the sound of a gun signalled our retreat down the shelter. I fancied I heard the whine of dive-bombers, most assuredly we heard the guns and crunch of falling bombs. I imagined this was the real commencement of hostilities against the British Isles.

After a few moments I again came up; I wanted to stay in the flat all the time, but for the sake of my parents I went down. Davis tried to keep me down, but my answer to him, if he tries again, is that I am eighteen years of age, old enough for military service and to fight and die for my country. Fellows only a year my senior are up there shooting the raiders down, and within a year I to hope to be there. That is good enough for him. I popped indoors and finished off my dinner, and went once again to the top floor, but the smoke had cleared, and nothing was to be seen. Evidently not a great deal of really substantial damage had been done. The 'all clear' sounded soon after, and we went back to cold chicken. Damn, the only time for months we have had a chicken and then the Nazis have to spoil it.

23 August

I was awakened in the early hours of the 23rd by the pom-pom-pom-pom of anti-aircraft fire. I lay as if in a far-off existence, snuggling down in my bed; half-consciously I remember thinking 'I suppose the sirens will go soon' and they did within the next minute. Instantly my drowsy brain cleared, and I recalled with clarity that it was the 23rd, and *my* prophesied date for invasion seemed quite plausible. The moon was magnificent, silvery and shimmering, and looking about me I saw the dark, sharp contrast of the houses of London. As the sirens rose and fell, I thought how queer, how unreal, how like a vivid novel portraying in wild, fantastic form events to come it all was. And as I watched the houses drain themselves of people, like water going down a sink, and as the dull, vibrating noise of 'planes became audible in the distance I knew it was real. In this perspective I saw how cheap, how frail our life is. Just a puff, and a life, perhaps a great man or an ordinary person who liked his pint of beer and his pipe, was snuffed out, for ever, just like that. And I wondered exceedingly about that 'ever.' The gunfire had ceased now, and it was cold outside, so I went down into the warm, sticky atmosphere of the shelter. It was one constant hub of noise, of old women and squeaking babies, and men in their ridiculously long, overstriped pyjamas. Somehow I fitted myself in but only for a few minutes. I was back again with Dad indoors making tea when the 'all clear' went about 4 am.

Wednesday, 28 August (night)

I cannot say how tired I am. I have never known how much sleep means. Since the early hours of Friday morning the Nazi bombers have been over continuously, in consequence we have had warning after warning. It is now 9.45 pm—the warning went at 9 sharp. I will indulge in a brief resumé of the whole raid.

During the first few warnings on Friday and Saturday everyone was alert, prepared. Prepared for intensive bombing raids. We took cover. I only did so when circumstances forced me—i.e. in the office where it is compulsory to evacuate to the basement. At home, however, I always went to the top floor to view the south. But during the last few nights single German raiders have been systematically crossing the Metropolitan area. These lone raiders have occasionally dropped bombs, deliberately on the suburban districts, with the result that now every time a raider is reported the sirens have to be sounded. It is obvious that these raiders are only sent to affect our nerves, and try to shake our morale. They are termed in the Press as 'nuisance' raiders, and indeed that is the most fitting title for them. It is these that are responsible for keeping all Londoners awake and in their shelters for hours every night.

I am wondering, not anxiously, just how we intend counteracting these 'nuisance' raiders, for sleep is imperative and it looks as though we are to have another sleepless night. I am (another German—two came over then and I can still hear their drone dying over London) dark-eyed, have a terrible head, and long for Hell's own blizzard which would keep these damn infernal droning machines away for a night.

Monday, 2 September

There is nothing glamorous about this war. It is not a war. It's a mass butchery. In the olden days the civilian population was far removed from the scene of battle, they were respected by both sides. Now the Germans think fit to rain down their loads of death on harmless, defenceless civilians. Thank God Churchill is firm enough to refrain from ordering a retaliation bombing upon the German civilians. I fear I shouldn't be.

I suppose one day the sirens will cease to wail—but I cannot imagine it. It was wonderful coming home in the tube tonight during the raid and reading the *Standard*'s most uplifting leader. 'London' it was entitled. I looked at the people around me as I read it—yes, they would uphold, with their smiling faces, the future of mankind.

Week-end: 7–8 September

This is the most momentous week-end. Yesterday I lived my most momentous day—so far.

I set out on my old bike yesterday afternoon and pedalled through Carshalton, Burgh Heath, and on to Collie Hill—that great viewpoint overlooking all Surrey and Sussex to the South Coast.

I managed to secure a grandstand post on the small foot-bridge over the main road, and from here I observed for half-an-hour the antics of our fighters—but there were no Jerries. I tired of this, and mounting my bike cycled along the deserted roads, past the Home Guards and their barriers, and along the country lane in the direction of Chipstead. All along this lovely lane, alive with the beauty of summer, every field seemed to have its squadron of British fighters high above it. I have never seen so many planes. The sky was full of these 'Birds of Freedom.' Here and there people on foot, in cars, on bikes, had deposited themselves under the screen of trees, away from the eyes of Messerschmitts. One and all remember the Nazis' machine-gunning zest. I continued, binoculars at the ready. An hour after the warning found me at the top of Chipstead Hill, lying full length in the thick grass, binoculars glued to my eyes, watching the many planes, and their landing on and off at a field some miles away. Suddenly I thought to make Croydon, and remembered a marvellous viewpoint overlooking the 'drome from a hilltop some miles distant. I got every ounce of speed from the old bike, and simply flew down Chipstead Hill. I kept skidding to a standstill every so often and I picked out fresh tangles of aircraft, but they were always British. I had just passed the bottom of the deep valley between Chipstead and Woodmansterne when from a hole in the ground an air-raid warden told me to take cover. I conveniently ignored him, and bent hard on my pedals to climb the very steep hill. I was no more than half way up, and already overlooking the whole of the district south of Croydon, when masses of planes roared above me. British I thought, and concentrated on climbing the hill—one solitary figure on an expanse of road. Suddenly to my astonished ears the thud, the crunch of bombs came ever nearer. I looked out over the country— but pressed more eagerly to get to the top of the hill, from where I knew a better view was obtainable. I had no chance though to progress more than three-quarters of the distance. Pandemonium broke loose right above me. I jumped off my bike and looked up. It was the most amazing, impressive, riveting sight. Directly above me were literally hundreds of planes, Germans! The sky was full of them. Bombers hemmed in with fighters, like bees around their queen, like destroyers round the battleship, so came Jerry. My ears were deafened by bombs, machine-gun fire, the colossal inferno of machine after machine zooming in the blue sky. As I watched, spell-bound, too impressed to use my glasses, a voice bellowed out 'Take Cover' and I realized then that it was the only sane thing to do. I jumped under a large and spreading oak, but no sooner was I under its protecting leaves than I realized the ridiculousness of my cover, and anyhow I could not control my burning desire to see what was going on, and as the noise became yet more intense I rushed out—twisting, twirling, spinning, zooming, the universe was alive with lean, silver shapes. It came home to me that in all probability it was the greatest massed raid the country had ever known, and I guessed they would be after Croydon. I remembered my viewpoint for the airport was only another mile away, so under that cloud of death I cycled furiously—but had got no more than into the village of Woodmansterne when I was compelled to dismount. Looking up—squadron after squadron of Spitfires and Hurricanes tore out of the blue, one by one they tore the Nazi formations into shreds. 'Planes scattered left and right, and the terrible battle came lower. As I stood on the neat grass verge of the row of suburban houses, transfixed, I saw one fighter (I very much fear ours) rush earthwards. With ever increasing speed it fell, silently, to its last resting ground, amongst the green of Surrey. I had no time to dwell upon the fate of that man—I could not look up—I just stood, and machine after machine rushed frantically, screaming, it seemed, at me. I had no cover, I held my glasses; I don't know what I felt, but I was proving my theory—that in danger one knows no fear, only a supreme feeling, indescribable. I would not disown those minutes for Life itself.

9 September: 3.30 pm

THE CITY OF LONDON

I look out of my window, down on Lothbury, across to the Bank of England. I see the beginning of Moorgate, Princes Street, and Gresham Street and Old Jewry. I look up into the sky—dull, cloudy, grey; I listen; the noise which is echoing in my ears is of a strange origin; it is banging and hammering, tinkling and squeaking. Lorries pass under my window laden with timber, cars stream by into Moorgate, great vans and powerful motor-cycles. Buses grate their gears, cars vomit huge clouds of exhaust. People surge through the streets, hurrying, dragging great parcels, gas-masks strapped round their bodies; this is London today—a London industrious, dutiful, a City of calm, of confidence, a City licking its hideous wounds in the lull of the storm, a storm of machines which fly through the air with the buzz of the bee, the sting of the wasp. They come by night, they come by day. They rain death upon the citizens of this, the greatest, most learned, foremost City of the World, the Civilized World!

How great an irony that strikes. Civilized indeed. Nightly London buries its head into the ground, turns out its lights, and sticks out its claws. Its long, tapering, fingers of light prick the universe, probe the darkness. They search for the birds of prey, the hawks of massacre who frequent our skies these September nights. The bark, the spit of her lungs echo across the starlit heavens and, turning yellow, orange, they flicker and dance and pierce the armour of those birds. And as the morning comes, as the people set forth into the light of another day, they survey the sting of the hawks, weigh up the damage showered upon their great, free City, note with hardened brow the bloody mess which once was their fellow man; this, these thoughts and sights are stored, locked away in their deepest cell, until, one day, in God's good time, they may without mercy exact from the nests of the prowlers of the night full and lasting revenge and fulfil that old and wisened proverb: 'An eye for an eye, a tooth for a tooth, a life for a life.'

So life goes on. As the clatter, the pounding of the labourer's tool becomes more incessant, I take leave of my meditation, I return once more into that which is London, Freedom, and I sigh, and breathe in the smoke, the smell of petrol fumes; I look at St Paul's and the figure of Justice, and I see myself looking back upon these long, dark, unreal days, when all the world seems mad, and lustful and sinful. I look back from a garden green, the sweet fragrance of red roses,

roses of a New England, and I hear different noises—the sound of children playing, so gay and happy, and the yap of a spaniel and the meow of a kitten, and as I sit there, so content, so utterly happy, I find I hold the hand of a woman, a very beautiful, good and keen woman, and I see the son of my blood, and hers, set forth upon a clean, straight trail, and he, righteous, shall make his mark upon the world until he is acclaimed by mankind as the advocator of a free and noble world, in which all mankind lives and works in peace.

But I have memories ...

10 September Later:

THE HEART OF A GREAT NATION

It is 1.10 pm on Tuesday, 10 September, 1940. I am sitting in my office on the second floor of the Royal Bank of Canada building in Lothbury. An air-raid siren sounded ten minutes ago. As I write under a grey sky, under a pall of 'acidy' smoke, within a few seconds' walk of wrecked and burning buildings, I take heart from the news I am to record.

I left the office this lunch hour at 12 precisely. I walked to the corner of King Street and Cheapside. My ABC was closed. Cheapside was a mass of charred debris; of firemen on ladders, hoses pouring jets of water into the charred and burning remains of elegant buildings of yesterday. Fire units, engines, troops in steel helmets move in the dense, choking clouds of smoke. Until the police move me along I stay and watch. The smoke rose high above St Paul's, obliterated the dome for minutes on end. Cheapside, in the heart of London, was stabbed. I moved along ...

I saw a crowd, milling, cheering, near the Mansion House

Station. More people rushed to the spot ... I tore headfirst. What a crowd. Throbbing with anticipation, I fought my way through, jumped a police barrier, and heading off the crowd found the core of the excitement. Winston Churchill! I cheered, I yelled. I fought harder, and finally established myself in between Winston and his escort of the Commissioner of Police and an Officer of the Army. The crowd pressed on either side, but whether they mistook me for one of the party or not I cannot say; the fact remains I kept next to Churchill the whole route from the Mansion House Station to the Bank. I had my photograph taken countless times, and once had my hand on Churchill's coat. He looked invincible, which he is. Tough, bulldogged, piercing. His hair was wispy, wiry, tinted gingery. As he made his way through the smoke, through the City workers all crying 'Good old Winston'— 'Give 'em socks'—'Good Luck'—and the culminating cry of 'Are we downhearted?' to the heaven-rising response of 'Nooooooo' which echoed round the City, round the world indeed, and warmed the 'cockles of our British hearts' and of all the free men in the world. It was magnificent, tremulous, stirring, dramatic. Amongst the 'ashes of London' stepped the man, his people, acclaimed, assured, and fulfilling the declaration that we will fight in the streets, in the fields, on the seas, in the air—that we would rather see London in ashes, but free and ours, than standing under the will of Hitler.

Churchill bought a flag outside the broken-windowed Mansion House, and I squeezed myself into the 'photo. He mounted the Mansion House steps and shook hands, presumably with the Lord Mayor; the people stood cheering themselves hoarse below, and we all stuck our thumbs up

and yelled louder than ever for the Press photographers—
and I guess I am in every one of their pictures. Next, Winston
crossed to the bomb crater outside the Bank of England, and
threw his cigar down upon the notice 'No Smoking—Danger
Escaping Gas.' I could easily have retrieved the butt, but I
had no desire to acquire such a souvenir—the sight, the
memory is sufficient, and, I hope, the pictures. Winston stood
on the bomb crater, waved, took off his bowlerish hat (how
typical of the Churchill of the Sidney Street siege), sported his
walking-stick, dug his left hand deep in his overcoat pocket.
Approaching once again the crowds a young boy dashed up
with an autograph album—Churchill signed. As he did so I
had my hand on his sleeve, indeed I could not help myself,
the crowd's pressure and enthusiasm was so terrific. Into his
car and away—my hat, I certainly do seem to wangle my
way into things—right by his side throughout his tour, the
records of which will find space in every future book of
history.

Tuesday, 24 September

Dad and I are on our own this week, Mother and Alan
being in St Alban's. I am more or less in the same position
as over a year ago when my people went to Cornwall and I
kept house for ten days. Yes siree, I am the housekeeper.
What fun!

Arriving home last night I set to work and made my tea,
then swept up the rooms, tidied all up, washed up the crocks,
tidied dirty corners. The sirens went at about 7.50 signifying
the nightly air-raid. But I stayed in as I always do and got
on with the housework. I cleaned out Joey, our canary, and
fed the goldfish. I washed handkerchiefs and pyjamas and

my favourite white shirt. As I washed these articles guns were howling all around me, and just as I had put the kettle on for my cocoa three bombs screamed down, shook the building which swayed distinctly, and blew up. German bombers roared overhead, searchlights lit the sky. Oh boy— I wonder what Lebkicher or even Kate would have said if they could have seen me—in my dirty old flannels, rolled-up blue open-neck shirt, hair ruffled, and washing clothes amongst those eggs of whistling death. I hung the clothes to dry in the bathroom, and as it is not blacked out I had to grope my way to hang the clothes, and my path was lit by constant gun flashes, flaming onions and bursting shells. Phew. But I must say I did enjoy myself, and I am extremely fond of housework, and if ever I get married, then my wife'll have to work like a Trojan and clean every nook and cranny in the place, for I cannot bear untidiness. Anyhow the German bombers did great damage last night, and over seven bombs were dropped in our immediate vicinity, and I hear Wandsworth Common Station has been hit and busted up.

This morning I have washed up, cooked breakfast—eggs and fried bread—washed up, washed kitchen floor, and bathroom, made beds, tidied up in general, washed walls in bathroom and again put things in ship-shape order. Ironed (I love ironing) handkerchiefs.

25 September

Last night and in the early hours of this morning we experienced our worst aerial bombardment. We anticipated this in view of the RAF's extensive four-hour raid on Berlin the other day.

The alarm was given early, and until 10.30 we had a great

deal of gunfire and bombs, in which period some fell exceedingly close. After 10.30 we had a comparative quiet period
and Dad and I retired to bed. I was awakened by Dad calling
at me to go in the hall at a quarter-to-one this morning.
Above, an enormous number of enemy planes were roaring;
our guns spoke I don't know how many times to the second.
Great powerful guns just near us. Suddenly there came a
whistle, shrill, followed by another nearer, yet a third, this
time seemingly on top of us. Bombs! As they thudded down
whistling, and then sudden silence, another salvo descended,
and the fourth fell the other side of our flat, so did a fifth
and sixth. In other words a stick of bombs had straddled our
building. Well, we got back into bed, and without exaggera-
tion it was undoubtedly our busiest night. I was awakened
almost hourly, and lay listening to the roar of jockeying
planes, the scream of bombs, and the terrific noise of our
guns which vibrated in my ears. I looked out—fires, searchlights, shells—a pandemonium.

Looking back this morning I am elated. Yes, elated. Last
night Wandsworth had its very worst raid. History will
prove that the area in which we live was the most frequently
bombed of all London, including the East End. Every other
area at least has its off and on nights, but we—well, every
night is an on. (I write this during a raid. The alert was
given ten minutes ago, but now the whistles telling of the
immediate presence of hostile aircraft have warned all London to take cover. But my journal comes first. London doesn't
all take cover—and I am not in the least degree perturbed,
merely curious, indifferent.)

9 October

What is the prospect of Youth to-day? Upon the distant horizon there is no break in the war clouds, no dawn of respite from death. Youth can only see wars and sorrow, destruction and annihilation. Their ideals they see already cast down, trampled upon. There is no incentive to urge them to study for the higher extremes. Guns, bombs, planes are imprinted in our minds.

Myself, 18: I am able to see all the tangles and perplexities. I know that my whole life will be altered utterly, that my dreams of youth will not materialize as I had planned. I no longer see my path with my company, progressive, ambitious, but I see a void to which I drift the nearer. I know that soon I shall be in the fighting services, and am glad. But my worry is that perhaps my people will have to remain in the battle of London, and I feel confused, and cannot concentrate. It is one thing to go to war, and another to have the war come to you and yours.

Monday, 14 October

I look around me as I write: at the beer bottles, the match boxes, the newspapers and pictures, the radio, goldfish and canary—they are all symbols so secure which make bombing seem so utterly fantastic. Yet a German bomber roared overhead and I knew at any instant death and rubble may mark this spot. I hate to see canaries and goldfish; it brings home to me the futility of their lives, so completely devoid of anything but isolation. They cannot attain any end. It would drive me mad.

Near midnight there was an enormous red glow; it lit the whole of London. It was ten times brighter than the brightest summer's day. Then a series of explosions, more and still more, and the redness made us wonder. It was the new bomb I spoke of yesterday. A basket full of splitting death. Very near too. London is grotesque, insane. I cannot describe it— it's all too enveloping. Yet I live here in this city of death, of shocking reality and see my people's homes and persons killed and razed to the ground. I know any moment my turn may come. Yet, paradoxically, I know it won't. I know that despite the blood, the death, the absurdity of this life I shall survive. And I feel not one atom of fear or perturbance as I contemplate my future. Last night I slept as usual.

HELL

Sunday night, the 13th, saw one of the heaviest raids of the war upon South London. Balham, the suburb of ordinary people, was again bombed. One bomb has fallen in the centre of the High Road (obviously aimed for the railway close by) and I do not know whether the bus which I saw sunk in the crater this morning drove into it or whether it was blown there. Whatever, only a few inches of the double-decker is peeping above the roadway.

This bomb I think penetrated to the steel-encased Tube below the ground, and I hear too that something, by a million to one chance, went down the ventilator shaft of the Underground Station. The water main was burst and the flood rolled down the tunnels, right up and down the line, and the thousands of refugees were plunged into darkness, water. They stood, trapped, struggling, panicking in the rising black invisible waters. They had gone to the tubes for safety, instead they found worse than bombs, they found the unknown, terror. Women and children, small babes in arms, locked beneath the ground. I can only visualize their feelings, I can only write how it has been told to me, but it must have been Hell. On top of this there came a cloud of gas. People not killed outright were suffocated, the rest drowned, drowned like rats in a cage.

GOD

I have only heard this from a friend, and I can therefore only say that I believe it to be true.

A boy went to bed during the nightly raid. He awoke suddenly in the middle of the night to find no walls surrounded him, no staircase by which he could walk downstairs. Instead his bed was open to the four winds, resting on a floor held together only by girders. A bomb had struck his home and opened it completely, yet he lay in his bed, unharmed.

16 October

To-day I stand on the crossroads of my life. I can remain as I am, secure as these days will allow, or go forth into the unknown, ahead into the course of my life.

Amidst this City, wrecked by air-raids, I have to choose my destiny. My roads are varied, wide and narrow; one is bumpy, stoney, the other broad and smooth. At the end of one of them lies peace and happiness, supreme content, the other leads to an awful abyss; I can not see whether it be life or death. But I am done with the smooth. I want the uncertain, because without struggle I shall never be content. But here I will summarize the choice of my roads.

I can stay at this desk, with my firm when they move. Can enjoy luxury, change and new faces. I can walk in the Oxfordshire countryside for the office is moving away from this City. I can leave all the bombs and the guns, the 'planes and all this death and destruction. My bank book, too, can swell with ease and my aim of wealth be achieved. And after a while I can see my way to money, security and a foreign land. But I hate the thought of leaving my City in her hour of peril and need. I have lived in her so long, been bored with her ways, that if I should go when at last she has changed I feel that I should be running away. And, therefore, I shall not quit.

Yet I cannot stay so very long for despite it all I've had my fill, and conquered all and every fear, and I have once more become impatient with all this routine. The Merchant Navy is a very tough job, but one I cannot hope to see as much different from home; for these nightly bombs offer nothing worse than a torpedo out in the middle of sea. By doing so I can fulfil my ambition, of travelling around this world, in insecurity, by dint of slogging, roughing it, that is the trail I cleave.

But I do want to feel the speed of an aeroplane. I want to fly, and shoot the Nazi eagles. I want to be a pilot in the RAF.

Yet I must make a name for myself if I do want to write a book and write of all my childhood, of high ambitions, frustrated hopes, and all my enigma of thought. I want to lead this very world unto a better way of life, and point out all our futile ways and make a name for the very brave.

18 October

I SWEAR

Churchill promised us 'blood, sweat and toil'—how true he was. I have already sampled sweat and toil. Last night I sampled blood.

Just gone 8 last evening, Dad, Miller, Judd and myself were sitting in the dining room, comfortable in front of a roaring fire. I had just finished sweeping out the rooms and washing up my dinner things, and was just about to settle myself in *The Distant Drum*, a novel. Dad and the others were debating a Holmbury Court Register, to be filled in nightly showing which tenants were down in the shelter and who remained in their flats. This was to be handed to G.65 at midnight, thus in event of a bomb the rescue parties would know where to commence digging. As this procedure was going on a German bomber growled overhead. Off-handishly I listened, subconsciously, as one always does. I started to read my novel. He, that Jerry, had gone, I thought. Suddenly there was a roar like an express train, a hurtling, a tearing, all-powerful, overwhelming rush. Together we sprang to our feet. We got no further. The earth seemed to split into a thousand fragments. A wrenching jar I thought signified the splitting of our outside wall. The subsiding rush of materials took, it seemed, all off the back. We reached the hall. We all thought the bomb had fallen just a few yards outside the back, in Scotia's scrapyard. I quickly but calmly donned my suitcoat, put my keys in my pocket and my wallet in my inside pocket. I did this groping in the dark for I saw at a glance our blackout was no more. Strangely I found myself contemplating all this with a very aloof mind, almost of indifference, and I quietly smiled to myself; I was very unimpressed and for all the world it appeared to me as though this bomb was a normal occurrence. Ninety-nine people out of a hundred would, and did, complain of a turning of the stomach; not so me. Yet I knew then that death had nearly come to us. Outside there was a stifling, forbidding atmosphere. I stumbled over two masses of debris, clattered over piles of glass. The moon shone wanly upon this uncanny nightmare. Women in the hall were dizzy. I rushed outside in the front. I saw at once all the windows of the flats had been blasted open or out. This I pointed out to Dad and Miller who together went down to the shelter, which since the explosion had rapidly filled, and told all the tenants to be extremely careful when they went into their flats in view of the torn down blackout. I meanwhile pelted headlong under a barrage of bursting shells along the Upper Tooting Road, past shopkeepers resignedly clearing up their smashed shop fronts, up Beechcroft and so into Fishponds Road, which as the crow flies lies not fifty yards at the back of us. It was a turmoil of rushing, calm, tin-hatted wardens. Two demolition squads and rescue parties roared up. I counted ten ambulances. I quickly entered into the centre of the crowd, a crowd only of nurses, wardens, firemen. And there, amidst the dark suburban street, standing on charred debris of every description, I found a new Perry. I confronted war in its most brutal savagery, I beheld blood, wounded, dying. I stood transfixed. My stomach did not turn, but from afar, yet so intimately, I found my brain dully registering sights of gore; I found I stood by the side of a little boy, his head a cake of blood, his arms—I knew not where they were. A small, plump, efficient voluntary nurse put her arms round him. He cried, every so often, very sobbingly for his Mummy. His Mummy was not to be seen. Quietly the nurse fingered his wounds—in a concise, firm, business-like voice, as if she was talking to a Mothers' meeting, 'Take him away immediately. Hospital case,' and turned her attention to the next. That nurse was in complete charge, she swayed her audience.

The little boy, head wrapped in towels, was gently laid upon a stretcher, passed softly along inside the waiting ambulance, still sobbing, though fainter, for his dear Mummy. I turned from that pathetic, heart-rending scene. I was oblivious of the falling shrapnel, of the clamouring guns, of the German bombers still roaring overhead. I heard from afar the wardens tell me to get under cover, for I was the only one without a steel helmet. Yet somehow that seemed very silly and petty to me then. I moved under the shielded light of a warden's torch; so shielded for we knew instinctively that the bombers might at any moment rain fresh death upon us. I saw through the waning moon the wrecked dwelling-houses, saw a warden rush headlong up the stairs of one of the doomed houses. I moved nearer to death—sitting on a chair, sobbing, convulsing, making distant moans, was a stout old lady; I judged that by her red and yellow spotted dress. By her side stood a quiet and silent girl, holding her arm, as if the contact would assure this wounded, bloody carcase that she was in the hands of God. Her face I could not see. It was covered with a huge piece of cloth, slitted for the nose to breathe. Underneath seeped streams of blood, and as I watched the blood clotted itself into little mounds. I shut my eyes tight for one instant. I wanted to shriek defiance at those bombers prowling even now above our heads. Then, as suddenly, this passion left me. I felt weak, impotent at the sight. My mind flashed back—if only—but I knew no first-aid, and I had never before so much wanted to be a doctor. The wardens formed a protective barrier around this slowly heaving woman, and under the light of a torch I saw her legs, cut and bleeding. A two-inch-long red mark signified where a piece of metal had embedded itself into her leg. They lifted her skirts—I did not look. I walked across to a young, it seemed, and slim woman. She was sitting so patiently on a chair, drinking water. I saw only the back of her head—it was enough. Blood, blood, blood, it oozed from her scalp, formed cakes on her skin. Oh God ... I breathed a soft prayer. All this while I had bit hard upon my pen which I had been holding in my hand, and after I had put it into my pocket I could not find it, and next to those wounded, smashed bodies I felt in all my pockets and in my wallet. I found my pen ... I wondered how I could trouble about such a trifle when around me lives were being fought for. I turned, I spoke to Mr Humphreys the post warden of G.65, now in supreme command. He asked me to stand by ready to take a message after I had volunteered my service. I was amazed at his efficiency: I admire the man. Some minutes later I ran back along the soft moonlit road, soft due to the mist which hung on the evening, as if a cloak to hide this wounded City. I went up to the flat, and surveyed the damage. But firstly I stood and said a prayer, to ask God to relieve their suffering and to give us strength to fight this war. I then looked at the photograph of Binnie, then at my own—it dawned upon me that death had struck just fifty yards away, in a straight line with our flat, the other side of Scotia's—that's how near. War had come to Tooting, to Holmbury Court, to me. War? nay murder, worse. Just a second later or a second earlier and that bomb would have struck at me, and I saw those blood-caked people ... I thanked God, and wondered if I had deserved to have been spared. After all, was I so good and righteous as those people across the way? They were an ordinary family, probably never been out of London in their lives; they had been no doubt just happily, as present conditions would allow, eating their supper, thinking the war very remote from them—and then, their lives were cut, they were victims of Hitler's massacre. I SWEAR that I'll revenge them, I swear I will! I will not be a member of a bomber crew—never! If I thought for one moment I was a cog in bringing about such terrible tragedy I would rather be shot. My job is clear. I will be a fighter pilot, and I will shoot mercilessly the bloody Hun from out of the skies. I will fire callously at their bombers' crews, I will know no pity. I will blast these murderers, assassins, devils of all that is evil from out of the skies. May God grant me strength. For I have experienced the horror of war, the blood which has to be paid. If they had been soldiers—different. But women, children, my breed—I will not rest until I have fulfilled my vow.

The Unknown Brother and Sister of Lodz Ghetto

POLAND ∞ UNKNOWN AGE AND

12 YEARS OLD

*I*t is likely that many more children wrote about their *suffering at the hands of the Nazis than we will ever know. With little to do, and their playmates and family members taken from them, how better to comfort themselves than to write about what they were going through. Sadly, although hundreds of children may have written them, few diaries survived the bombings, the fires, and the Nazi pillaging and made their way into the hands of future generations.*

In honor of the children who wrote but whose work has been lost forever, this anthology concludes with the diaries of a brother and a sister whose names, like so many child diarists', will remain unknown.

Orphaned by the Nazis, the children lived in the Lodz

Ghetto in Poland, where they were forced into slave labor. The little girl was twelve years old when she began her diary in July of 1944, several weeks after her older brother started his. The little girl's diary itself was never found, but her brother copied the first two entries of it into his own diary, which is reproduced here.

Amazingly, the boy wrote in four different languages, all scrawled into the margins of an old French novel, presumably because he did not have access to any other paper.

After the war was over, a man named Avraham Benkel, who had miraculously survived Auschwitz, returned to his home in the Lodz Ghetto, where he and his murdered family had lived. His and all surrounding houses had been systematically plundered by vandals looking for "Jewish treasure." In the house next door to his, he found that only one thing had been left behind—a tattered copy of an old French novel in which he discovered the boy's diary written in the margins.

There were no clues about who the boy was, but Avraham Benkel treasured his writing and took it with him when he moved to Israel in 1949. There, he turned it over to the historical archives of Yad Vashem, the Jewish Remembrance Authority in Jerusalem, where it remains today in a locked vault as a memorial to the unknown children of the Holocaust.

The following entries from the children's diaries were published in Yad Vashem News in 1970.

Unknown Girl
(AS COPIED INTO HER BROTHER'S DIARY)

July 11, 1944

Many a time in the past I began to write my memoirs, but by unforeseen circumstances, I was prevented from putting this mind-easing and soul comforting practice into reality, to begin [to write] of those days when cares and sufferings were unknown to me. I must look back to those bygone days, for my today is quite dissimilar to those which went away.

> Childhood, dear days,
> Alas, so few they were!
> That dimly only I remember them.
> It is only in my dreams that I'm
> Allowed to imagine days bygone.
> Short indeed is human happiness
> In this world of ours!

Unknown Boy

May 5, 1944

I committed this week an act which is best able to illustrate to what degree of dehumanization we have been reduced. Namely, I finished up my loaf of bread at a space of three days, that is to say on Sunday, so I had to wait till the next Saturday for a new one. [The ration was about 33 ounces of bread a week.] I was terribly hungry. I had a prospect of living only from the ressort soups [the soup ladled out to forced laborers] which consist of three little potato pieces and two decagrams [three-quarters of an ounce] of flower [sic]. I was lying on Monday morning quite dejectedly in my bed and there was the half loaf of bread of my darling sister.... I could not resist the temptation and ate it up totally.... I was overcome by a terrible remorse of conscience and by a still greater care for what my little one would eat for the next five days. I felt a miserably helpless criminal.... I have told people that it was stolen by a supposed reckless and pitiless thief and, for keeping up appearance, I have to utter curses and condemnations on the imaginary thief: "I would hang him with my own hands had I come across him."

[Several days later]

After my fantasy of writing in various languages, I return to my own tongue, to Yiddish, to *mammelushen*, because only in Yiddish am I able to give clear expression, directly and without artificiality, to my innermost thoughts. I am ashamed that I have for so long not valued Yiddish properly.... Yet even if I could rob Homer, Shakespeare, Goethe and Dante of their muses, would I be capable of describing what we suffer, what we sense, what we experience, what we are living through? Is it humanly possible? ... It is as possible to describe our suffering as to drink up the ocean or to embrace the earth. I don't know if we will ever be believed ...

[End of May]

Despair increases steadily as does the terrible hunger, the like of which mankind has never yet suffered. With complete assurance we may say that they have not left us even a jot of that which is called body or soul.

In truth, the world deserves only that we spit in its face and do as Arthur Zygelboim did. [He committed suicide.] ... Sudden death, hunger, deportation, interrogations, labor, queues, etc., etc. wreak havoc in the ruined vineyard of Israel, among the poor remnant. Will you, O God, keep silent? How can you, having seen it? Send your wrath against these savages, against this scum of humanity, and wipe them out from under your heavens. Let their mothers be bereaved as they have caused Jewish mothers to be bereaved for no cause at all, guiltless Jewish mothers. Let the verse come to pass: "Blessed is he that seizes and smashes on the rock those that have tortured you."

Eli, God, why do you allow it?
Why let them say
You were neutral?
In the heat of your anger
The same that makes
A harvest of us,
Are we the sinners
And they the righteous?
Can it be?
Is that the truth?
After all, you have enough
Intelligence to understand
That it is not thus:
That we are the sinned against
And they are the guilty.

[Undated]

We are suffering so much. The old man was savagely beaten up by Biebow. [Hans Biebow, German commander of the ghetto, hanged for his crimes in April 1947.] He had to be taken to the hospital. Five hundred people are to be deported. Again a kind of uncertainty overwhelmed everyone. Have we all gone through all this suffering in order to be liquidated now in their infamous way? Why didn't we die in the first days of the war? My little sister complains of losing the will to live. How tragic. She is only twelve years old! Will there be an end to our suffering? When and how, great heavens! Humanity, where are you?

[Undated]

We are so tired of "life." I was talking with my little sister of twelve and she told me: "I am very tired of this life. A quick death would be a relief for us." O world! World! What have those innocent children done that they are treated in such a manner? Truly, humanity has not progressed very far from the cave of the wild beast.

Thank heavens that I'm no realist for to be a realist is to realize and realizing the whole horror of our situation would have been more than any human being could endure. I go on dreaming, dreaming about survival and about getting free in order to be able to "tell" the world, to yell and "rebuke," to tell and to protest.

July 31, 1944

My after all human heart is cut to pieces when I perceive how terrible my little sister is tormented. She lost literally everything—no stockings, no clothes ... no tenderness. O you poor orphan, and what you have to suffer by my unjust treatment, because of my destroyed nerves. You, poor being, must help yourself with substitutes: instead of stockings some rags, instead of boots some wooden contrivance. . . . God seems to have abandoned us totally and left us entirely to the mercy of the heartless fiends. Almighty God, how can you do this?

August 3, 1944

When I look on my little sister my heart is melting. Hasn't the child suffered its part? She has fought so heroically the last five years. When I look on our cosy little room tidied up by the young intelligent poor being I am getting saddened by the thought that soon she and I will have to leave our last particle of home.

Oh God in heaven, why didst thou create Germans to destroy humanity? I don't even know if I shall be allowed to be together with my sister. I cannot write more. I am resigned terribly and black spirited.

[Last entry. Undated.]

Although I write a broken and hesitant Hebrew, I cannot but write Hebrew, for Hebrew is the language of the future, because I shall use Hebrew as a Jew standing proudly upright in the Land of Israel!

Bibliography

CHILDREN'S WRITINGS IN THE HOLOCAUST
AND WORLD WAR II

GENERAL REFERENCE

Dwork, Deborah. *Children with a Star: Jewish Youth in Nazi Europe.* New Haven and London: Yale University Press, 1991.

Eisenberg, Azriel. *The Lost Generation: Children in the Holocaust.* New York: The Pilgrim Press, 1982.

We Are Children Just the Same: "Vedem," The Secret Magazine by the Boys of Theresienstadt. Philadelphia and Prague: Jewish Publication Society, Aventinum Publishing House, 1994.

Volavkova, Hana, ed. *I Never Saw Another Butterfly.* New York: Schocken Books, 1978.

ADDITIONAL CHILDREN'S DIARIES

Bauman, Janina. *Winter in the Morning: A Young Girl's Life in the Warsaw Ghetto and Beyond.* New York: The Free Press, 1986.

Frank, Anne. *The Diary of Anne Frank.* New York: Doubleday, 1989.

Ginter, Maria. *Life in Both Hands.* London: Hodder and Stoughton Ltd., 1964.

Gissing, Vera. *Pearls of Childhood.* New York: St. Martin's Press, 1988.

Kosterina, Nina. *The Diary of Nina Kosterina.* Translated from the Russian by Mirra Ginsburg. New York: Avon Books, 1968.

Solomon, Charlotte. *Charlotte, A Diary in Pictures.* Brought to press by Paula Solomon Lindberg. New York: Harcourt Brace, 1963.

Urman, Jerzy Feliks. *I'm Not Even a Grown-Up: The Diary of Jerzy Feliks Urman.* London: Menard Press, King's College, 1991.

Zuker-Bujanowska, Liliana. *Liliana's Journal: Warsaw 1939–1945.* New York: Dial Press, 1980.

Berg, Mary (pseudonym). *Warsaw Ghetto: A Diary*. S. L. Shnei-
derman, ed. Prepared by Norbert Guterman and Sylvia
Glass. New York: L. B. Fischer Publishing Corporation,
1945.

Fishkin, Sarah. Excerpt from her unpublished diary. Translated by E. Dobkin. Presented for publication by Sarah's
brother, Jacob Fishkin, from whom Sarah's diary is available at: 26 Cass Place, Brooklyn, New York 11235.

Flinker, Moshe. *Young Moshe's Diary: The Spiritual Torment of
a Jewish Boy in Nazi Europe*. Shaul Esh and Geoffrey Wi-
goder, eds. Jerusalem: Yad Vashem, 1965 and 1971. Original edition was in Hebrew: *Ha-Na'Ar Mosheh* (romanized
form). Shaul Esh, ed. Jerusalem: Yad Vashem, 1958.

Galnik, Werner. "Diary of a Ghetto Boy," in *Jewish Life*, Vol.
6, #4, April 1947. © by Jewish Currents 1947.

Heshele, Janina. "Excerpts from Janina Heshele's Diary of
Lvov." Translated and edited by Azriel Eisenberg from
Hebrew translation of original Polish edition. This excerpt
appeared in *The Lost Generation: Children in the Holocaust*,

New York: Pilgrim Press, 1982. (The excerpt in Hebrew that Azriel Eisenberg used to make his translation into English was in the following book: Bartura, Abraham. *Hayelad Vehonoar Bashoa Ugvurah (Children and Youth in the Holocaust and Resistance)*. Israel: Kiryat Sefer, 1965. I have been unable to locate any reference to the title or whereabouts of the original Polish edition, which may have been only privately published.)

Heyman, Eva. *The Diary of Eva Heyman*. Translated by Moshe M. Kohn. Jerusalem: Yad Vashem, 1974. American edition: New York: Shapolsky Publishers, 1974 and 1988.

Kinsky-Pollack, Helga. "Excerpts from the Terezín Diary of Twelve-Year-Old Helga Kinsky of Vienna." In *Terezín*. Frantisek Ehrmann, Otta Heitlinger, and Rudolf Iltis, eds. Prague: Council of Jewish Communities in the Czech Lands, 1965, pp. 103–05.

Konstantinova, Ina. "Diary and Letters." In *The Girl from Kashin: Soviet Women in Resistance in World War II*. K. Jean Cottam, Ph.d., editor and translator. 1st edition from MA/AH Publishing, 1531 Yuma, Box 1009, Manhattan, KS 66502-4228. Originally published in Russian: *Devushka Iz Kashina*. Molodaya gvardiya (the publishing house of the Young Communist League), 1947. Latest Soviet edition: *Devushka Iz Kashina: Dnevnik I Pis'Ma I. Konstantinovoy, Vospominaniya I Ocherki O Ney*. [*The Girl from Kashin: The Diary and Letters of I. Konstantinova, Reminiscences and*

Sketches Concerning Her.] Moscow: Moskovskiy Rabochiy Publishing House, 1974.

Lazerson, Tamarah. "Extracts from Tamarah Lazerson's Diary." Excerpt edited by Azriel Eisenberg from the Hebrew edition of Tamarah's diary. In *The Lost Generation: Children in the Holocaust.* New York: Pilgrim Press, 1982. Original edition: *Tamarah's Diary.* Tel Aviv: Beit Lohamei Haghetaot (Ghetto Fighters' House), 1966.

Malthe-Bruun, Kim. *Heroic Heart: The Diary and Letters of Kim Malthe-Bruun, 1941–1945.* Vibeke Malthe-Bruun, ed. Translated by Gerry Bothmer. New York: Random House, 1955. From *Heroic Heart: The Diary and Letters of Kim Malthe-Bruun,* by Kim Malthe-Bruun. Copyright © 1955 by Random House, Inc. Reprinted by permission of Random House, Inc. Original edition: *Kim: Uddrag af Dagbog og Breve Skrevet af Kim Fra Hans Syttende.* Copenhagen: Thaning & Appel, 1945.

Perry, Colin. *Boy in the Blitz.* Originally published in Great Britain by Leo Cooper Limited, 1972. (Copyright Colin Perry, 1972.) Corgi edition published in 1974. Colin A. Perry Limited Edition published in 1980.

Phillips, Janine. *My Secret Diary.* London: Shepheard-Walwyn (Publishers) Ltd., 1982. German edition: *Polen, Mai 1939: Ein Tagebuch.* Ravensburg: O. Maier, 1982.

Rolnikas, Macha. *Je Devais Le Raconter.* Paris: Les Editeurs Français Réunis, 1966. Translated from the French for this book by Christine Lienhart Nelson.

Rubinowicz, Dawid. *The Diary of Dawid Rubinowicz.* Translated by Derek Bowman. Edinburgh: Blackwood, 1981. The book remains in print from Laing Communications/Laing Research Services, Redmond, Washington, original packagers of the 1982 American edition by Creative Options Publishing. © Laing Communications Inc., Redmond, WA.

Rudashevski, Yitskhok. *The Diary of the Vilna Ghetto: June 1941–April 1943.* Translated by Percy Matenko. Israel: Beit Lohamei Haghetaot—Ghetto Fighter's House, 1973.

Senesh, Hannah. *Hannah Senesh: Her Life and Diary.* Translated by Marta Cohn. London: Vallentine, Mitchell, 1971. American edition: From *Hannah Senesh: Her Life and Diary* by Hannah Senesh, trans. by Marta Cohn. Intro by Abba Eban. (Text) copyright © 1971 by Nigel Marsh. Introduction copyright © 1972 by Schocken Books Inc. Reprinted by permission of Schocken Books, published by Pantheon Books, a division of Random House, Inc.

Shtenkler, Ephraim. "What Happened to Me in My Childhood," in *Commentary* (May, 1950): 442–446. Reprinted from Commentary. All rights reserved.

Unknown Brother and Sister. "The Unknown Diarist of Ghetto Lodz." *Yad Vashem News,* No. 2 (1970): pp. 8–11.

Van der Heide, Dirk (pseudonym). Translated by Mrs. Antoon Deventer. *My Sister and I.* New York: Harcourt, Brace, and Co., Inc., 1941.

Veresova, Charlotte. "Notes from the Ghetto—Excerpts from

the Terezín Diary of Fourteen-Year-Old Charlotte Veresova of Prague." In *Terezín*, Frantisek Ehrmann, Otta Heitlinger, and Rudolf Iltis, eds. Prague: Council of Jewish Communities of the Czech Lands, 1965, pp. 110–12.

Weissova-Hoskova, Helga. "Excerpts from the Diary of Helga Weissova-Hoskova." In *Terezín*, Frantisek Ehrmann, Otta Heitlinger, and Rudolf Iltis, eds. Prague: Council of Jewish Communities in the Czech Lands, 1965, pp. 106–09.

Wyndham, Joan. *Love Lessons: A Wartime Diary*. London: William Heinemann Ltd., 1985. By permission from Reed International Books, London, England. 1st American edition: Boston and Toronto: Little, Brown and Co., 1985.

EUROPE IN 1942

1. Janine Phillips
2. Ephraim Shtenkler
3. Dirk Van der Heide
4. Werner Galnik
5. Janina Heshele
6. Helga Weissova-Hoskova
7. Dawid Rubinowicz
8. Helga Kinsky-Pollack
9. Eva Heyman
10. Tamarah Lazerson
11. Yitskhok Rudashevski
12. Macha Rolnikas
13. Charlotte Veresova
14. Mary Berg
15. Ina Konstantinova
16. Moshe Flinker
17. Joan Wyndham
18. Hannah Senesh
19. Sarah Fishkin
20. Kim Malthe-Bruun
21. Colin Perry
22-23. The Unknown Sister and Brother

■ TRANSPORT CAMP

○ *Concentration Camp*

▲ *DEATH CAMP*

Border of Greater Germany 1942

250 Km

250 Miles

Designed by Jeffrey L. Ward

NETHERLANDS
Amsterdam
WESTERBORK
The Hague
BARNEVELD
Rotterdam
Antwerp
○*Vught*
MALINES
Brussels
BELGIUM

North Atlantic Ocean

Dublin
IRELAND

North Sea

U. K.

SEE INSET ABOVE

London

English Channel

NETHERLANDS
BELGIUM

DRANCY
Paris
Strasbourg
PITHIVIERS
Natzweiler-Struthof ○
BEAUNE-LA-ROLANDE
Bern
FRANCE
SWITZERLA

Lyon
VENISSIEUX

GURS
NOÉ
LES MILLES
AGDE
RIVESALTES
ARGELÈS
SPAIN
Marseille

Madrid
Barcelona

Mediterranean Sea